SHOCKING CONTRASTS

In the fourteenth century, the Black Death killed as much as two thirds of Europe's population; in the fifteenth, the introduction of moveable-type printing rapidly expanded Europe's supply of human capital; between 1850 and 1914, Russia's population almost tripled; and in World War I, the British blockade starved some 800,000 Germans. Each of these, *Shocking Contrasts* argues, amounted to an unanticipated shock, positive or negative, to the supply of a crucial factor of production. It also elicited one of four main responses: factor substitution; factor movement to a different sector or region; technological innovation; or political action, sometimes extending to coercion at home or conquest abroad. This book examines parsimonious models of factor returns, relative costs, and technological innovation. It offers a framework for understanding the role of supply shocks in major political conflicts and argues that its implications extend far beyond these specific cases to any period of human history.

Ronald L. Rogowski is a Distinguished Research Professor of Political Science at University of California, Los Angeles. He has taught at Princeton, Duke, and Minnesota. He was elected as a Fellow of the American Academy of Arts and Sciences in 1994 and has held research appointments at the Center for Advanced Study, the Wissenschaftskolleg zu Berlin, and Harvard University. His previous books include *Rational Legitimacy* (1974), *Commerce and Coalitions* (1990), and *Electoral Systems and the Balance of Producer-Consumer Power* (2010; co-authored).

SHOCKING CONTRASTS

Political Responses to Exogenous Supply Shocks

RONALD L. ROGOWSKI
University of California, Los Angeles

CAMBRIDGE
UNIVERSITY PRESS

CAMBRIDGE
UNIVERSITY PRESS

Shaftesbury Road, Cambridge CB2 8EA, United Kingdom

One Liberty Plaza, 20th Floor, New York, NY 10006, USA

477 Williamstown Road, Port Melbourne, VIC 3207, Australia

314–321, 3rd Floor, Plot 3, Splendor Forum, Jasola District Centre,
New Delhi – 110025, India

103 Penang Road, #05–06/07, Visioncrest Commercial, Singapore 238467

Cambridge University Press is part of Cambridge University Press & Assessment,
a department of the University of Cambridge.

We share the University's mission to contribute to society through the pursuit of
education, learning and research at the highest international levels of excellence.

www.cambridge.org
Information on this title: www.cambridge.org/9781316510704

DOI: 10.1017/9781009039444

First published 2023

Printed in the United Kingdom by TJ Books Limited, Padstow Cornwall

A catalogue record for this publication is available from the British Library.

A Cataloging-in-Publication data record for this book is available from the Library of Congress

ISBN 978-1-316-51070-4 Hardback

Continued on page following index

For my wife and daughters

Karin Margaret Best

Emma Lynn Best Rogowski

Clare Brigitte Best Rogowski

We . . . need to become comfortable in thinking about the economic activity of the human race, not merely in terms of gradual movements of technical and economic progress occurring by insensible degrees, but also as shoved on occasion by shocks, many barely noticed, some easily absorbed, and a few with cataclysmic consequences.

Larry Neal, "A Shocking View of Economic History"

Contents

Figures

Maps

Tables

Preface and Acknowledgments

Just as I was finishing up work on this book's chapter on the Black Death, the COVID-19 pandemic broke out.[1] Suddenly, even the front page of the *New York Times* was discussing supply shocks; and, while the plague of 2020–2021 was (despite its shocking toll) trivial compared to the Black Death's loss of some two-thirds of Europe's population, it brought home how greatly an unanticipated and exogenous change can affect economic and political life – and how greatly countries can vary in their responses to such a shock.

The puzzle of varying responses to pandemics led me to search out other cases in which some unanticipated and exogenous event had sharply increased or decreased a region's supply of some crucial factor of production. I had also long been interested in how, or even whether, a new factor-biased technology could alter the supply and relative price of factors. And, of course, unforeseen openings or closings of trade routes, and with them increases or decreases in the effective supply of essential factors of production, were an old interest of mine.

I had originally thought only to consider how such exogenous changes affected inequality within societies; but a pair of criticisms – one by Jim Robinson over a decade ago, and the other by my former student Thomas Flaherty in late 2019 – convinced me that the more interesting question was how and why different governments or societies responded to the same shock in such different ways (with, of course, usually very different consequences for inequality).

[1] I gave a talk on that chapter at Princeton University on March 9 – which turned out to be the last talk in that series before everything closed down. People sensed what was coming, and the after-talk dinner was peppered with dark humor about its being "the last supper."

Those criteria thus became my *leitmotif* for case selection: (a) a clearly exogenous, severe, and unforeseen change, positive or negative, to the supply of some factor of production, which (b) had elicited responses that differed sharply between or within societies. The classic case was of course the Black Death of the fourteenth century. The acute labor shortage that it occasioned elicited almost polar opposite responses in Western and Eastern Europe: ending serfdom and decreasing inequality in the West; enserfing the peasantry and sharply increasing inequality in the East. In Chapter 4, I offer a new conjecture, which attributes the divergent responses to differences in soil and climate.

Thinking about the Black Death, which had reduced Europe's population by 1420 to one-third of its early fourteenth-century levels, put me on the search for a case in which some exogenous shock had *increased* a country's population by a factor of three. I instantly recalled Keynes's offhand comment in *Economic Consequences of the Peace*, that the tripling of Russia's population between 1850 and 1914 had been a major cause of the Bolshevik Revolution. But was that increase in any meaningful sense exogenous? Wasn't it a standard early stage of demographic transition? I thought I was being clever and original in speculating that the construction of Russia's railway network might have somehow contributed; but then I learned in a conversation with Nathan Nunn (with whom I carry a shamefully negative balance on current intellectual account) of the Burgess and Donaldson paper showing that railway construction had alleviated famine and spurred population growth in colonial India (Burgess and Donaldson 2012). Once I learned that Russia's railroads, like those of the Raj, had been routed chiefly for the exogenous reason of military advantage, I warmed to Keynes's twin questions: Had railways spurred Russian population growth, and were they somehow connected to political unrest in the late Czarist period? Here, the question was one of contrasting reactions *within* a country – some regions rebelled, others remained quiescent – rather than between nations. I offer possible answers in Chapter 5.

In teaching an undergraduate course on Fascism over several years, I had come to accept another of Keynes's conclusions, amplified by the crucial work of Adam Tooze on the German wartime economy (Tooze 2008): that the supply shock that faced Europe during and after World War I was its loss of ready access to the fertile lands of the New World. Here, not only did reactions differ across countries – Germany clearly differed from France and the United Kingdom – but within Germany: a substantial minority supported the Nazis' genocidal answer, the pursuit of nutritional self-sufficiency through the conquest and settlement of

Lebensraum, while a majority, even as late as the last free elections of 1932, did not. One obvious possibility was that Germany had suffered actual mass starvation in World War I, while other European states had not; and that, within Germany, the incidence of hunger had varied strongly across regions. I pursued that hunch with the invaluable help of Professor Jürgen Falter, who kindly provided me with his datasets on Nazi membership, Nazi voting support, and demographic characteristics of Germany's cities and regions in the interwar period. Results are presented in Chapter 6.

My reading in international political economy and development economics had convinced me of the crucial importance of human capital. Were there cases of exogenous and unanticipated increase or decrease of this essential factor of production? Every case of decrease that I could find was endogenous: rulers deliberately drove out or massacred persons of skill and talent, or civil wars forced them to flee. To the regions that received those refugees, on the other hand, the accretion of human capital was, in at least a few cases, unexpected and unsought. The clearest such case in modern European history was Louis XIV's impetuous expulsion of the French Calvinists – the Huguenots – in 1685; and one of the receiving areas that benefited the most was Protestant Germany, most notably the Electorate of Brandenburg-Prussia (Hornung 2014). It became clear, however, that Protestant German cities and principalities had differed widely in their receptivity to the Huguenot influx: some, such as Brandenburg, had actively recruited them with subventions and privileges; others, such as Weimar or most of the Hanseatic cities, had either rejected them or treated them as inferiors by, for example, not allowing them to own property, join guilds, or become citizens. What could explain these varying responses? I suggest, in Chapter 7, that a combination of new ideas (about guilds and economic growth) and proximity to trade routes mattered most.

Next, I wanted to examine at least one case of a technologically induced supply shock. Only a few of these were truly exogenous and unexpected, but in some cases an originally endogenous innovation so overshot the initial need as to become an unexpected multiplier of one or more crucial factors of production. Here, the leading historical example seemed to me to be the invention of moveable-type printing around 1450, which had led to an unanticipated explosion of literacy and knowledge. Why had it arisen when it did, and why had different states and regions within and beyond Europe responded to the invention in ways that varied from enthusiastic acceptance (the Netherlands) to outright prohibition (the Ottoman Empire)? I suggest, in Chapter 8, that new opportunities in commerce and state-building provide most of the answer – and shaped a stark difference between southern and northwestern Europe.

Last of all, I sought to discern common features that influenced how people and societies responded to such supply shocks. People, I assumed, were rational enough to seek the least costly response that could avert major loss. Coercion – violent resistance to change – would normally be the costliest route; factor substitution, using less of a newly costly factor and more of a newly abundant factor, the cheapest. I tease out these implications in Chapter 2. Chapter 3 covers the intermediate route discussed almost a century ago by Hicks [(Hicks 1963); 1st edition 1932], namely a factor-saving technological innovation: When and why does such an innovation arise, and why – at least until the last two centuries – were such innovations so rare?

This book would not have been possible without the unstinting help of my friends, students, family, and colleagues (and those categories do not mutually exclude one another). I inevitably will overlook some important ones here, but a partial list will include the following:

Three institutions housed me during research leaves: in Berlin, the Wissenschaftskolleg and later the Hertie-Universität; in Cambridge, MA, the Weatherhead Center at Harvard University. I am grateful to my hosts at each: at the WiKo, Joachim Nettelbeck and Luca Giuliani; at the Hertie, Mark Kayser and Mark Hallerberg; at the Weatherhead, Kathleen Molony – who did especially heroic work shepherding us all through the pandemic – along with Ted Gilman, and Erin Goodman. Financial support came from New York University, Abu Dhabi (where I was also an occasional visiting professor) and the Division of Social Sciences at the University of California, Los Angeles (UCLA). During my stay at the Hertie, I exploited the generous hospitality of Uli and Marta Mayer, whom Karin and I are now privileged to count among our dearest friends.

The unfailingly helpful advice of two graduate students saved me from many (but by no means all) errors: at UCLA, Caleb Ziolkowski; at Harvard, Brendan McElroy. Caleb, who completed joint degrees in Political Science and Statistics, moved on to a post-doctoral appointment at Princeton University; Brendan, whose knowledge of serfdom and state-building in both the German lands and Russia is unparalleled, took up a post-doctoral appointment at the University of Michigan and, in Fall 2022, became an assistant professor at the University of Toronto. The three of us have already begun coauthorship on two papers.

I benefited also from the expert advice and criticisms of many colleagues in many countries and specializations: leading citizens of our twenty-first century Republic of Letters. In naming them, I implicate them in none of my mistakes; indeed, several persist in their inability to be persuaded by my pellucid and irrefutable arguments. In each category, I list alphabetically. On Russia, Scott Gehlbach (Chicago), Timur Natkhov (HSE University, Moscow), and Imil Nurutdinov (Institute for Advanced Study, Toulouse; also my former student). On the Black Death and/or European serfdom: Carles Boix (Princeton), Daniel Gingerich (University of Virginia), Margaret Peters (UCLA), Tom Raster (Paris School of Economics), and Jan Vogler (University of Konstanz). On German mortality and disease in and after World War I: Bettina Hitzer (Free University of Berlin and Max Planck Institute for Educational Research). On skeletal and archaeological evidence, especially regarding the Black Death: Gundula Müldner (University of Reading) and Mike Richards (Simon Fraser University). On the NSDAP, the unrivalled master of that daunting subject, Jürgen Falter (University of Mainz). On European political and economic history generally, the most deeply learned and wittiest writer I know, Josef Joffe (Hoover Institution and *Die Zeit*).

None of the empirical work would have been possible without the dedicated and untiring service of a platoon of undergraduate research assistants, some compensated, the majority volunteers: at Harvard, Catherine Liang, Can Yesildire, and Alvin Zou; at UCLA, Brandon Zhao (the team boss), Nina Groeneveld, Stephanie Inchaustegui, Aidan O'Sullivan, Ragini Srinivasan, and Matthew St. Geme; at the London School of Economics and in Vienna, Arthur Krön. Some were expert in R, others in Python; their range of languages included Arabic, Basque, Cantonese, Dutch, German, Mandarin, Romanian, Spanish, Tamil, and Turkish. Can, Brandon, and Aidan, working under Caleb's tutelage, gained greater facility in advanced statistics and modeling. Aidan, whose expertise extends beyond degrees in political science and computer science to art history, suggested the Albers painting that illustrates the cover. Nina did heroic work in indexing the volume. They have been an astonishingly impressive and dedicated bunch, to whom I cannot express enough gratitude. At a later stage, a CalTech graduate student, Jacob Morrier, whipped the maps and illustrations into a sufficiently high-resolution format to satisfy the demands of Cambridge University Press; and Tom Raster (see above; now spending two years at Harvard) generously recast his map on 1816 Prussian landholdings to meet the Press's specifications and gave me permission to use it.

I have presented various parts of this work at different stages of its development at the regular Tuesday seminars of the Wissenschaftskolleg, the International Relations Faculty Colloquium at Princeton University, the Harvard Political Economy Luncheon Group, the Quantitative Collaborative at the University of Virginia, and the Weatherhead Scholars Seminar and the Weatherhead Forum. I am grateful for the many helpful criticisms and pointers – to literature, datasets, historical episodes, and much else – that participants in those groups were kind enough to give me.

For wise and witty counsel, warm friendship, and unfailing encouragement, I owe much to my fellow Weatherhead Scholars of the academic years 2019–2021 and to members of the Tuesday Political Economy (PE) Luncheon group at Harvard. With advance apologies to those whom I will inevitably have overlooked, I extend particular thanks (again, in alphabetical order) to: among the Weatherhead group, Wolfgang Aschauer, Adam Dean, Bernhard Fischer-Appelt, Yossi Harpaz, Michael Harsch, Annette Idler, Friederike Kelle, Henrique Pacini, Anna Skarpelis, Matt Swanson, and Thijs van Dooremalen; in the PE lunch group, James Alt, Robert Bates, Peter Buisseret, Bill Clark, Jeffry Frieden, Richard Grossman, Carl Müller-Crepon, Pia Raffler, Kenneth Shepsle, Artur Silve, Daniel M. Smith, and Dustin Tingley.

The early chapters received thorough and exceedingly helpful reviews from three readers for Cambridge, one of whom – Bill Clark, at Texas A & M – has since outed himself and continued to provide wise and trenchant critiques. My editors at Cambridge, Erika Walsh, Robert Judkins, Franklin Mathews Jebaraj, and especially my fellow Nebraskan Robert Dreesen, have also labored diligently, professionally, and compassionately on this project. At a later stage, Fiona Cole proved to be the kind of copy-editor of which most authors can only dream.

The notorious difficulty of finding decent and affordable housing in Cambridge, Massachusetts, was unexpectedly solved for us by the family of the late Frederick Levy, who generously accepted us as house sitters during the year between Fred's death and their putting his spacious and beautifully furnished home on the market. I am especially grateful to Jody Garber and Joanna Levy, who could not have been more gracious and accommodating. We will carry fond memories of that home, including our storybook Christmas in it, for the rest of our days.

My deepest debt, however, is to my family: my wife Karin Margaret Best and my daughters Emma Lynn Best Rogowski and Clare Brigitte Best Rogowski, to whom this book is dedicated. They have borne with me through all the false starts, crippling doubts, and intense labors that have attended this work's long gestation. I cannot thank them enough, except by trying to be less irritable in the future.

Introduction

This is a book about *supply shocks* and *technological shocks*, and about how societies react politically to those shocks. By supply shocks, I mean any sudden, exogenous, and unanticipated increase or decrease in a society's supply of some essential input, or *factor of production*; by a technological shock, I mean more precisely what economists would call an unanticipated *factor-biased* technological change, that is, one that allows a more efficient use of some factor of production.

While it is often useful to consider more fine-grained categories of inputs, I will focus on the traditional "big four" factors of production: *labor*, *land* (including *natural resources*), *physical capital*, and *human capital* (also known as "skill"). To these I will occasionally add the "lubricant" of means of *transportation and communication*, which bring geographically separated products or factors of production into useful proximity to each other, or to markets.

Examples of shocks to the supply of one or more of these should come readily to mind:

- Plagues and major wars, as Walter Scheidel's pathbreaking book reminds us, can suddenly decrease the supply of *labor*, as can large-scale emigration (Scheidel 2017); but unanticipated immigration from abroad, or unexpected population "explosions" at home, can increase that supply almost as rapidly.
- States and empires have often gained *land* and *resources* from, or lost them to, conquest; less than a century ago, Nazi Germany and Fascist Japan fought cataclysmic wars in pursuit of oil, ores, and *Lebensraum*.
- Wars can also destroy, and a flood of investment from foreign or domestic sources[1] can rapidly create, *physical capital*.

[1] Communism's "forced draft" investment, in which savings were extracted from the population by terror, was an extreme example. Cf. Frieden (2006, 217–218).

- Immigration can rapidly expand, or emigration rapidly deplete, a society's supply of *human capital*: industrious Huguenots in the seventeenth century, highly skilled Russian Jews in the late twentieth.
- Various "revolutions" in *transport and communication* are well known, prominent among them: Roman roads and harbors (Dalgaard et al. 2018); canals, railroads, and steamships; and the telephone, telegraph, radio, and internet. Such breakthroughs are, with rare exceptions, endogenous; we encounter more frequently unanticipated technological breakdowns or interruptions of established trade routes. An example, which I exploit in Chapter 6, is the blockades and lasting effects of World War I.

Even more familiar, indeed a staple of high-school history texts, are episodes of *factor-saving technological innovation*: Labor was made more productive by the Industrial Revolution, land by new crops from the Colombian Exchange (chiefly potatoes and maize), physical capital by Henry Ford's assembly line, human capital by computers.

So why do shocks to supply and technology matter? First of all, because they change (or, at the very least, threaten to change) the *returns* that factors earn: the wages of labor, the prices of land and resources, the rent of physical capital, the "skill premium" that goes to human capital, the cost of transportation.[2] Since we are talking about *unanticipated* changes, the owners of the affected factors will not have redeployed: They will enjoy unanticipated gains or suffer unanticipated losses. Second, these changes *ramify*: They usually also affect the owners of other factors, engender technological change, sometimes even reshape language or gender relations. When low-skill labor suddenly becomes either scarcer (as in times of war or plague) or more productive (as in the Industrial Revolution), wages rise and workers gain; but capitalists, landowners, and the highly skilled must suddenly pay more for any labor they employ. When grain from the New World entered European markets, European workers gained cheap food, but European farmers lost. Third, long-established patterns of *inequality* often change quickly: Plagues and mass warfare serve as what Scheidel pithily calls "levelers," that is, they make

[2] One still encounters the (to me) strange view that "traditional" societies lack markets, or that people in them do not respond to incentives. Admittedly, as a farm boy, I find this view patronizing; but I also regard it as refuted by a wealth of historical evidence. Curtin for example notes that "markets and fluctuating prices could be found in Mesopotamia at least as early as the end of the fourth millennium BC" (Curtin 1984, 64). For a comprehensive overview, see also Bernstein (2008).

society more equal; but low-wage imports make advanced labor-scarce economies (see the extensive literature on the "China shock") more unequal.

And, finally, these prospective gains and losses, and looming changes to inequality, often *mobilize people politically*: The winners seek at least to let the market prevail, and often to expand their political influence; the losers pursue measures to stem or reverse their losses, and sometimes to restrict other groups' influence. In the later nineteenth century, the import of cheap New World food, coupled with massive emigration, raised real wages, diminished inequality, and impelled wide-spread democratization throughout much of Europe; but landowners sought protective tariffs, and large landowners opposed democratization or sought to restrict the existing franchise. In our own age of stagnating wages and rising inequality, low-skill workers demand limits on imports and immigration, while the high-end beneficiaries of globalization pursue (at least in the US) lower taxes and voter suppression.

All of this excites, or at least should excite, little controversy. As I show in Chapter 1, the conclusions about factor returns and inequality follow directly from rudimentary economics; and the political implications are no less common currency among students of comparative politics and history. What will, I hope, prove controversial are the following three claims:

1. Supply and technological shocks are no rarity but have induced many episodes of political mobilization and contestation – in both democratic and non-democratic regimes.
2. Previously underappreciated economic considerations powerfully affect, and in some cases appear to determine, the outcomes of such conflicts and why those outcomes vary among and within states.
3. Political institutions are less determinative of how societies respond to supply shocks than we often imagine, indeed are largely endogenous. What matters more is such physical factors as soil and climate, such economic ones as labor markets, and the unforeseen consequences of technical innovations.

I will try to sustain the first of these assertions through a series of historical case studies, all involving a supply or technological shock that simultaneously affects two or more countries or regions and, even more to the point, a divergent response among the affected regions. One example, familiar to most students of comparative politics and history, is the Black Death that begins in Europe in 1348. It created acute labor shortages everywhere, yet the response in western Europe was rising wages and the end of serfdom, in eastern Europe declining wages and an intensified "second serfdom."

To understand my second assertion, and hence to explain why regions can differ so greatly in their response to a common shock, I will invoke three main, closely related, factors: *elasticity of substitution*; *factor mobility*; and *exit options*. Again to use the Black Death as an example of how elasticity of substitution matters: In much of western Europe, and most clearly in England, agriculture (despite much resistance by landowners) shifted with only modest difficulty from labor-intensive to land-intensive production: Grain-growing gave way to pasturage and forest, meat and dairy consumption increased, and people wore woolen rather than flaxen garments. In short, land could readily substitute for labor in agricultural production, and landlords could adjust to higher real wages by using less labor. In eastern Europe, for reasons I will try to elucidate, such substitution was highly inelastic: A move from labor- to land-intensive production proved to be almost impossible, and in any event highly unremunerative. The higher wages that the labor-scarce market demanded would have driven landowners into penury. Hence, despite the high costs (in monitoring, collusion, coercion, and even absolutism) of doing so, landowners tied peasants to the land and forced them to work for wages far below their marginal product – or, more precisely, forced them to work much of each week on the lord's land for no wage at all.

Even where factor substitution is difficult, owners can sometimes adjust by shifting the factor in which they are invested to a different use or sector. A worker in agriculture may, for example, move into some urban occupation; a person with skills in finance may find that those skills are almost as valuable in marketing. As Peter Hall, Torben Iverson, David Soskice, and other students of modern capitalism have noted, to some extent factor mobility is endogenous (Hall and Soskice 2001): An educational system may impart sector- or firm-specific skills, or more general and adaptable ones; factories may be built specifically for a single use, or with a profile that allows them to switch to other kinds of production. An additional reason that landowners often cling to political power is that most land can be used only for agriculture; it cannot readily be shifted to some other sector.

Finally, owners threatened by some adverse change in their society or region may, in some circumstances, limit their losses by moving what they own to some other jurisdiction less affected by the given shock to supply or technology. Labor, the highly skilled, and some kinds of capital can simply emigrate; land (and most deposits of natural resources), at least until recently, could not.[3] Again, openness to exit is partly endogenous: People often invest in skills rather than physical capital because the former are more easily transported (Becker et al. 2020); and even some forms of physical capital (factories, mobile homes) may be constructed to guarantee ease of exit (O. E. Williamson 1985, 35–38).

Hence, in opposition to an extreme solution like enslavement, I will posit a more nuanced array of responses, ordered by rising cost and dictated by increasing elasticity of substitution, factor mobility, or availability of exit (encapsulated under the rubric of "ease of adjustment").

1. Where adjustment is easy: Accept the verdict of the market, perhaps after initial resistance.
2. Where adjustment is slightly more difficult: Adapt by substituting the newly abundant factors for the newly scarce one, or by moving the abundant factor to a different sector or jurisdiction.
3. Where adjustment is yet more difficult: Seek a *technological or institutional remedy* that makes more efficient use of (and hence requires less of) the factor or factors whose relative price has increased.[4] If such a new technology can be found, again accept the verdict of the market.
4. Where adjustment would be extremely difficult, and assuming no adequate institutional or technological response: Resort to political action, collusion, coercion, conquest, or some combination of these to inhibit or reverse the market-dictated change in relative prices.

A crucial issue under (3) is what determines the likelihood that a technological "fix" will be found. Part of the answer lies in how strong the incentives are, as in, how desperate is the need for (and the commensurate rewards to) a technological answer. But at least as important, I will argue (following Michael Kremer), is the sheer size of the affected population – or, I will add,

[3] Freeman and Quinn note that Argentine landowners can now securitize their holdings on foreign (chiefly London and New York) exchanges and, in consequence, have become less concerned about holding political power (Freeman and Quinn 2012, 62).

[4] In economic thinking, institutions, and particularly property rights, are often treated as a species of technology: E.g., the shift from manorial strip farming to enclosed fields at the end of the Middle Ages made for a more efficient use of land, just as did the change from ox- to horse-drawn plows (which itself depended on the invention of the horse-collar).

of the linguistic group among whom a newly invented solution might be readily transmitted.

As the foregoing discussion suggests, I will propose to treat most factor-saving technological innovations as *endogenous*: That is, they arise as a market-incentivized or politically dictated response to some shortage of a particular factor. One clear, if perhaps almost too pat, example: the German introduction, early in World War I, of the Haber-Bosch process to fix nitrates from atmospheric nitrogen, as a desperate answer to the British blockade of saltpeter and guano imports from the New World – crucial for both munitions and agriculture (Smil 2001, esp. 103–107). But the endogenous can become exogenous via *overshooting*: when the technological "fix" to some scarcity then renders the scarce factor so cheaply available that the consequences ramify far beyond. Examples include the printing press (1450; see Chapter 8), improved navigation and ship design (1490), and railroads (1830).

A few technological innovations, nonetheless, appear to be genuinely exogenous. So far as economic historians can tell, neither the introduction of New World food crops into Europe, and then the world, nor the construction of railways (particularly in Russia and India), was an intentional response to land scarcity or recurrent famine. Potatoes and maize, initially only curious artifacts of exploration, made land so much more productive that population exploded; and railroads, often introduced chiefly for military purposes, so reduced the high variance in local food availability as to mitigate, or actually eliminate, recurrent famine.

I will address these issues, and more, in a separate chapter on technology. A particularly important aspect is what facilitates or impedes the spread of some productivity-magnifying new technology. Why were some regions of the world so slow to adopt more abundant crops, or the Industrial Revolution, or (a somewhat different example) firearms (Hoffman 2015)?[5]

[5] Military technology raises a separate set of issues. Too often treated as determinative (e.g., feudalism arrived full-blown with the introduction of the stirrup, or Greek democracy arose only because of the turn to *hoplite* warfare), and surely spurred on by rivalry among rulers, it nonetheless also responds to factor abundance or scarcity: A society with abundant labor and scarce capital (human or physical) will prove particularly prone to adopt a labor-intensive military technology (the age of mass warfare between roughly 1870 and 1960); one abundant in human and physical capital, but scarce in labor, will likelier adopt high-tech, i.e., capital-intensive, modes of combat. See fuller discussion in Chapter 3.

If, however, neither factor substitution nor technological innovation provides an adequate response – one that allows production on roughly the previous scale to continue – the owners of factors harmed by the unanticipated shock to supply or technology will likely resort to some form of coercion (using, where possible, existing institutions of government, but if necessary creating new ones); while the beneficiaries of the unanticipated shock will resist, or resort to counter-coercion.

This, it seems obvious, is what happened in the eastern European reaction to the labor shortages that attended the Black Death. Abetted to some degree by rulers' policy but relying chiefly on their own economic and military power, landowners invented and imposed a new institution: They forbade peasants to leave, bound them to the land, and thus enserfed what had been a free peasantry. By way of contrast, when the Great Migration of African Americans out of US southern agriculture into northern (in most cases, wartime) industry deprived cotton growers of their sharecropping workforce, the landowners could simply adopt mechanical cotton harvesters – which, in turn, pushed more sharecroppers off the land and into migration.

More often, those threatened with loss can employ or adapt existing institutions. When the technological breakthroughs of railroads and steamships made cheap grain and meat from the New World available on European markets, and when even more intensive methods of farming (including extensive use of fertilizer) failed to make European agriculture competitive, landowners throughout Europe sought (and in most cases won) tariffs that eliminated the imported products' price advantage. When, only slightly later, industrially produced goods and modern retailing threatened the existence of German small business (the *Mittelstand*), Bismarck enacted legislation that granted the small enterprises local monopolies and inhibited industrial competition (Blackbourn 1977, 411–412).

These are only illustrative examples. Subsequent substantive chapters will present relevant historical cases in detail. I begin, however, by presenting and elaborating the theory. In Chapter 1, I examine how supply shocks arise, often as the unintended by-product of some change in technology. Chapter 2 addresses the three main ways in which societies can adjust to such a shock, and why they sometimes cannot adjust. Chapter 3 asks how factor-saving technological adjustments arise (or, more often, fail to arise); and how these can in turn occasion supply shocks of their own. Chapters 4–8 detail cases in which a common shock induces differing responses across various regions of the globe. Chapter 9 concludes.

Throughout, but especially in the opening theoretical Chapters (1–3), I invoke basic economics to elucidate crucial parts of the argument. My treatment will likely appear patronizing to economists, obscure to some non-economists. On either score, I ask the reader's indulgence and patience. I have found that purely verbal exposition invites confusion on fundamental points, for example, about whether the acute labor shortage after the Black Death should have raised wages or left them largely unchanged. Expressing things mathematically, even in the simplistic way I employ here, at least yields clear results – which, if they are wrong, lead us to question fruitfully the underlying assumptions.

At several points, I also offer statistical tests of some of the hypotheses. These cannot be in any sense conclusive; rather, they are intended to demonstrate the plausibility of the explanations I advance. They invite, and may well be refuted by, further testing.

I

How Supply Shocks Arise and Why Political Responses to Them Vary

When will men accept the verdict of the market,
and when do they attempt to alter it?

E. R. Walker, *From Economic Theory to Policy*.[1]

Suppose that some exogenous shock unexpectedly increases or decreases a society's supply of one of its major factors of production.[2] How does such a shock affect wages and returns on investment (in capital or land)? Create winners or losers? Make the society more, or less, equal? Change the "mix" of inputs used by producers? And, finally, precipitate political conflict and challenge (and perhaps change) existing institutions?

From a simple economic standpoint, a shock to supply changes relative returns to factors of production: the pay of workers, the rents of landowners, the returns to physical and human capital. In a competitive market economy, each unit of a factor earns its marginal product, that is, the value that one additional unit (hour of labor, hectare of land, year of education, dollar invested in new machinery) would create.[3] It follows that the relative returns to each factor will – again, in a *competitive* economy– be proportional to the relative abundance of each factor in the given economy.[4]

[1] Walker (1943, 109), slightly paraphrased by Kindleberger (1951, 42).

[2] I focus on unanticipated shocks, because actors can often adjust their actions or investments to compensate for a shock that is foreseen, or foreseeable.

[3] The logic is simple: If an employer is thinking of hiring one additional worker, the most that she will pay is whatever that additional employee will add to the employer's bottom line – i.e., that employee's marginal product. While the employer will of course want to pay less than this, in a competitive market, other employers will bid up the wage, until it reaches exactly the maximum, i.e., the full marginal product of that additional worker.

[4] I consider below the possibilities of monopoly, monopsony, regulation, or coercion – which are, indeed, among the most frequent political reactions to supply shocks.

Take, as an illustrative example, a purely agricultural economy, where the only factors of production are land (T) and labor (L). In a standard "workhorse" Cobb–Douglas production function,[5] output Y is given by

$$Y = AT^{\alpha}L^{1-\alpha} \qquad (1.1),$$

where α is some fraction greater than zero and less than one and A (usually denoted "total factor productivity") is a technology parameter, to be considered at greater length below. In the real world, as illustrated by many share-cropping arrangements around the globe, including on the farm I grew up on in Nebraska, α is usually around 1/3: Therefore, a third of the crop goes to the landlord, two-thirds to the tenant farmer.[6] Whatever the actual value of α, the laborer's wage will be the marginal product of an additional hour worked, the landlord's rent the marginal product of an additional hectare of land. In standard notation (the marginal product being the derivative), we have then

$$w = MPL = Y_L = (1-\alpha)A(T/L)^{\alpha} \qquad (1.2),$$

$$r = MPT = Y_T = \alpha A(T/L)^{\alpha-1} = \alpha A(L/T)^{1-\alpha} \qquad (1.3).$$

Wages, in other words, rise monotonically (holding technology constant), and rents fall, as the land-labor ratio rises.[7] Moreover, falling rents entail falling land prices, since no rational buyer will pay more per hectare than that hectare will return in present value of anticipated future revenue.[8]

Four important things follow, in a competitive market, if the land-labor ratio increases:

[5] This version of Cobb–Douglas is just the simplest of many possible production functions characterized by constant returns to scale (i.e., doubling all inputs exactly doubles output) and constant elasticity of substitution (explained below). We assume constant returns to scale for a simple reason: If returns to scale were decreasing, firms would be too large and smaller ones would have a competitive advantage; if returns were increasing, firms would be too small and larger ones would prevail (up to, possibly, monopoly domination of the market). This implication about optimal firm (or, in this case, farm) size in equilibrium is often regarded as an illustration of the Coase Theorem. Cf. Medema (2020).

[6] Footnote 37 explains why these exponents translate into shares of total production.

[7] Note that the exponent in the final expression in both (3) and (4) is fractional but positive. It should also be obvious that all these results would hold analogously if we were thinking of capital and labor in a more advanced economy.

[8] If the ratio of prices to rents remains unchanged (and historically that ratio has been about 20, implying an annual return on investment of about 5 percent), land prices will of course decline by the same percentage as rents.

- Workers *gain*, and owners *lose*;
- Society becomes *more equal*;
- Production becomes, to the extent possible, *more land- and less labor-intensive*; and
- Incentives to invent or adopt a *labor-saving technology* increase.

Exactly the reverse happens in each case when the land-labor ratio *decreases*: owners gain, workers lose; society becomes more unequal; agriculture becomes more labor-intensive; and incentives to create a technology that uses land more efficiently expand. Let's consider each of the first three aspects in turn, reserving discussion of technology to Chapter 3.

GAINS AND LOSSES

As the land-labor ratio increases, so that wages rise and rents fall,[9] owners must pay more for the labor they employ, and their revenues shrink – again, *if* both parties must strike their bargains in something approaching a competitive market. As we will see below, in times of extreme labor scarcity, owners may find it in their interest to collude against, or even to coerce, labor (acting on their own, through government, or by some combination of the two), compelling workers to accept less than their marginal product. Workers, by contrast, will want to preserve or expand the competitive market. Political conflict ensues.

Equality vs. Inequality

Economic historians often take the ratio of wages to rents, w/r, as a measure of equality (i.e., what does a worker earn relative to an owner?); or, conversely, r/w is treated as an indicator of economic *in*equality.[10] For consistency with other conventional measures (see below), let us for now focus on the latter ratio, r/w. That turns out by simple algebra to be

$$r/w = \frac{\alpha}{1-\alpha}(L/T). \qquad (1.4)$$

[9] Relative to each other, and in real rather than nominal terms. For reasons that we will see shortly, a sudden decrease in the labor supply is often accompanied by high inflation.

[10] See, for example, O'Rourke and Williamson (1999).

In words, the more abundant that labor is, or the scarcer land becomes, the more unequal will such an agricultural society be. Indeed, in this extremely simplified Cobb–Douglas setting, the ratio of land rents to wages increases linearly with the labor/land ratio.

As I show in an appendix to this chapter, other frequently used measures of inequality, such as the Gini index or the share of total income that accrues to the top decile or 1 percent (or arbitrary top × percent), vary monotonically with this ratio: As r/w rises, so does the Gini index or the share of total income accruing to the top earners.

Both increasing and decreasing inequality are likely to provoke resistance, but experience suggests paradoxically that *decreasing* inequality creates greater friction. The previous elite often resents its loss of status (signaled by fewer luxuries, less exclusivity, more modest dwellings) even more than its diminished income. Elites have, moreover, the social and political influence to resist such leveling, by such varied measures as sumptuary laws, ethnic or religious segregation, or (in the direst cases) pogroms or enslavement. [11] At a minimum, some form of political resistance seems almost inevitable.

Generalizing to Multiple Factors and Indirect Shocks

We focused earlier on a two-factor model of a purely agricultural economy, touching only briefly on more complex and realistic scenarios in considering factor mobility between sectors. The basic logic outlined above extends readily to a more industrial two-factor economy or sector, where the inputs are physical capital and labor, to a so-called knowledge economy (Iversen and Soskice 2019) that relies on labor and human capital, or to a three- or four- (or more) factor economy.[12] As indicated in the Introduction, we'll consider almost exclusively the "big four" factors: *land, labor, physical capital, and human capital.* As any one of these becomes more abundant, while the others hold roughly constant,

[11] Here, institutions matter, if only as a kind of friction. If we assume that elites control political institutions, they can employ these to retard their decline. As we will see in the case of the Black Death, their efforts may find only short-term success.

[12] The canonical Cobb–Douglas constant-returns production function readily generalizes to more than two factors, so long as the exponents continue to sum to one. For example, if one wanted to consider, in additional to land (T) and labor (L), physical capital (K) and human capital, or skill (S), the production function would simply be written as

$$Y = AK^{\alpha}T^{\beta}S^{\gamma}L^{!-\alpha-\beta-\gamma}.$$

returns to that factor decrease; as one factor becomes scarcer relative to the others, its earnings grow.[13]

Summary

Supply shocks, whether positive (increasing the supply of some factor of production) or negative (constricting it), change relative prices, affect inequality, and incentivize factor substitution and often – to be explored in Chapter 3 – technological innovation. Both directly and through those channels, such shocks usually present profound challenges to existing political and institutional arrangements. As the detailed studies in later chapters will show, societies often respond to a common shock in quite different ways. Our task will be to explain and predict the pattern of those responses.

ILLUSTRATIVE EXAMPLES

I propose to examine first of all supply shocks in the narrower sense of actual gains or losses of supply within a country. At the end of this section, I will consider briefly the indirect shocks that can arise from trade in goods and services.

Labor

Decrease The pool of available labor can rapidly contract (thus making incomes more equal) from plague- or war-induced *mortality*, or through emigration. In one extreme case, treated in detail in Chapter 4, the Black Death (bubonic plague), which struck Europe in 1348 and returned in subsequent waves until about 1420, may have reduced that continent's population by as much as two-thirds.[14] The Thirty Years War (1618–1648) is generally agreed to have reduced the population of the German-speaking lands by between a quarter and a third: The prewar

[13] Human capital, as we'll discuss more fully below, may be a partial exception. Because, as even Adam Smith noted (Thomas 2018, 110ff.), its social return exceeds its private return, and because of resultant strong agglomeration effects, accumulating more human capital may actually raise the returns to skill. Cf. Lucas (1990, 93–94).

[14] It seems certain that Europe in 1420 had barely a third as many inhabitants as in the early 1300s (Herlihy, 1997, p. 17); English population peaked in 1310 at about six million and fell by 1450 to just over two million (Clark, 2007, p. 30).

total of between 15 and 17 million inhabitants was reduced, at the end of the war, to between 10 and 13 million (Schmidt 2003, 91).[15]

Even more fatal than the Black Death may have been the first exposure of the indigenous peoples of the Americas to such common European diseases as smallpox, measles, and influenza, to which (unlike the Europeans) they had no acquired immunity. There, up to 95 percent of the population may have perished (Diamond 1997, chap. 11), facilitating the European colonization and contributing both to high wages in parts of North America and – for reasons we shall explore – to enserfment and slavery in much of the rest of the two continents.

Finally, the two World Wars and the influenza pandemic of 1919–1920, all of which decimated especially adults – in the case of the two great wars, males – of prime working age,[16] probably contributed significantly to the liberation (including enfranchisement) of women, the strengthening of labor unions, the rise of working-class militancy, and the great decline of inequality that began in the 1920s but reached its modern nadir between 1945 and 1975.

Large-scale *emigration*, however, albeit largely endogenous, was the engine that raised wages and lowered rents in nineteenth-century Europe (O'Rourke and Williamson 1999, chaps. 7 and 8). When up to a third of their population emigrated in the space of a few decades,[17] wages in such previously impoverished areas as Ireland, Denmark, Sweden, and Norway rose, between 1870 and 1913, from as little as a quarter, to over 90 percent, of British levels.[18]

[15] Wars of course are endogenous, and sometimes even anticipated. What is often unanticipated is the war's duration or the extent of its damage. No more in 1618 than in 1914 was the catastrophically long and destructive struggle anticipated that actually ensued.

[16] World War I killed some 9.5 million combatants and at least an equal number of civilians; about 13 percent of the males of military age (15–49 years) died in combat in both Germany and France, 12 percent in the Central Powers as a whole (Winter, 2001). World War II entailed some 60 million deaths, and in the worldwide influenza epidemic of 1918–1919 at least 30 million perished (Patterson & Pyle, 1991).

[17] Between the 1840s and World War I, a total of some 60 million emigrated from Europe, the pace rising from some 300,000 annually in the late 1840s to almost 800,000 annually in the later 1880s, and then to 1.3 million annually in the last years before World War I (Torp 2005, 43). In the single decade of the 1880s, over 14 percent of Ireland's population and over 9 percent of Norway's emigrated (O'Rourke and Williamson 1999, 119 and 122).

[18] Local wages as a percentage of UK wages, 1870 vs. 1913: Sweden, 28 vs. 98; Norway, 32 vs. 93; Denmark, 36 vs. 102; Ireland, 49 vs. 90 (O'Rourke and Williamson 1999, 17).

Increase The supply of labor can grow almost as rapidly, chiefly through population "explosions" or waves of immigration. Population for example increased rapidly in much of the world in the eighteenth and nineteenth centuries , in Russia throughout the second half of the nineteenth century (see Chapter 5), and in Asia and Africa from the middle of the twentieth century.[19] Such an expansion of numbers rarely happens because of an increased birth rate, but rather when pre-existing high fertility encounters a sudden *decline in mortality* – a weakening of the "positive checks" to population that the Rev. Mr. Thomas Malthus memorably extolled, chiefly famine and disease.

Famine receded for two reasons: the introduction of more nutritious and land-efficient crops from the New World,[20] above all potatoes and maize (Braudel 1981, I: 163–172; Nunn & Qian, 2011); and better transport, above all railroads, that allowed the alleviation of local famines[21] – which, as Amartya Sen has noted, most famines are (Sen 1982, chaps. 4 and 10). Disease similarly yielded to improvements in sanitation, immunizations, and (probably least important, in terms of lives saved) antibiotics (Gordon 2016, 215).

Beginning even before Neolithic times, population has also increased rapidly in some areas through **immigration**, voluntary or forced, peaceful or violent. The earliest agriculturalists, as Jared Diamond has observed, regularly displaced or exterminated pastoral or hunter-gatherer groups.[22] Every ancient state captured and transported slaves, and the Roman Republic sometimes compelled free citizens to settle on newly conquered land (W. Scheidel 2004). In the thirteenth and early fourteenth centuries, west European settlers, facing growing population pressure, moved in large numbers to the thinly populated areas of central and eastern Europe (the original "Drang nach Osten"). And, of course, the nineteenth-century European emigrants mentioned earlier became immigrants into those parts of the New World now styled "areas of recent settlement."

19 India's population more than tripled between 1951 and 2011, from 361 million to 1.2 billion, while China's more than doubled, from 557 million to 1.34 billion. Navaneetham 2011, 13; Jan Lahmeyer, "populstat," www.populstat.info/Asia/chinac.htm , accessed 3 November 2019.

20 As noted earlier, this was a rare instance of a genuinely exogenous technological shock.

21 For convincing evidence on the importance of railroads in bringing about convergence of regional food prices and reducing the incidence of famine in India, see Burgess and Donaldson (2012) and Donaldson (2018).

22 A striking example is the almost complete displacement, probably in the third and second millennia BC, of Khoisan and Pygmy peoples in Africa by Bantu farmers (Diamond 1997, 376–401).

Barring any compensating change, these sudden augmentations of the labor pool will hold down wages and increase inequality – as, indeed, econometric estimates suggest resulted from the nineteenth-century waves of immigration into the USA.[23]

LAND

Societies typically gain or lose land through conquest and annexation; more rarely, through reclamation (e.g., from wasteland or the sea or from natural or man-made disasters [flooding, erosion].[24])

In predominantly agricultural economies, a higher land/labor ratio meant more product and higher per capita production.[25] For precisely this reason, pre-industrial rulers often sought to conquer or to colonize more territory. Eighteenth-century Europe saw recurrent warfare, shifting of boundaries, and even partition of some states (notably Poland); as late as the 1840s, the USA seized by conquest over half of the territory of Mexico. In the eighteenth and nineteenth centuries, European settlers colonized the Americas, Australia, New Zealand, and substantial parts of Africa.[26] As detailed in Chapter 6, Hitler's genocidal dream of *Lebensraum*, which (as concretized in the *Generalplan Ost*) would have expelled or exterminated some 40 million Slavs to gain land that German peasants were to settle, may be regarded as the last gasp of an already obsolete European colonialism (Tooze 2008, 462ff.)

To be sure, as Frederick Jackson Turner famously noted in the US case, the availability of seemingly unlimited land – an "open frontier" – entailed low levels of inequality (Turner 1993, chap. 2), that is, a high w/r ratio (above, Equation 1.4). But that was true only to the extent that a society's production remained predominantly agricultural. In 1890, the point at which Turner regarded the frontier as closed, American agriculture constituted for the first time less than half of both total production and total employment and was waning rapidly in importance. *(Historical*

23 "Had there been no US immigration over the forty years between 1870 and 1910, it has been estimated that the unskilled real wage would have been higher in 1910 by 34 percent ..." (Williamson 2005, 24).

24 A wide-ranging overview of reclamation from the sea (and, often, of renewed loss to the sea), from Etruscan times to the modern Netherlands, is Wagret (1968).

25 See above, Equation 1.1; from which it follows that per capita production, Y/L, is equal to $A(T/L)^{\alpha}$.

26 The European empires were of course more extensive; I count here only the territories that were taken for settlement, for example, South Africa and Rhodesia.

Statistics of the United States, 1789–1945, chap. D, 1949, 63). By the year 2000, farmland rents in England, which had still constituted almost a quarter of national income in 1760, had fallen to 0.2 percent (G. Clark 2007, 198); and today, agriculture accounts for less than 1 percent even of US GDP (Bureau of Economic Analysis 2019, 11). While in earlier epochs it was decisive, today it is only in the poorest countries that the land-labor ratio still matters for overall inequality.[27] In an industrial economy, defined by high capital investment, the ratio of human and physical capital to low-skill labor influences (but by no means determines) the level of inequality. And, as Gregory Clark has emphasized, the strong complementarity of those two factors of production means that they are highly correlated, both across societies and intertemporally within them (G. Clark 2007, 204–207).

PHYSICAL CAPITAL

Gain

Marx described capital as "stored-up labor": By devoting some share of current effort to the creation of implements or infrastructure, future labor is made more productive. Even in foraging societies, time spent on the production of axes, bows and arrows, weirs, or baskets made future hunting, fishing, and gathering more efficient. In early Neolithic societies, time devoted to the manufacture of hoes and primitive plows, or simply to the clearing of land, meant that a future hour of labor would produce a higher yield. More complex early agrarian societies invested in elaborate irrigation systems, roads, harbors, ships, and wagons that again multiplied the output per unit of labor – and, additionally, facilitated the drastically improved productivity that (as Adam Smith memorably apostrophized) flowed from specialization. Well before the Industrial Revolution, enterprises began to acquire physical capital on credit, that is, by "renting" the purchasing power of others' stored-up labor. We have evidence for elaborate systems of banking, borrowing, and lending in antiquity (Renger et al. 2003), and the systems of finance and credit became even more elaborate during the European Renaissance, especially in the northern Italian city-states. In all ages, lenders have sought the

[27] Agriculture constitutes a little over 6 percent of world GDP; it makes up over 40 percent of GDP in only nine countries, among them Chad, Somalia, and Mali. (Central Intelligence Agency 2018).

highest rate of return, to be found where capital was most scarce relative to labor (high L/K ratio), or technology most advanced, since the return on capital (cf. Equation 1.3) is simply

$$r = Y_K = \alpha A(K/L)^{\alpha-1} \equiv \alpha A(L/K)^{1-\alpha} \qquad (1.5).$$

Physical capital accumulated for most of human history slowly and in waves, with great gains (e.g., in the Roman Imperial period) followed by massive losses. The transformation to steadily accelerating gains began during what de Vries has called the "industrious revolution," in mid-seventeenth-century Europe (De Vries 2008): first in transportation and agriculture, then in manufacturing, and centrally in the Netherlands and England (Neal and Cameron 2016, chaps. 5 and 7), which gave birth to the Industrial Revolution of the eighteenth century.

The Industrial Revolution meant, almost by definition, that machinery, especially when powered by fossil fuels, became the most productive form of physical capital. While in the earliest phases, for example, in England, most investment came from domestic sources, foreign loans, ownership claims (portfolio investment), and direct investment soon flowed across political boundaries. In some cases, market-driven investment failed to satisfy rulers' political or strategic needs; and then either state-led investment (e.g., in Imperial Germany and Meiji Japan) or the terror-fueled "forced draft" industrialization of Stalinism curtailed consumption and conscripted domestic savings to create new physical capital at break-neck speed. By either route, from the eighteenth until the last quarter of the twentieth century, the world separated increasingly into a few countries or regions with high capital-labor ratios, high standards of living, and (at least by world standards) low levels of inequality; and the great majority of "less developed" countries (LDCs), with far less capital per worker and higher levels of poverty and inequality: what Lant Pritchett may have been the first to call the "Great Divergence" (Pritchett 1997). This violated economic theory, which held that, if similar technologies were available to all countries, returns to capital would be far higher in countries that had little of it (see again Equation 1.4); hence the poor countries should attract more investment (Lucas 1990), grow more rapidly, and quickly achieve roughly the same level of output and wages as the wealthier ones (so-called convergence theory) (Barro and Sala-I-Martin 2003, 462–465). Political instability, and consequent insecurity of investment, was usually invoked to explain the poorer countries' failure to attract investment; and the spectacularly rapid "catch-up" of countries like South Korea and Taiwan has seemed to validate the point.

An equally significant factor may have been a lack of human capital (see below), the increasingly essential complement of physical capital.

Resistance from existing owners of scarce capital, often augmented by ideology or mistaken economic theories, sometimes led governments to wall out foreign investment and to seek some form of "import-substituting industrialization" (Frieden 2006, chap. 13) – thus forgoing the higher wages that an increased K/L ratio would have guaranteed. Fortunately, since about 1980 much of the less developed world, beginning with China but including much of South and Southeast Asia, Latin America, and significant parts of Africa, has begun (or resumed) the importation and accumulation of physical capital. In consequence, global inequality has fallen significantly (Bourguignon 2015, 42).

Loss

War is a major destroyer of physical capital. Artillery and aerial bombing in our own age, sieges and plunder in earlier ones, have rapidly annihilated arduously constructed houses, buildings, factories, equipment, roads, harbors – even, as in the infamous case of ancient Alexandria, libraries. More rarely, natural disasters obliterate physical capital: For example, a volcanic eruption and an ensuing tsunami appear to have destroyed the palaces and harbors of the ancient Minoan civilization on Crete (Antonopoulos 1992); the great Japanese Kantō earthquake of 1923, and the resultant tsunami and fires, are supposed to have destroyed some 90 percent of the structures in Yokohama and 45 percent of those in Tokyo (Schencking 2008, 296). More slowly but no less certainly, failures of upkeep, in many cases attendant on state failure (e.g., in the declining Roman Empire) (Ward-Perkins 2005, chap. 6), erode and eventually render useless what had been highly productive investments.[28] The destruction of capital causes wages and the standard of living to fall (indeed, that is often the aim in wartime[29]), surviving capital commands

[28] Present-day Venezuela is a vivid, but fortunately an isolated, present-day example. See, for example, "Cutbacks, Disrepair, and Bacteria Plague Venezuela's Water System," New York Times, October 20, 2018, p. A8.

[29] Probably the first example in modern warfare was Sherman's famous "march to the sea," from Atlanta to Savannah, in the US Civil War. In proposing the action, "Sherman assured Grant he would accomplish 'the utter destruction' of Georgia's roads, houses, and people . . . . He aimed to shift the whole calculus of the war, . . . not to hunt down an army but to destroy the civilian foundations of the war." (Chernow 2017, 447).

a higher return, and inequality normally rises. While in a modern economy the loss of physical capital can often be made good, so long as human capital survives (Barro and Sala-I-Martin 2003, 244), in earlier ages advanced civilizations often simply succumbed to such losses.

HUMAN CAPITAL

Gain

By far the quickest way to accrue human capital is – as with physical capital – to import it, i.e., to encourage high-skill immigration. During and after Europe's sixteenth- and seventeenth-century wars of religion, some nascent states (the Netherlands, Switzerland, Prussia) eagerly recruited talented refugees: The Elector Friedrich Wilhelm's Edict of Potsdam (1685), welcoming and subsidizing the immigration of persecuted French Huguenots to Prussia and Brandenburg, is a particularly famous (and opportunistic) example (Dölemeyer 2006, 84–91), covered in more detail in Chapter 7. The early Latter-day Saints (Mormons) put a high premium on bringing to their "Zion" (Utah) skilled converts (carpenters, blacksmiths, miners, gunsmiths, millwrights, even buttonmakers: (Taylor 1965, 102)) from the United Kingdom.[30] In Israel, massive Russian immigration in the 1990s greatly augmented that country's pool of scientific and technical talent: By 1997, they had increased Israel's working-age population by 15 percent, and 60 percent of the Russian immigrants (as opposed to roughly 30 percent of native-born Israelis) had a university education (Cohen and Hsieh 2001, 3). Even today, high-skill immigration remains surprisingly uncontroversial in most countries (e.g., Hainmueller and Hiscox 2010), likely because, alone among major factors of production, its positive externalities often outweigh any depressing effect on high-skill wages.[31]

[30] In the Census of 1870, one-quarter of Utah's inhabitants were immigrants from the United Kingdom, and their Utah-born children constituted at least another quarter (Jensen 1994). As Taylor notes, " . . . the Mormons had every reason to try to record accurately the skills of their emigrants"; their ledgers show that at least two-thirds were skilled or professional, with the largest single contingents being miners (15 percent), metal and engineering workers (10 percent), textile workers (9 percent), and carpenters (7 percent). Only a fifth were classified as "general laborers." (Taylor 1965, 150).

[31] Lucas famously estimated that "a 10 percent increase in the average quality of those with whom I work increases my productivity by 3.6 percent." (Lucas 1990, 94). Barro and Lee also find a high rate of social return on human capital: Each

Governments however sometimes engage in "crash" investment in human capital no less than (or simultaneously with) investment in physical capital. The USA moved from elite-only to almost universal high-school education in the space of thirty years, affording it technical skills that proved crucial in World War II industries (Goldin 1998). The USSR, even as it was pouring investment into new industrial plants, achieved almost universal literacy and a high degree of expertise in the physical sciences and technology in an even shorter span of time.[32] Normally, however, human capital, like physical capital, accrues gradually, as more in each generation are exposed to education and accumulate more years of training (Barro and Lee 2013).

Loss

In a few cases, domestic revolutionaries or foreign conquerors have sought deliberately to destroy human capital by what might be called (to coin an ugly term) "intellicide," i.e., the annihilation of a nation's or an ethnicity's best educated and most talented people. The Nazis targeted the Polish intelligentsia, the Khmer Rouge the Cambodian educated classes (Nhem 2013).[33] In other cases, an ethnic or religious minority abundant in human capital has been driven into exile; or a long-running civil war, as in present-day Syria, induces the most talented to flee first. The effect, and sometimes the aim, has been to raise returns to the remaining owners of human capital. Much more rarely, disease kills or disables disproportionately the highly educated. As we'll see later, because learning in the Middle Ages centered on the monasteries, and monks lived in close proximity and daily contact, the Black Death seems to have sharply reduced the numbers of scribes capable of reproducing manuscripts by hand. More often, human capital, like physical capital, simply deteriorates from lack of new investment in it. Neglect or outright

additional year of education, according to their estimates, has a rate of return of between 5 and 12 percent (Robert J. Barro and Jong-Wha Lee 2010, 39).

32 According to census data, 30 percent of the Russian population was literate in 1897; by 1939, literacy in the USSR was 87 percent (B. Mironov 1991, 245). On scientific education, see Graham (1993).

33 "... during the war Poland lost [to German executions] 45 percent of her physicians and dentists, 57 percent of her attorneys, ... 40 percent of her professors, 30 percent of her technicians, and more than 18 percent of her clergy." Richard Lukas, *The Forgotten Holocaust*, quoted in Piotrowski (1998, 23). The Nazis actually denoted this part of their Polish mass murder the *Intelligenzaktion*.

collapse of a nation's educational system – think again of contemporary Venezuela – leads to a rapid loss of human capital. Even where the failure is temporary, as in the closure of most of China's schools and universities during the "Great Proletarian Cultural Revolution" (Giles et al. 2019), or of elementary and high schools during the recent pandemic, the loss of human capital is never fully made good. Like loss of physical capital, depletion of human capital leads to greater inequality, lower wages, and – because of its strong complementarity with physical capital – slower economic growth.

TRADE SHOCKS

When trade opens between one region and another with different factor endowments – whether through the opening of a new trade route, the overcoming of some previous geographic or political obstacle, or a technological innovation that makes transport faster and cheaper – the effect is exactly the same as if the importing region had acquired more of a factor of production, or the exporting one had lost some of that factor. Trade in products, as Heckscher and Ohlin saw over a century ago, amounts to trade in the factors that are used intensively in creating those products. Importing grain or meat, both land-intensive products, has exactly the same effect as would acquiring more land; exporting agricultural products, the same effect as losing some land. In the importing region, land prices fall (and wages, at least relative to land rents, rise); in the exporting one, land prices rise and the relative wage of labor falls. In the importing region, inequality decreases; in the exporting one, inequality grows.

By the same token, a region that exports goods that are intensive in low-skill labor sees rising wages and falling inequality; while in one that imports such goods, wages fall and inequality rises.[34] In effect, the exporting country "loses" some low-skill labor – instead of exporting the workers, it exports products that embody their labor – and the importing one "gains" low-skill labor. In the exporting country, labor becomes relatively scarcer; in the importing one, more abundant.

That of course is not the whole story. As David Ricardo first showed the world two hundred years ago, specialization according to comparative advantage makes both regions better off. As we shall see in the case of

[34] From this standpoint, the rise in inequality in many labor-abundant countries over recent decades is puzzling. For one suggested answer, see Zhu and Trefler (2005).

nineteenth-century Russia, even opening easier trade among the regions of a single country can also foster specialization and thus improve productivity.

The "first globalization" of the late nineteenth and early twentieth centuries brought the abundant prairies and pampas of the New World to land-scarce Europe, as surely as if some tectonic shift had enlarged Europe's land mass. Some European governments opened their economies to such imports, i.e., took advantage of the newly available land, and prospered; but many did not, responding to farmers' pressures by erecting tariff barriers that effectively "walled out" the new land.

That same first globalization brought the abundant capital of Europe – or, chiefly, of the United Kingdom – in the form of investment and capital-intensive goods, into such capital-scarce regions as India and the Americas. India as a colony could not, and South America under pressure from its agricultural exporters would not, erect barriers to the importation of Britain's capital-intensive goods. The opening, at the end of the twentieth century, of China, the former Soviet Empire, and South and Southeast Asia to the world economy created a new abundance of labor in the developed economies of the globe. And the opening of the internet made the human capital of Silicon Valley, but also of many other talent-rich areas around the globe, available to the whole world. In each case, trade has improved the lot of all the participating countries and regions – perhaps unequally, but nonetheless significantly (Bourguignon 2015, chap. 2).

Similarly, sudden closure of a trade route amounts to an abrupt reduction in access to an imported factor – or to goods whose production is intensive in that factor. Among the chief causes of unanticipated closures are wartime blockades (e.g., of Germany in World War I, discussed in detail in Chapter 6) and natural disasters (e.g., hurricanes, earthquakes, volcanic eruptions).[35] Depression-induced waves of protectionism, as in the 1930s (Frieden 2006, chap. 9), are a borderline case: The crash was mostly unanticipated, but at least in the larger economies – pre-eminently the United States – the choice to erect protectionist barriers (the infamous Smoot-Hawley Tariff) was endogenous.

[35] The volcanic eruption and tsunami that are believed to have destroyed most of Minoan civilization's physical capital (above, p. 19) also destroyed the ships in and near its busy harbor apparently irreversibly choking off trade throughout the region.

Bear in mind, however, that I want to focus here on *unanticipated* shocks – or, at a minimum, ones that are far from fully anticipated. International agreements that lower barriers to trade are endogenous and, hence, usually anticipated: People see them coming and can, at least in principle, adjust.[36] The same is true of the building of new roads or canals. By contrast, trade is opened exogenously in two principal ways: the unanticipated discovery of a new trade route (e.g., Vasco da Gama's opening of sea route between Europe and Asia), or some radical innovation in the technology of transport or communication: for example, railroads, steamships, containerization; the transatlantic telegraph cable (Ejrnaes and Persson 2010; Steinwender 2018) or the radio. As I will discuss more fully in Chapter 3, such innovations almost always originate endogenously: They address some pressing social or economic need and relieve some troublesome bottleneck. What makes them exogenous is their "overshooting": They lower transport costs more radically or quickly than even their inventors or early adopters could anticipate.

An exogenous shock that either curtails or expands trade *is*, then, a supply shock. The sudden opening of the Atlantic economy in the nineteenth century through the largely unforeseen introduction of railroads and steamships, by making it possible for Europe to export labor-intensive goods, curtailed the relative supply of European labor almost as surely (if far less tragically) as had the Black Death of the fourteenth century. It presented the same kind of political opportunities and challenges: Should the market be allowed to operate, wages to rise, inequality to decline, and the power of the "lower orders" to grow? Or would existing elites manage to stifle the working of the market? And, above all, what would determine the outcome of such a struggle?

CONCLUSION

Supply shocks unavoidably present political challenges. They threaten, or promise, sudden changes in returns to the owners of land, labor, and human and physical capital; sudden increases or decreases in inequality; sudden shifts of political power and alterations of political institutions. Indeed, as I will try to show in subsequent chapters, they have been the

[36] Apparently the Cobden-Chevalier Treaty of 1860, often credited with beginning the nineteenth-century period of free trade and globalization, was an exception: To frustrate protectionist interests in France, negotiations were kept secret until the actual signing of the agreement.

underlying cause of surprisingly many fundamental political conflicts. More to the point, what determines the outcome of such conflicts are the three crucial factors I have outlined above: elasticity of substitution, exit options, and the possibility of a technological remedy. To see this in greater detail, I will examine an array of cases in which exogenous supply shocks have caused political and social upheavals, to which governments in similar situations have responded very differently, essentially either allowing the market to work its changes or acting to stymie the market and preserve (or intensify) the existing order.

First, however, we must analyze in greater detail what determines the strength with which a supply shock is embraced or resisted. That will be the task of the next chapter.

Appendix to Chapter 1 The Equivalence of Major Measures of Inequality

Recall that in our illustrative Cobb–Douglas world, where the only factors of production are land and labor (Equation 1.1 in the main text), the share of total income that accrues to capital will always be α; and, necessarily, labor's total share will be the remainder, $1 - \alpha$.[37] Recall that the Gini index represents the area between the 45° line and the Lorenz curve, which represents cumulative share of total income, starting with those who earn the least.[38] Since, in our simplified world, each unit of labor receives exactly w and each unit of land exactly r, and we assume $w < r$, the Lorenz curve consists of two straight segments, intersecting at the point $(L, 1 - \alpha)$ (Figure A1.1). Now suppose that L increases, i.e., L becomes relatively more abundant. We have already seen that an increase in L raises the rent-labor ratio, r/w. But it is intuitively obvious that, as L increases, for example, to L^*, while labor's share of total income

[37] Consider the case of labor: If, as already shown, the wage per unit of labor (hour, person-year, etc.) is $(1 - \alpha)A(T/L)^{\alpha}$(above, Equation 1.2), then the total income of labor must be simply the total units of labor L times the wage per unit of labor, i.e., $L(1 - \alpha)A(T/L)^{\alpha}$; but, since $L^1L^{-\alpha} = L^{1-\alpha}$, the product $Lw = (1 - \alpha)AT^{\alpha}L^{1-\alpha}$; but this is just the same as $(1 - \alpha)Y$, i.e., share $(1 - \alpha)$ of total production (see again Equation 1.1).

[38] If everyone earns exactly the same income, the cumulative share is the 45-degree line; hence the more the actual distribution deviates from it, the greater is the inequality of incomes.

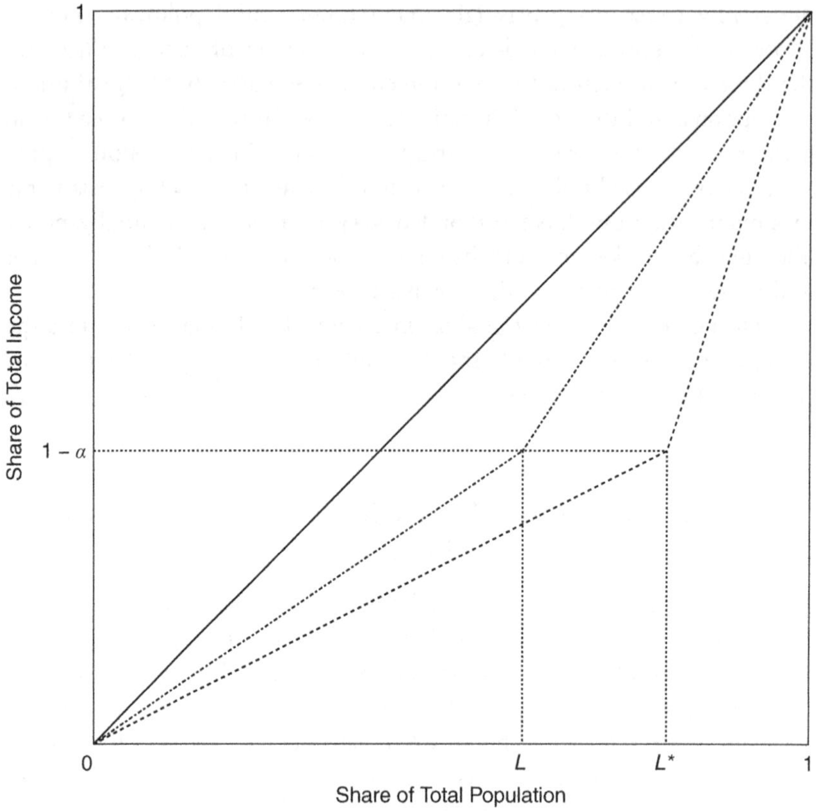

Figure A1.1 Gini index in a two-factor world[39]

remains at 1–α, the area between the Lorenz curve and the 45° line, i.e., the Gini coefficient, must also increase.

Similarly, consider the case where the top decile (or, by extension, other top percentile) includes all, and only, landowners. Then the top decile will receive total income αY. If the class of landowners expands, to encompass, say, 20 percent of the entire population, the r/w ratio will decline; but the top decile will receive only half the share that it did before. If the class of landowners shrinks to, let us say, 5 percent of the total, raising the r/w ratio, the top decile will still receive all of αY, plus some share (to be exact, 5/95, or a little over 5 percent) of (1–α)Y. In other

[39] All of the population who are not laborers (i.e., all to the right of L or L*) are landowners, whose share of total income is α. The Gini is the area between the Lorenz curve (consisting here of only two line segments) and the 45-degree line.

words, as the class of landowners expands, holding all else equal, the r/w ratio falls and the top decile's share of total income shrinks; as the class of landowners contracts, increasing r/w, the top decile's share increases.

The logic extends readily to an economy of more than two factors. If, as is true in the great majority of settings, labor (by construction, low-skill labor, high skills being captured under the heading of "human capital") is the least well compensated, we can continue to take the ratio of wages to the returns on the other factors (or to some composite of the others) as the index of equality: As that ratio declines, inequality rises.[40]

[40] The strong complementarity, and the high empirical correlation, of human and physical capital (Clark 2007, chap. 10) often makes it useful to treat these as a single factor; while the relative insignificance of land in most advanced economies (Clark 2007, 198–199) means that it can often be safely ignored. Thus we may wind up with a model in which there are only two inputs, namely labor and "augmented capital," i.e., a composite of human and physical capital.

2

Who Adjusts to a Supply Shock and Who Resists It

Three Determining Factors

Why, faced with a supply shock, do some societies adjust with seeming ease, while others are riven by conflict? Why do the losers from a supply shock – owners of factors that have unexpectedly become relatively more abundant, and therefore cheaper – accept the reallocation of incomes and wealth with relative grace (often after initial resistance), while others resist to the point of changing institutions, coercing, or expropriating (or even liquidating) the presumptive winners, or seeking to conquer from other lands more of the factor that is suddenly pricier and in short supply?

The governing principle is simple economy of effort (Zipf 1949): resistance is costly, extreme resistance extremely costly; and rational actors will bear that cost only to the extent that it promises a commensurate reward or will avert some yet costlier loss. Elites in nineteenth-century Britain, faced with growing wealth and power of the masses, offered only slight resistance to extending the parliamentary franchise; but contemporary elites in Wilhelmine Germany increasingly restricted the franchise or resorted to electoral manipulation to entrench their disproportionate power (Ziblatt 2009). While other factors were at work, it was hardly irrelevant that British elites were moving smoothly from landholding into industry and commerce, while German Junkerdom remained wedded to the agrarian income of their East Elbian estates (cf. Schonhardt-Bailey 1991).

Our prior question, therefore, is just this: Why do some supply shocks threaten only moderate losses in some countries or regions, while the same shock portends catastrophic deprivation elsewhere? Nor are only elites affected. The present-day "China shock," by in effect radically expanding the developed countries' supply of low-skill labor, threatened to lower the wages of those countries' low-skill workers. In the USA and the UK, those workers responded with furious resistance (Colantone and Stanig 2018; Jensen et al. 2017); in much of northern

Continental Europe, by contrast, similarly situated workers have adjusted with relative ease.[1]

To move the question back one step farther: Why does the same supply shock threaten radical alteration of returns to factors in some countries but have much less impact in others? I will suggest that four variables determine the extent of threat and, consequently, the difficulty of adjustment: elasticity of substitution; factor mobility (among sectors); availability of exit (to a different region or jurisdiction); and availability of a factor-saving technology. I reserve the issue of technology for a separate chapter, focusing here on the solutions that require no leap of innovation. Once again, to fix ideas, I will focus on the simple case of a two-factor agrarian model, where the only factors of production are land and labor.

FACTOR SUBSTITUTION

As labor becomes more expensive relative to land (or, equivalently, land cheaper relative to labor), farmers will of course seek to substitute land for some labor in production. We can perhaps see the problem more clearly set out in Figure 2.1.

Again invoking essential economics, the curved line is an *isoquant*; it represents all of the various combinations of labor and land that can be used, under prevailing technology, to produce a given quantity of a good, for example, a ton of wheat or a thousand kilocalories.[2] The two dotted lines depict factor prices, that is, the rate at which labor trades for land. Along the shallower, more finely dotted, line, labor is cheap relative to land: one unit of land trades for more than one unit of labor. Along the steeper line, labor is expensive relative to land: one unit of labor trades for more than one unit of land. The profit-maximizing farmer produces at the point on the isoquant where the slope of the isoquant (more technically, the marginal rate of technical substitution) is equal to the slope of the

[1] One important variable appears to be a society's preexisting economic inequality. For reasons that remain unclear, greater economic equality predisposes present-day economies to adjust more smoothly (Flaherty and Rogowski 2020).

[2] In a typical two-factor production function, we obtain the isoquant simply by holding the quantity of production constant at some level we will denote Y_0, and solving for T in terms of L. Thus, if $Y_0 = AT^{\alpha}L^{1-\alpha}$, we can simply re-state this as $T^{\alpha} = (Y_0/A)L^{\alpha-1}$ and, taking both sides to the power $1/\alpha$, obtain $T = (Y_0/A)^{1/\alpha}L^{1-1/\alpha}$. But since Y_0 and A are in this context both constants, we can set $k = (Y_0/A)^{1/\alpha}$ and obtain $T = kL^{1-1/\alpha}$. This gives us the kind of convex isoquant shown here, e.g., if $\alpha = 1/3, T = kL^{-2}$.

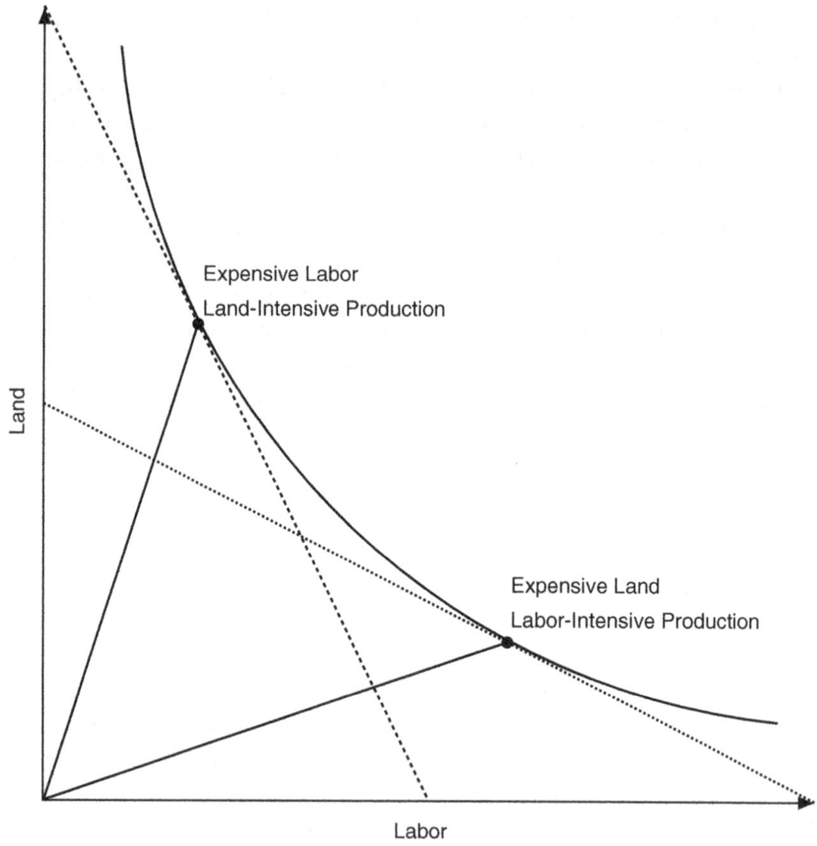

Figure 2.1 Factor substitution: Expensive land vs. expensive labor

price line: when labor is cheap, the farmer uses more labor than land; when labor is dear, more land than labor. Finally, at the given point of production, the actual ratio of land to labor inputs is given by the slope of the ray (the solid line from the origin) that connects the point of production to the origin. As illustrated here, cheap labor entails the use of more than one unit of labor for each unit of land, whereas expensive labor uses several units of land for each unit of labor.

Under the production function whose isoquant is sketched here, it is moderately easy to substitute land for labor; but it will sometimes be easier, sometimes harder. How can we measure this adaptability? Starting in the 1930s, the economists John Hicks and Joan Robinson, working independently of each other, developed a precise measure of substitutability for any given production function: its *elasticity of substitution*. This measure asks, in essence, by what percentage factor proportions change in response to a 1 percent change in the factors' relative price. In the case we are considering here, if the price of labor in terms of land (in Figure 2.1, the shallower line) increases (grows steeper) by 1 percent, by what percentage does the ratio of land to labor used in production (the slope of the ray from the origin in Figure 2.1) rise?

Although it is far from evident at first, elasticity basically measures the *curvature of the isoquant*: As an isoquant becomes more curved, elasticity (i.e., factor substitutability) declines. Were the isoquant a straight line, that is, not curved at all, elasticity would be infinite: the slope of the factor-proportions ray would change as one moved higher on the isoquant, but the relative price of the two factors would not change at all. The denominator of our defining ratio would be zero, and one factor would be a perfect substitute for the other. At the other extreme, an isoquant that was "curved" to the maximum extent, forming an L-shaped right angle,[3] would have zero elasticity: no matter how great the increase in the relative price of labor (the steepness of the price line), the proportion of the factors used in production (the ray from the origin) would not change.

The constant-returns Cobb-Douglas production functions that we have used for illustration have, by design and for convenience, a constant elasticity of substitution of one: at every point on any of its isoquants, a 1 percent increase in the relative cost of labor would raise the ratio of land to labor actually used in production by exactly 1 percent. Cobb-Douglas, however, is merely a special case of a larger family of production functions characterized by *constant elasticity of substitution* (c.e.s.), and one can easily generate c.e.s. production functions with elasticities greater than one (hence flatter than Cobb-Douglas) or less than one (more curved).

This matters politically because, where producers can easily substitute one factor for another – where substitution is highly elastic – they can adjust with ease, even to an unexpected change in relative factor prices. They face a milder threat and are far likelier to accept the verdict of the market. In contrast, where substitution is inelastic, an unexpected change in the relative price of factors will far likelier provoke political resistance. Owners of the factor that is losing value, and producers who use intensively the factor whose price is rising, have augmented incentives to employ political action, collusion, regulation, or coercion to obstruct the working of markets; while owners of the newly scarce factor, and

[3] These are conventionally labeled Leontieff production functions.

producers who use the newly abundant factor intensively, will often combine to oppose such obstruction, forcefully if necessary. Such conflicts can easily morph into challenges to existing institutions of governance, especially where these empower (as is often the case) the holders of the previously scarce factor or production.[4] Institutional conflict often focuses on a widening or narrowing of the effective franchise, or what some have called the "selectorate." In the most extreme cases, rulers seek to expand supply of a newly scarce factor through conquest.[5]

The sudden and extreme labor shortage that followed Europe's fourteenth-century Black Death – an example to be discussed in greater detail in Chapter 4 – created pressure for wages to rise and land values to decline. In England and much of western Europe, landowners responded, after initial resistance, by switching from labor-intensive to more land-intensive production: meat, milk, and wool displaced grain and flax. As we will see, climate and soil worked against such factor substitution in eastern Europe. Compelled by nature either to remain labor-intensive or to abandon production, east European landowners turned to costly coercion, enserfing their peasants and forcing them to accept compensation far below their marginal product.

FACTOR MOBILITY

We have implicitly been considering a single-sector economy, devoted only to agriculture. In a more realistic multi-sector setting, owners of a factor threatened with declining returns, and with inelastic factor substitution in its current employment, have at least a hypothetical possibility of putting that factor to a different use – of moving it to a different sector. If agriculture contracts in the face of imported foodstuffs, agricultural labor may be able to move into manufacturing or services; land devoted to farming, on the other hand, can rarely move so easily into another

4 E.g., in premodern agrarian societies, where land was typically the scarce factor of production, political institutions normally empowered landowners.

5 A fictional but all too plausible depiction was Clancy (1986), in which the Soviet Union's sudden loss (due to a terrorist attack) of a large part of its petroleum supply impelled a desperate effort to conquer supplies. The last century's most catastrophic real-world case, discussed in detail in Chapter 6, was Hitler's explicit effort to conquer, depopulate, and resettle eastern *Lebensraum* (Hitler 2003 (1928); Tooze 2008).

sector: it is usually an *immobile* factor.[6] Owners of factors characterized both by low elasticity of substitution and low factor mobility are likelier to resist any fall in the returns to their asset – unless, that is, they have some possibility of exit.

EXIT

As Bates and Lien first argued, and Boix expounded more fully, owners of a threatened factor sometimes have a third possibility of adjustment: mobility not just among sectors, but among regions or jurisdictions; they can physically move their imperiled asset to an environment where it still commands a higher return (Bates and Lien 1985; Boix 2003). The most obvious examples are *labor* and *human capital*, which (depending on transport costs and political barriers) can emigrate. The nineteenth-century "Atlantic economy" saw massive migration from densely populated Europe to the thinly populated Americas (Torp 2005, 43ff.), which also proved a magnet for the abundant labor of Asia; the later twentieth and early twenty-first centuries have witnessed powerful migratory pressures, only partly caused by war or crime, out of the Middle East, Africa, and Central America.

These are usually drastic and costly solutions, hence resorted to only when neither factor substitution nor factor mobility seems possible. Even moving to a different region of the same country, speaking perhaps a different dialect or practicing a different religion, can be costly: the German East–West migration of the later nineteenth century, the Great Migration of Black Americans out of the postbellum South into northern industry, and the Italian South–North movement after World War II are familiar examples. Especially in previous centuries, migration to a different country often entailed evading capture (in the land of emigration, that of immigration, or by authorities or predators in between), learning a new language, adapting to a new culture, and severing most ties to one's closest friends and relatives.[7]

6 The main alternative uses for land are housing and tourism. The first depends highly on proximity to densely populated areas; the second, on advantages of scenery or wildlife.

7 The costs and risks, and the reasons for bearing them (in this case, poverty and religious persecution) are portrayed movingly in Jan Troell's twin films of the early 1970s on Swedish emigration to Minnesota in the nineteenth century, *The Emigrants* and *The New Land.*

At the same time, such a shock incentivizes the potential losers to erect obstacles to exit: for example, to forbid emigration or impede foreign investment. In the most infamous example, discussed at length below, fifteenth-century Eastern European landowners met labor scarcity and the threat that their tenants would migrate to the higher wages of western Europe by simply "binding" tenants to the land – that is, using juridical and physical force to block their exit. Much more recently, Soviet-era elites erected physical walls and invented the crime of *Republikflucht* ("flight from the [East German] republic") to hold their scarce workers captive and keep wages suppressed.

But "entry" options also matter. Owners of a factor devalued through some unanticipated sudden surplus may seek to recruit (usually from abroad) more of the complementary factor that has become relatively scarce. Where labor is rapidly becoming more abundant, as in most of nineteenth-century Europe, workers may emigrate, but at the same time physical or human capital can be lured from abroad to increase the overpopulated society's ratio of capital to labor (K/L) or skill to labor (S/L) . Alternatively, or in addition, new lands may be opened, or land-intensive products may be imported, effectively increasing a labor-abundant society's stock of land.

Less obviously, but an aspect on which both Boix, and Bates and Lien, focus much of their analysis, some forms of *physical capital* can move across boundaries. What is loosely called "capital flight" depends, even more than migration, on political barriers and physical characteristics.[8] As Frieden noted in some of his early work, physical capital invested in extraction of natural resources (e.g., mining) was totally immobile, thus incentivizing both domestic and foreign owners to counter political threats to those assets with organized violence or military intervention (Frieden 1994). Steel mills and automobile factories are almost equally immobile; but garment-making sweatshops, whose main capital consists of sewing machines, can rather easily move to another jurisdiction, for example, from China or Thailand to Vietnam. As these examples suggest, geographical mobility of physical capital affects, and is affected by, the political and economic environment; that is, mobility is partly endogenous. Insecurity discourages investment in immobile capital, but the

[8] "Capital flight" often denotes movement of liquid capital out of a country, or only a cessation of new investment in physical capital. I mean here something narrower: the ability of existing physical capital to move to a different jurisdiction.

possibility that capital will flee incentivizes governments to provide greater security.[9]

Land, of course, cannot be moved, although boundaries sometimes can.[10] For this reason, landowners often provide some of the most obdurate resistance to supply shocks that threaten their incomes and wealth. As Ansell and Samuels were only the most recent to notice, the existence of a class of large landowners has historically been a source of strong resistance to democratization (Ansell and Samuels 2014, 12 and 71ff.).

TECHNOLOGICAL OR INSTITUTIONAL REMEDIES

Finally, if factor substitution, factor mobility, or exit cannot cushion the impact of a relative shortage of one factor, or where these provide only partial relief, incentives will increase for the introduction of some new technology (or new institutional arrangement) that allows more efficient use of the newly scarce factor. Robert Allen explains the English origins of the Industrial Revolution through two simple facts: in England, "labor was expensive and coal was cheap" (Allen 2009, 2). English labor scarcity provided the incentives that prodded inventors like Newcomen and Watt to perfect, and British manufacturers to adopt, the radically labor-saving device of the steam engine. Similarly, labor scarcity in the nineteenth-century United States – along with, as we will see in Chapter 3, the sheer size of its domestic market – inspired the rapid adoption of such labor-saving inventions as the mechanical reaper and binder, the sewing machine, and the steam-powered threshing machine (Romer 1996).

New crops and fertilizers, and the ensemble of innovations known as the "green revolution," compensated for local and global shortages of

[9] What Nathan Nunn calls "relationship-specific" investment proves possible, regardless of other advantages, only where the rule of law guarantees property rights and contract enforcement (Nunn 2007).

[10] A notorious example, albeit one not directly connected to a supply shock, is the US annexation of the formerly independent Kingdom of Hawaii. Owners of sugar plantations, faced with ruin from the high duties that the 1896 Dingell tariff placed on imported sugar, found a simple remedy. If they orchestrated a coup that overthrew the monarchy, petitioned the USA for admission as a Territory, and were successful in their petition, their sugar would be of domestic origin and hence not subject to the tariff (Grandy and Lacroix 1995). A contemporaneous report suggested that annexation roughly quintupled the value of stocks in Hawaiian sugar companies ("Booming Sugar in Hawaii" 1898).

arable land.[11] Gutenberg's printing press, at least in part, responded to an acute shortage of human capital, namely the plague-induced high mortality in monastery-based late Medieval *scriptoria* (Herlihy 1997, 49–50; cf. Chapter 8); and "Fordist" production technologies, including the assembly line, made far more efficient use of expensive physical capital.

On the institutional side, as noted earlier, enclosures encouraged investment in, and more efficient use of, land (North and Thomas 1973, pt. III); and government provision of clear title to land and structures unlocks credit and makes physical capital easier to accumulate (Soto 2000).

More often than not in history, no such technological or institutional "fix" has emerged; or, even where such a remedy was available, entrenched interests or obdurate governments have blocked its adoption (Acemoglu and Robinson 2012). We will consider in Chapter 3 what influences the likelihood of such an innovation and, perhaps even more importantly, how such a change can itself ramify to induce further supply shocks. For now, it is enough to observe that, where no such remedy succeeds – and where, additionally, factor substitution is inelastic under existing technology, factor mobility among sectors is low, and possibilities of exit are foreclosed – intense political, social, and institutional conflict is almost certain. Subsequent chapters will be devoted to tracing through examples of such conflicts, and of how they have eventuated differently in different states and regions.

First, however, we must deal with the puzzle of why, when the other routes prove inadequate, factor-saving technological solutions so rarely arise – or, more precisely, what affects the probability that they will arise.

[11] Perhaps most crucial was the Haber-Bosch process, originally deployed by Imperial Germany as a desperate wartime measure to produce nitrates for explosives, but since World War II transformed into a source of fertilizer that makes possible the world's current agricultural abundance. "Haber-Bosch plants today consume 1 percent of all the energy on earth, and … [t]his huge, almost invisible, industry is feeding the world. Without [it], … about 40 percent of the world's population would starve to death" (Hager 2008, 271).

3

Why a Technological Solution Does, or Does Not, Emerge

A change in the relative prices of the factors of production is itself a spur to invention, and to invention of a particular kind – directed to economizing the use of a factor which has become relatively expensive.

John Hicks, *Theory of Wages*, 1932[1]

Supply shocks create incentives for technological solutions. Faced with a sudden shortage of some factor of production, owners of the other factor(s) will seek to alleviate their unexpected increase in costs (and the decline in relative returns and value of their suddenly more abundant factor). But if existing technology[2] allows little factor substitution, affords but limited mobility of factors among sectors, and leaves few possibilities for factors to exit to more rewarding jurisdictions, owners may find one other way, short of coercion or other drastic political intervention, to alleviate the shortage: adoption of a new technology that uses the now-scarce factor more efficiently, one that, therefore, can produce as much or more output using less of the scarce factor.[3] There will be strong demand, in short, for a factor-saving technological innovation. Where labor is scarce, owners of land or capital will pursue some labor-saving technology; where land is scarce, workers and capitalists will welcome some innovation (e.g., a new crop, better machinery, or different property rights) that increases per-hectare output. Where human or physical capital is rapidly depleted, demand will rise for a technology that can produce as much using less of those factors. In exactly the same way, a sudden influx of one factor

[1] (Hicks, 1963 (2nd edition), p. 124).
[2] As does much of economics, I use "technology" here in a broad sense that encompasses not only machines, but institutions (North 1991).
[3] Where no great leap from existing technologies is involved, the breakthrough may happen even where one or more of these other options is open.

(e.g., rapid immigration of human capital) will motivate owners of that factor to seek a technology (and to reward handsomely any such technology) that uses one or more of the other factors (now in relatively shorter supply) more efficiently. In a purely agricultural economy, for example, a population explosion produces powerful incentives to use land more efficiently, for example, by introducing a more calorie-producing crop (potatoes) or changing methods of cultivation (the so-called Agricultural Revolution of the seventeenth and eighteenth centuries in the Netherlands and England, discussed more fully below), or the more gradual innovations of the pre-Black Death thirteenth and fourteenth centuries (Epstein 2000, 45–46). On the other hand, a sudden shortage of labor, such as followed the Black Death, incentivizes the introduction of labor-saving technologies – as we shall see in Chapter 4.

Graphically, such a labor-saving innovation would appear as in Figure 3.1, which also portrays both the old and the new technology as characterized by zero elasticity of substitution (i.e., Leontief isoquants). If a sudden shortage moves labor from being inexpensive (the shallower dotted line) to being expensive (the steeper dashed lines) relative to land, the old technology would force producers to pay the higher wages; and, if we assume the conventional equilibrium in which profits were already zero, this would mean producing at a loss (or, likelier, simply going out of production). If some new technology that allows land (now cheap relative to labor) to be substituted for labor, and that perhaps is more efficient in its use of both factors, producers will readily shift to the newer technology. In consequence, the ratio of land to labor actually used in production will move from the slope of the lower ray from the origin to the slope of the higher ray (both portrayed here as solid lines). If, as depicted in Figure 3.1, the new technology can produce the same output using about a quarter as much labor and three times as much land, and if land is now far cheaper relative to labor, producers who adopt the new technology will obtain a windfall profit. The benefit will be even greater than might have been achieved from more elastic substitution. (Note, however, that no producer would have adopted this technology had labor remained cheap relative to land. Following an insight of Robert Allen, I generalize on this point below to explain why many seemingly high-productivity innovations fail initially to be adopted everywhere.)

Our central puzzle, then, shared with anthropologists and economic historians, is just this: What affects the likelihood that a technological solution to some sudden shortage will be found? What spurs invention, and (probably more important) furthers adoption, of a new technology?

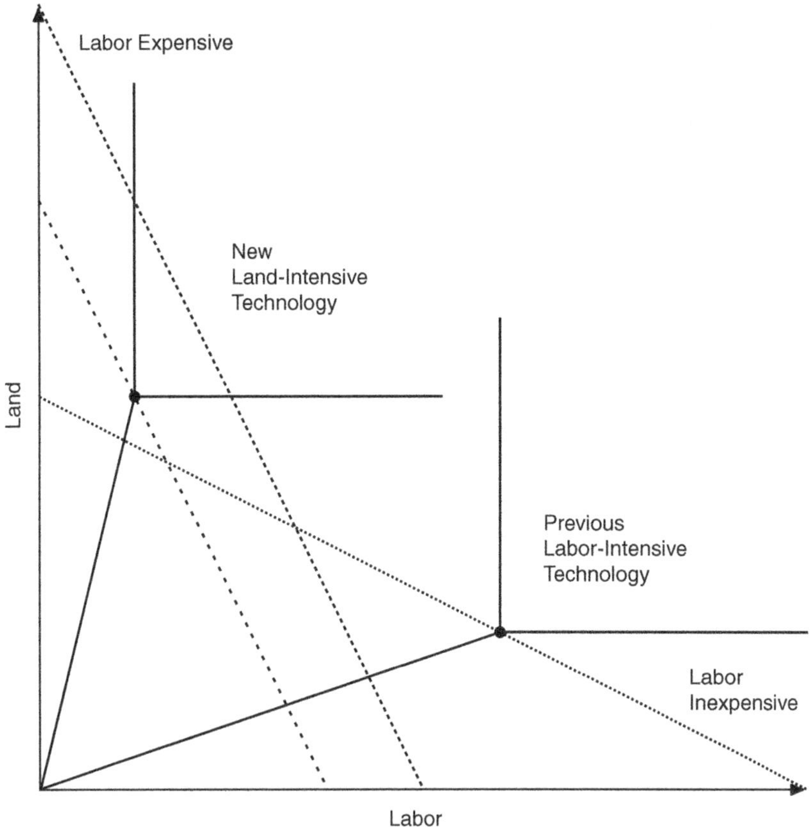

Figure 3.1 Introduction of a labor-saving technology in response to an increase in wages

Why did civilizations devise and adopt (or adapt) agriculture, iron, the wheel, or writing? How did they sometimes lose one or more of those arts, only to reinvent them later?[4] When the human capital of the Medieval *scriptoria* is destroyed by the Black Death, why (and where) does the printing press emerge? How, in the seventeenth century, do Dutch and then English farmers adopt new techniques of tillage, crop rotation, and fertilization that, by substituting capital and labor for land, allow each

[4] Ancient Greeks became illiterate after the collapse of Mycenean civilization (which used "Minoan" Linear B), only to re-learn writing (using a modified Phoenician script) some four centuries later (Desborough 1972, 21–23); and some Native American peoples abandoned agriculture in favor of hunting when Europeans introduced the horse and firearms.

hectare to produce a much higher yield; or secure the changed property rights (enclosures, freehold) that make such improvements pay off?

This way of posing the question ignores the simplistic and erroneous "folk" explanation, according to which innovations are the isolated work of such lone geniuses as Jethro Tull,[5] James Watt, or Thomas Edison. As Jared Diamond among others has shown, most innovations involve collaboration and refinement (Diamond 1997, 223–227), often of long pre-existing techniques. Nor, on balance, can we accept the more plausible scholarly hypothesis that inventions arise from a scientific culture or from Enlightenment rationality (Pinker 2018, chap. 1). As Robert Allen notes, France in the eighteenth century had a far more advanced scientific culture than England; yet it was England that midwifed the Industrial Revolution (Allen 2011, chap. 3). Moreover, many "inventions" involve simply the adoption, or slight adaptation, of technologies that had long been known. Innovations take hold only where demand for them is intense and the rewards to innovators correspondingly high. A labor-saving technology was strongly demanded in high-wage England, but not in low-wage France. Technological innovations that succeed are, in this sense, always *endogenous*: They respond to some acute social need, or more precisely to the incentives that such a need generates.[6]

At the same time, as discussed more fully below, such an endogenous innovation can rapidly become exogenous, through what I will call "*overshooting*." Introduced to alleviate some shortage, or some impediment in product or factor markets, the innovation can be so successful as to turn a shortage into a sudden, and unforeseen, surplus. A classic example is again steam-powered spinning and weaving, the first fruits of the Industrial Revolution. Introduced chiefly both to remedy a growing shortage of human capital (the skills of human spinners and weavers) and to answer the strong demand for textiles and apparel that the resultant bottleneck, coupled with rapid population growth, had induced over the previous century, the new methods quickly made textiles so cheap and plentiful that the human capital of the traditional spinners and weavers overnight became superabundant and hence superfluous. The railroad is

[5] As only my fellow farm kids are likely to know, Tull is credited with the invention of the seed drill – a method of planting that wasted far less seed than the broadcasting that had prevailed for centuries before. It substituted capital (the drill and the horses to draw it) for the human labor of the sower.

[6] That need, to be sure, may not be perceived by the inventors themselves. Edison, famously, thought that the phonograph would be used to record the words of the dying, not for mass entertainment.

an analogous case: Envisioned, like canals before it, as a marginal improvement to reduce the cost of overland transit (and thus to bring products and markets closer to one another), its rapid refinement wound up reducing transportation costs by at least 95 percent (Woytinsky and Woytinsky 1955, 310), alleviating local shortages and surpluses to a revolutionary extent that few in 1830 could have imagined (Kindleberger 1951, 31).

Back, then, to our essential question: Why do such innovations arise in some cases of acute need, but not in most?[7] What determines their likelihood? And why does an innovation, once introduced in one area of the world, not rapidly spread to others?

Start with the first basic question: What determines the likelihood that a technological answer, even where the need seems dire, arises at all? Two obvious aspects of any answer are (a) the intensity of incentives and (b) the "innovative fertility" of the given pool of potential inventors.

INTENSITY OF INCENTIVES

Think, as a potential inventor might, of the likely return (if any) on her investment of effort and ingenuity. At least three factors would have to be weighed: How extreme is the shortage, how big a technological leap (and hence how great an effort) is required, and how extensive is the potential market?[8] Imagine, difficult as it may be, that you are the goldsmith, blacksmith, and sometime minter of coins Johannes Gutenberg in Mainz in the 1430s, tinkering with ideas for various profit-making ventures. You know that the supply of hand-copied reading matter has stagnated or fallen[9] (the Black Death, which abated only around 1420,

[7] As we shall see in Chapter 6, Europe between the two World Wars desperately needed, but was unable to devise, technologies that would have made land produce more calories; yet a half-century later, first the Green Revolution and then genetically modified organisms (GMOs) provided exactly such innovations.

[8] The potential market must be quite large. Even under the well-developed patent system of the United States between 1940 and 2001, according to the estimates of Nordhaus, innovators captured only between 2 and 3 percent of the social benefit from their inventions (Nordhaus 2004, 22).

[9] While such estimates are inexact – they are based on surviving manuscripts, and hence on best guesses about how many have perished – it appears that the per capita production of hand-copied manuscripts fell between the thirteenth and fourteenth centuries in the British Isles and present-day Belgium, stagnated in France, Germany, and present-day Austria, but rose in the Netherlands, Central Europe, Italy, and Iberia. Finer-grained data for the German-speaking parts of Europe suggest a sharp decline in manuscript production up to about the 1390s, but a rapid increase in

particularly decimated the *scriptoria*, and the few lay scribes – mostly attached to universities – cannot adequately take up the slack), even as demand from an increasing literate and well-to-do public has risen (Barbier 2017, chaps. 2 and 3); hence books have become prohibitively expensive. You understand also that, under existing technology, substitution of some other factor (labor or physical capital) is highly inelastic – indeed, almost impossible.[10] You are acquainted with many extant technologies that might point you to an answer: woodcut and intaglio printing; screw presses, used both in winemaking and in the cloth trade; even movable type; and the many kinds of metals used in the mint and in blacksmithing. Just as important, the technology of paper-making has recently arrived in Europe, indeed in nearby Nürnberg (Sporhan-Krempel and Von Stromer 1960), offering a far less expensive medium than parchment for the written word.[11] It will prove an ingenious leap, but in fact not a very large one, to combine all of these to achieve readily castable metal, a printing press, improved inks, and printing on paper. Perhaps most important of all, you will want to know the size of the potential market: How numerous are the literate public, and in which languages do they want to read (Sasaki 2017)? It quickly became apparent that the commercial revival had produced a sizable readership, which demanded literature not in Latin, but in their own vernaculars.[12]

While it may seem a "just so" story, in fact all of these crucial variables fell into place: They indicated that high returns were likely, no large technological leap was required, and a sizable and remunerative market

subsequent decades, so that by 1450 output was roughly triple that of 1350. From about 1470, however, manuscript production dropped precipitously, stifled by the competition of the printing press (Buringh and Van Zanden 2009, 419–420).

[10] Low-skill labor, even if rudimentarily literate, could not reliably produce legible and accurate copies – and, worse, were likely to ruin the parchment and vellum still predominantly used by existing technology. Increased capital would have only made available more desks and quills – hardly likely to improve the output of the remaining scribes. The lone innovations that did speed hand-copying were the development of the less ornate "Bastarda" cursive and the *pecia* system, which divided the text into sections that were copied simultaneously by different scribes (Barbier 2017, 48 and 59–61).

[11] Paper-making itself involved substitution of a more capital-intensive method, using water-power and machinery to pulverize rags, for the extremely labor-intensive one (described in detail in Avrin (1991, 210–212)) of producing parchment. See below, Chapter 8.

[12] Barbier asserts that as early as the ninth century AD in Europe, "classical Latin was no longer understood or used beyond a very narrow group of educated men ... Most people now used the vernacular ..." Even before the advent of printing, a substantial market for works in the vernacular arose (Barbier 2017, 4 and 44–46).

stood open, for any innovation that could produce reading matter with fewer inputs of the expert human capital that had become suddenly scarce and expensive. Needless to say, the new technology of printing, even with the few refinements that it achieved over the next century, quickly overshot the initial need and became itself one of history's most powerful exogenous shocks (Dittmar 2011). It made many kinds of human capital (e.g., the near-monopoly of literacy previously enjoyed by priests, scholars, and a few of the secular elite) suddenly abundant and cheap, increased returns to (and lowered the costs of acquiring[13]) literacy and divided the world into defenders of the old monopolies of learning and acceptors of the new abundance of scholarship and vernacular literature. To make a large leap: It divided Europe into Catholic realms that defended the priestly and Latin monopoly, and a Protestant part that (hardly by accident) embraced the "priesthood of all believers" and the doctrine of *sola scriptura*, a faith that could be defended only by reference to the scriptures, which were now available to all. But that is a story I reserve to Chapter 8.

INNOVATIVE FERTILITY

We owe to the Nobel Laureate Michael Kremer the startlingly simple insight that innovative fertility depends on the size of the pool of potential inventors and the ease with which news of an innovation, or of progress toward that innovation, can be transmitted. In essence, we assume that each person has the same, very small, probability of coming up with a brilliant solution. We assume also that, within some relevant population, whether because of shared language, physical proximity, literacy, or existing information technology (to name only a few possibilities), the brilliant idea, once arrived at, can be transmitted instantly and universally.[14] Then the likelihood that a technical solution will be found increases monotonically (albeit at a declining rate[15]) with the size of the

[13] The cost of books fell by about two-thirds between 1450 and 1500 (Dittmar 2011, 1133). See Chapter 8.

[14] This is obviously an abstraction, not a description of the real world. I relax the assumption below.

[15] If p represents the (very small) probability that any given individual will have a brilliant idea in a given span of time, then the probability that nobody among n individuals has such an idea is $(1 - p)^n$; and therefore the probability that at least one person has such an idea (label that probability b) is $b = 1 - (1 - p)^n$. $1 - p$ must be a number less than, albeit very close to, 1; hence, as n increases, in the limit $(1 - p)^n$

population linked by those means of communication (Kremer, 1993).[16] It follows that technological innovations become ever likelier to emerge as the relevant population becomes larger and denser, means of cheap and rapid communication multiply, and linguistic barriers fall.[17] If this is correct, technological solutions to sudden factor shortages will be likelier among large and literate populations that share one or more common languages and swift means of communication: for example, the Roman Empire, where literacy was surprisingly widespread, even among the soldiery (Wilkes 2001); the USA in the later nineteenth century (Romer, 1996); or Europe or China today.

Ease of transmission, including linguistic facility, is of course in part endogenous: European scholars of the early Renaissance often learned Arabic, and citizens of eighteenth-century Europe's "republic of letters" mastered French, to gain access to valued knowledge. In late seventeenth-century England, even many of the country gentry, and most urban merchants, were conversant enough in other languages to be avid readers of French (and sometimes Dutch) newspapers and books (Pincus 2009, 308–309). Learned societies and scholarly and technical journals arise to meet the perceived need for rapid transmission of new knowledge.

Even so, a solution that is swiftly adopted in one region of the world, even if it becomes rapidly known and available, is often not adopted everywhere. This is the fundamental puzzle that underlies the "Great Divergence": Why was modern industrial technology, once it had demonstrated its potential in places like Britain and North America, not immediately adopted everywhere? Why did some regions remain desperately poor, or indeed become poorer, even as the industrialized countries became rich? Or, at yet a simpler level, why was the potato, whose nutritional advantages were widely known, not cultivated in all regions where population was outrunning available land?

The basic answer is pre-existing factor endowments. The case of the potato, as Nunn and Qian have shown, is easy: It simply could not grow in many soils and climates (Nunn and Qian 2011, 609–615); nor did it

goes to zero, and b goes to one. It will probably be intuitively obvious that b increases with n, but at a declining rate. One such function (with $p = 10^{-4}$) is plotted in Appendix Figure A3.1.

16 Kremer attributes this insight to Kuznets and Simon; he uses it to develop a more complex and innovative model than is sketched here.

17 In the High Middle Ages, Epstein argues, "By exposing a larger proportion of the population to new technology, market integration may also have increased the rate of invention" (Epstein 2000, 65).

attract much interest where land was abundant. Similarly, Diamond argues, humans failed to domesticate large mammals (cattle, horses) where there were few such mammals suitable for domestication (Diamond 1997, chap. 9). It was crucial to the Industrial Revolution that England possessed ample endowments of coal. Demand also matters: China failed to adopt firearms at the same time as Europe, Hoffman contends, because firearms were of little use in the kind of combat (chiefly against steppe barbarians) that Chinese civilization faced (Hoffman 2015). The failure of modern industry to spread is trickier, but Robert Allen has offered a convincing answer to the puzzle (Allen 2009, 152) – which, again, is more easily seen if we resort to graphical exposition and isoquants (Figure 3.2).

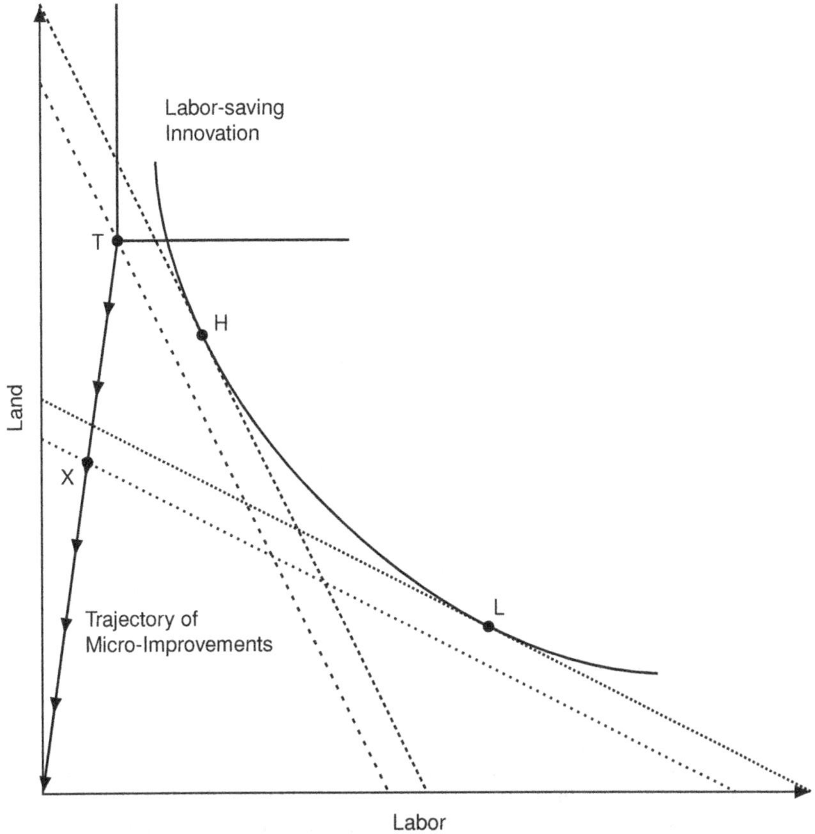

Figure 3.2 Delay of labor-abundant economy in adopting labor-saving technology. (From Allen 2009)

Allen supposes an isoquant common to two countries, with the labor-abundant one producing at L, the labor-scarce one at H. The rate at which capital trades for labor is represented by the two sets of price lines, with of course the steeper ones characterizing the labor-scarce economy. Suppose that some new technology allows the same quantity to be produced at point T, which we can usefully regard as the vertex of (as before) a Leontief production function (i.e., one with zero elasticity of substitution). Producers in the labor-scarce economy will adopt that technology at once; but it will have no appeal in the labor-abundant country, which can still produce more cheaply using the old technology. Only when a series of what Allen calls "micro-improvements," in which the new technology maintains the same ratio of capital to labor in production but successively needs less of both, brings costs to a point like X, will producers in the labor-abundant economy find it worthwhile to adopt the innovation. We saw essentially the same argument in Figure 3.1, where the new technology would never have been adopted so long as wages remained low.

OVERSHOOTING: WHEN THE ENDOGENOUS BECOMES EXOGENOUS

Factor-saving technological innovations, then, ordinarily emerge and take hold only in response to some intense social need, usually arising from a sudden relative shortage of one or more factors of production.[18] Many, perhaps most, of these endogenous innovations do little more than alleviate the (relative) shortage that occasioned them: That appears to have been true, for example, of the many incremental improvements in Medieval agriculture – increased use of manure, introduction of the wheeled plow, the shift from biennial to triennial crop rotation, increasing use of water- and windmills, etc. (Barbier 2017, 7; Duby, 1998, esp. pp. 103–112; Epstein 2000, 44–45). These were gradual, and they simply compensated for the growing shortage of land (as population expanded up to the Black Death) by making each hectare yield more.[19]

[18] Some innovations, it is worth re-emphasizing, have been totally exogenous, among them the New World crops that entered the rest of the world, and the horses and firearms that came to the Americas, through the Columbian Exchange.

[19] More land was also brought into production, as forests, swamps, and waste land were cleared, and land-hungry peasants migrated into the relatively vacant lands of central and eastern Europe (the original *Drang nach Osten*). In both developments, the Cistercian monks played a significant role.

The "revolutionary" innovations that history records, however, vastly overshoot the original need and become themselves sources of supply shock. Ones intended to alleviate shortages of: human capital (the printing press and computers); labor (mechanized manufacturing, powered by fossil fuels); land (railroads and steamships); or physical capital (the assembly line and Fordist production techniques) – instead made available each of those factors in previously unimagined quantity, unleashing large shifts in relative prices and precipitating even larger political conflicts.

If we go back much farther in human history, even such innovations as agriculture, writing, hierarchy, government, the wheel, the plow, metallurgy (copper, bronze, and iron), and coinage met specific needs but rapidly occasioned supply shocks of their own: Agriculture, to take perhaps the most prominent example, yielded not just a modest increase in productivity but at least ten and as much as 100 times per hectare what foraging had provided (Diamond 1997, 54). Property rights in land suddenly became important, which in turn created incentives to establish hierarchy and government. The more efficient use of land provided, moreover, what the Marxists call an "appropriable surplus," capable of financing priests, bureaucrats, and soldiers – possessors of highly specialized forms of human capital.[20] Not least, as a far more labor-intensive method of production, it created incentives to increase the supply of labor – usually by conquest or enslavement.

SHOCKS OF SUDDEN ABUNDANCE

Following Hicks, I focus here on instances in which the supply of some crucial factor is suddenly curtailed. It is important to bear in mind that no less powerful a shock can arise from a sudden expansion of one factor, making the other(s) *relatively* scarcer. A sudden influx of human capital makes labor, physical capital, and land relatively less abundant, and creates incentives for labor- or capital-saving innovations. The trade-induced sudden augmentation of land (i.e., the import of land-intensive products) in nineteenth-century Europe incentivized the introduction of technologies that could use labor and capital more efficiently. And, however paradoxically, the vast expansion of the developed world's effective supply of labor occasioned by the "China shock" has increased the

[20] But see also J. C. Scott (2017), who suggests that nascent states may have fostered agriculture, or at least the cultivation of grain, rather than the other way around.

rewards to technologies that can economize on human and physical capital. The same change that has depressed low-skill wages in the advanced economies, as we often fail to see, has increased the skills premium within those societies and encouraged the "revolutions" of information technology and robotics that employ now relatively scarce human and physical capital more efficiently (Acemoglu and Restrepo 2019, 2020).

INSTITUTIONS AS TECHNOLOGY

Systems of land tenure have often adapted (but more often failed to adapt) to shocks in supply (North and Thomas 1973). Rome's sudden abundance of slaves, and of Egyptian grain, after the Second Punic War displaced peasant smallholdings in favor of latifundia (Scullard 1970, 19–20);[21] the sudden decline in population that accompanied the fall of the western Roman Empire (coupled, to be sure, with a decline in security) gave rise to the manorial system; and the population surge of the seventeenth century occasioned, at least in the most densely populated parts of western Europe, the enclosures that ended the manorial system and alone made possible the soil improvements and intensified cropping that constituted the Agricultural Revolution.[22]

The opening or deepening of trade routes, with new opportunities for commerce, raises the returns to systems of law and adjudication – in other words, to institutions – that facilitate such exchange. An early and influential example was the development, in the expanding Roman Republic, of a rationalized and mutually acceptable system of commercial law. What came to be called the *jus gentium*, or "law of peoples," evolved through the successive edicts of the *praetor peregrinus* (literally, the magistrate who "moved around"), which successively melded Roman commercial law with what appeared the best and most sensible features

[21] It is reasonable to conjecture that the sudden abundance of land, and the consequent relative shortage of labor, human capital, and physical capital, encouraged innovations – in transport, agriculture, and not least combat – that economized on the use of all three.

[22] Controversially, North and Thomas attribute the demographic crises of the fourteenth century, culminating in the Black Death, to a failure of institutional innovation: The population, in their view, had simply outgrown the ability of the manorial system to feed it, and chronic malnutrition rendered people more susceptible to plague. For a well-argued dissenting view, which views constricted markets rather than institutions of land tenure as the relevant constraint, see Epstein (2000, chap. 3).

of the pre-existing legal systems of newly conquered provinces. This resembled, as the eminent historian of Rome H. H. Scullard observed, the English system of common law, also shaped through successive judicial rulings; except that, instead of relying on eclectic precedents, the praetor's edicts effectively codified the relevant precedents into a unified body of law, readily accessible to all parties (Scullard 2013, 337–338).

Institutional innovations may, but need not, originate with governments (Ostrom 1990). The coercive power of the state makes compliance likelier; but often reputational concerns suffice. From the "law merchants" of the Medieval trade fairs to the sophisticated arbitrators of present-day international commerce and sovereign defaults (Casella 1996), non-coercive institutional solutions have arisen and succeeded – albeit usually among relatively few actors, who interact repeatedly (Landa 1981).[23]

THE ROLE OF GOVERNMENT

Rulers can foster innovation, chiefly by guaranteeing intellectual property rights and subsidizing research; but patents and copyrights are themselves fairly recent creations (Bottomley 2014; Epstein 2000, 67), and over millennia governments have spent most freely on military research (cf. the next section on military technology).[24] Sharply focused efforts to solve a specific technological problem, for example, prizes offered by the British government in the eighteenth century to find a reliable ship-borne indicator of longitude (Sobel 1995, chap. 6), have usually failed.

Once a factor-saving innovation begins to be adopted, however, a government can often simply stand aside and allow the market to prevail; it can adopt (or decline to adopt) institutional changes that the new technique may require (again, enclosures are a relevant example); or it can support opposition to the new technology or itself act to suppress it (Frieden and Silve 2022). Improvements in transportation (roads, canals, railways) often required an aggressive use of eminent domain, which paradoxically English "limited" governments employed much more freely than the French "absolutist" monarchy (Allen 2011, 29). British governments of the late eighteenth and early nineteenth centuries, moreover, acted decisively

[23] Avner Greif, building on Landa's work, found that Genoan traders relied on reputational enforcement only so long as their number remained small and their interactions frequent (Greif 1993).

[24] Perhaps the earliest example, and certainly one of the most successful, was Hippocrates' commission to Archimedes to devise ingenious technologies for the defense of Syracuse against the Romans: Polybius, *The Histories*, VIII.3–7.

in support of the Industrial Revolution: They deployed significant military force and no small amount of judicial terror to crush machine-breakers in industry (the Luddites) and agriculture (the Swing riots) (Bailey 1998, 41–43 and 73ff.; Hobsbawm and Rudé 1973, 220–225).

More often, or perhaps only more prominently, governments have intervened to block innovations that threatened powerful groups of factor owners (Acemoglu and Robinson 2006). Tokugawa Japan banned firearms to preserve the samurai monopoly of the means of violence; in many countries owners of canals and turnpikes were able to impede the growth of railroads, and railroads in turn later won restrictions on long-haul trucking (Seely 1986; Woytinsky and Woytinsky 1955, 339); and small-scale retailers in many countries (France, Germany, more recently India) have won governmental restrictions on competition from supermarkets and department stores.

What induces governments to adopt one or another of these courses is a larger subject, addressed in the theory of regulation that has grown up around the fundamental Stigler-Peltzman model (Chang et al. 2011). The main arguments of that theory are the benefits and costs to consumers, and to industry, of action to impede or to retard the innovation; and the support that government will gain or lose, from consumers and from the relevant industrial interests, by any action that it may take.

MILITARY TECHNOLOGY

Even the earliest organized societies (tribes and chiefdoms) sometimes warred against each other; and, indeed, external threats powerfully stimulated greater organization, specialization, and hierarchy. Early warfare created incentives to the introduction of militarily more effective technologies, from bronze and iron to chariots, saddles, and stirrups. As Aristotle may have been the first to note, particular military technologies often correlated with political and social structures: Heavy armor went together with kingship and cavalry with oligarchy, whereas "light infantry and naval forces are an entirely democratic element" (Politics 1297b and 1321a). Nineteenth- and early twentieth-century historians of ancient Greece, chief among them George Grote and Victor Ehrenberg, turned correlation into causation, arguing that the "hoplite revolution"[25] and Athenian reliance on naval power (Hale 2009, chap. 7) had in essence created Greek democracy.

[25] Hoplites were lightly armed infantry, into which virtually all adult male citizens were conscripted. Formed into phalanxes they proved superior to the traditional heavily armed cavalry portrayed in the *Iliad*.

Later historians and sociologists have boldly extended to many other eras the attribution of major social and political change to "revolutions" in military technology. Gaius Marius's replacement of Rome's citizen army with well-drilled professional legions allegedly caused, or was at least necessary for, the rise of Caesarism and Rome's subsequent transformation from Republic to Empire (Scullard 1970, 58–59). The introduction of the stirrup into western Europe around AD 750, by reestablishing after centuries the dominance of heavily armed cavalry over infantry, single-handedly created feudalism (L. White 1962, chap. 1),[26] while the introduction of firearms, as part of the larger "military revolution" of the sixteenth and seventeenth centuries (Eltis 1995) (Parker 1996), supposedly doomed feudalism and forced the creation of larger armies of professional infantry – whose fiscal burdens in turn gave rise to the modern Westphalian state (Tilly 1990, chap. 3).[27] And, most recently, Ferejohn and Rosenbluth have argued, mass armies – of the French Revolution, the US Civil War and two World Wars – by conscripting and arming virtually all able-bodied adult males, gave rise to modern democracy (Ferejohn and Rosenbluth 2017, chaps. 10 and 11).

Alluring as Ockham's Razor, or our innate human love of simplicity, makes such monocausal theories, historians have cast doubt on the seeming centrality of military revolutions. Sparta also relied on hoplites but was hardly a democracy; the stirrup had been known for centuries in China and the Near East without giving rise to feudalism; Ming China's already strong state was unaffected by (and indeed found little use for) firearms; and mass warfare appears to be neither a necessary nor a sufficient condition for democratization: Switzerland and the USA in the nineteenth century demonstrate the first point, the USSR in and after World War II the latter one.

It seems likelier that the link between military innovation and regime change is endogenous – that both the military innovations and the social and governmental adaptations respond to some radical change in factor supply.

26 To elaborate White's intriguing thesis in greater detail: Mounted knights, to be effective, required expensive armor and years of training, only possible in an agrarian economy if they were sustained by the revenues of large, landed estates. Hence Charles Martel granted his nascent cavalry revenue from, and control over, tracts of land seized from the Church; and his example was quickly emulated by rival rulers. All else – benefice, commendation, vassalage, subinfeudation, ultimately parcelization of sovereignty – supposedly followed as the night the day.

27 Hintze, echoing Aristotle, argued at the end of the nineteenth century that powers dependent on large armies (e.g., Germany) necessarily inclined toward authoritarian rule, while ones that could rely on naval power (Britain) or mountain defenses (Switzerland) were likely to develop democratic institutions (Hintze 1906).

As most historians of the period will now argue, both Athenian democracy and Athenian hoplite armies stemmed from rapidly growing Athenian prosperity, which in turn owed to the sudden opening of new land (via trade with the grain-growing Black Sea regions and Magna Graecia[28]) that allowed overpopulated Athens to specialize in high-quality manufactures.[29] The new wealth of Athens (and of such similarly situated Greek cities as Corinth) allowed its middle and lower classes to purchase the light armor and spears that formed the essential equipment of the hoplite soldier.[30]

Similarly, feudalism was an inventive adaptation to the depopulation, technological retrogression, and general insecurity that characterized late Roman and post-Roman Europe. The infantry-based legions of Rome would have found but slight use for the stirrup, or for that matter for the heavy armor of the Medieval knight; but in thinly populated and locally autarkic Carolingian Europe, a land-intensive and equestrian technology of combat made perfect sense.[31] It was the growing wealth and population of Europe that made possible the military revolution of the sixteenth and seventeenth centuries, and the mass armies of the late nineteenth and twentieth centuries could be fed and transported only after the Industrial Revolution and the introduction of the railroad (Onorato, Scheve, and Stasavage 2014).

To be sure, military competition, especially during time of actual combat, speeds the introduction of new technologies of warfare – the *levée en masse* of revolutionary France; the airplanes, radios, and tanks of World War I (Münkler 2013, 526–545); the radar, heavy bombers, and nuclear weapons of World War II – but these radical adaptations are conditional on the factor endowments of the combatants. Pre-industrial powers do not produce railroads or tanks, and only countries with abundant labor mount "human wave" attacks. The USA succeeded in the Manhattan Project, while Nazi Germany abandoned its quest – despite being at least as advanced in

28 Sicily and southern Italy, which in turn (much like nineteenth-century Argentina) grew wealthy on its agricultural exports. Our adjective for extreme luxury, "sybaritic," derives from the legendary wealth of the Sicilian city of Sybaris in present-day Calabria, Italy.

29 Scheidel estimates that the per capita GDP of Athens had risen by around 330 BC to "four to five times minimum physiological subsistence, similar to fifteenth-century Holland and sixteenth-century England" (Walter Scheidel 2017, 85).

30 Sparta financed its legendarily obedient hoplite soldiers without trade, but by conquering the extensive lands of neighboring Messenia and enslaving its inhabitants.

31 A useful thought-experiment is to imagine pitting the valiant knights of the *Song of Roland*, against a Roman legion in its prime, for example, under Augustus. Even with stirrups and heavy armor, the knights would be unlikely to prevail.

nuclear physics as the USA – not because of Roosevelt's superior insight or Einstein's famous letter, but because the USA had the wealth and infrastructure (e.g., electrical power) to do so more quickly (Tooze 2008, 510–511).

Military revolutions, in short, usually follow supply shocks; and the alleged consequences of military revolutions – as regards economic equality, political participation, or property rights – are themselves mostly engendered by radical changes in the supply of crucial factors of production. While they will play a role in some of the analyses that follow, they will rarely prove to be determinative.

CONCLUSION

On a principle of "economy of effort," the least costly way to adjust to a supply shock is to substitute the suddenly more abundant factor(s) for the one(s) that have become scarcer and more expensive. The second least costly is to move the newly abundant and devalued factor into another sector or region where it commands a higher price. Where both of those routes are blocked, demand will rise, and potential rewards will increase, for a factor-saving technological innovation: one that permits the same or greater production with fewer inputs of the newly scarce factor.

In most historical cases, no such innovation, or only a marginal improvement, has emerged; hence the attention that historians devote to the rare cases of "revolutionary" factor-saving innovations. As Kremer observed, however, the frequency of such technological breakthroughs rises as the pool of potential inventors expands and barriers to communication fall. However much we may regret the extinction of some languages and the increasing neglect of others, the world's growing ability to communicate needs and findings in a single language, be it French, English, Chinese, or Esperanto, has powerfully expanded its innovative fertility. Innovation, however, also feeds on itself: Had Gutenberg not been able to draw on prior advances in intaglio, metallurgy, and ink- and paper-making, he would likely have abandoned any thought of so radical a method for economizing on human capital as the printing press. In the labor shortage that followed the Black Death, as we shall see, effective labor-saving technologies in agriculture (better plows, harrows, seed drills, and mechanical reapers) had to wait until many intermediate hurdles had been passed; in the circumstances of the fourteenth century, such a technology was unimaginable. By contrast, physicists of today can draw on centuries of advances in physics, code-writers on decades of successful (and of failed!) efforts, economists on the advances that began with Adam Smith.

This implies, rather radically, that future supply shocks are increasingly likely to find a technological solution;[32] and, hence, that societies are likelier to adjust to such shocks, even with initial dislocations and frictions, without radical political controversies. The chapters that examine specific cases of supply shocks will shed some light on that conjecture. I propose to return to it in the conclusion of this book.

Appendix to Chapter 3

Example: $b = 1 - (1 - 10^{-4})^n$

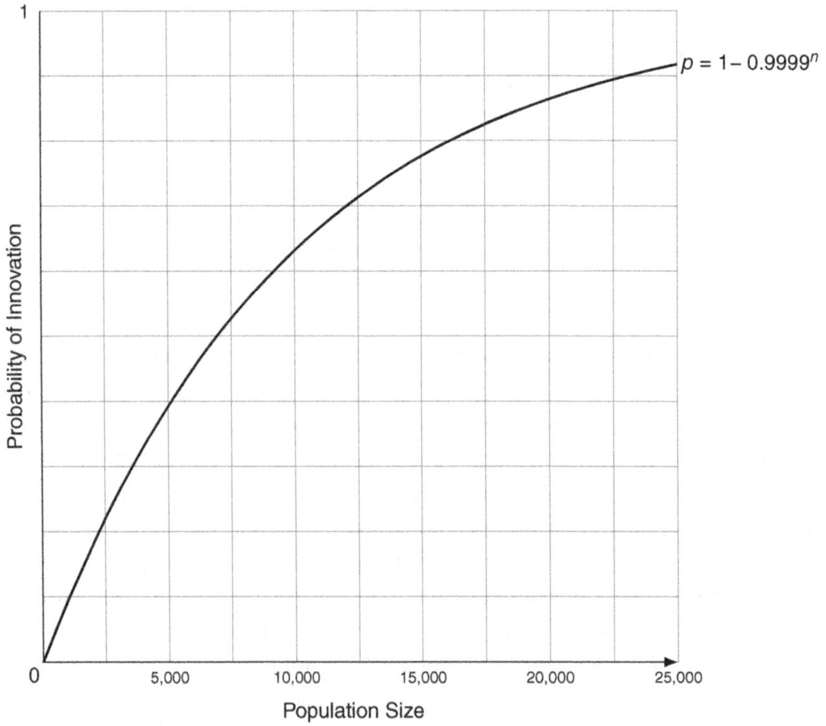

Figure A3.1 Probability of innovation as a function of population size

[32] A tangential example has been the rapid, if not altogether smooth, transition to "virtual" classes and meetings in response to the COVID-19 pandemic.

4

Exogenous Loss of Labor

The Black Death in Fourteenth-Century Europe

By the dawn of the fourteenth century, Europe's population had risen from its medieval nadir of perhaps 25 million in the time of Charlemagne to between 70 and 100 million (Fischer 1996, 44; Herlihy 1997; Russell 1976, 36). The Great Famine of 1315–1322 and, even more, the Black Death of 1347–1352 and its subsequent recurrences had by 1420 reduced Europe's population to at most 35 million (Herlihy 1997, 17).[1] Since the region's endowments of land, physical capital, and specie barely changed, the capital-labor and land-labor ratios roughly tripled, and the same money was soon chasing two-thirds fewer goods.[2]

Standard economic models, as outlined in Chapter 1, predict the outcome with some precision: Wages should rise (in real terms, probably by at least 40 percent), rents on land and capital would fall (probably by about half, again in purchasing power), per capita output (and thus the average standard of living) would increase, and nominal prices would roughly triple. Land-intensive foodstuffs would cheapen relative to more labor-intensive products (manufactures, construction, hand-copied literature). Inequality, which had reached extremes in thirteenth-century western Europe, should decline drastically: The rental-wage ratio would

1 Bendedictow suggests, on the basis of an exhaustive survey of the available (if inevitably fragmentary) evidence, that the first wave of the Black Death (1347–1353) likely killed some 60 percent of Europe's population, rather than the one-third conventionally estimated: 50 million, he conjectures, out of a total population of (again, by his estimate) 80 million. The subsequent waves merely prevented population from rebounding until sometime between 1420 and 1450 (Benedictow 2004, chap. 33).

2 One form of physical capital does appear to have dwindled: livestock. Cattle, sheep, and pigs proved to be also susceptible to the plague, and their high mortality temporarily reduced the meat and wool supply – also, doubtless, further incentivizing the shift to meat, wool, and dairy production described below.

likely fall to less than a third of its former level, leading to political and social equalization.[3]

WESTERN EUROPE

This, at any rate, is what would be expected to happen in an economy subject to market pressures, that is, one in which neither elite collusion nor governmental action impeded adjustment.[4] The available data suggest that change in much of western Europe was even more radical than the standard models would suggest. Between the 1320s and the 1380s, Gregory Clark's standard time-series (G. Clark 2005, 1324) shows, the purchasing power of English craftsmen's daily real wages rose by 55 percent (from an index of 41.3 to one of 63.9), while helpers' (i.e., unskilled laborers') real wages rose by over 90 percent (respective indices of 32.5 and 62.4). At their post-plague peak in England, between 1440 and 1460, craftsmen's real wages had increased by 90 percent over their pre-plague nadir; helpers' wages, by an astonishing 145 percent.[5] Herlihy observes more generally of Europe in this period that "wages in the towns soared, to two and even three times the levels they had held in the crowded thirteenth century" (Herlihy 1997, 48).

These increases in real terms were accompanied by skyrocketing nominal prices – an inflation not experienced since the later Roman Empire's debasement of its currency (Jones 1953). Matteo Villani, writing in 1363, noted of Florence immediately after the plague, when it was estimated

[3] If, in a standard Cobb-Douglas setup, where T is land, L is labor, and A is total factor productivity, $Y = AT^{\alpha}L^{1-\alpha}$ and α approximates one-third, a tripling of the land-labor ratio would imply about a 45 percent increase ($3^{1/3} = 1.44$) in per capita output ($Y/L = A(T/L)^{\alpha}$). Wages would rise by the same amount, and the rent of land would go to $(1/3)^{2/3}$ of its former level, or about half. The rental-wage ratio, being linear in the labor-land ratio, declines by the same amount as L/T, or to one-third of its former level.

[4] A recent comparative study finds that these effects have been typical, at least in western Europe and North America, of all high-death-rate pandemics since the Black Death: Wages have risen and the return on capital has fallen. The effect typically persists for some forty years (Jordà et al. 2020).

[5] Pamuk's estimates are somewhat lower: Wages of skilled construction workers in London increased between 1350 and 1450 by about 45 percent, while those of unskilled workers roughly doubled. The general pattern throughout western Europe, and indeed as far away as Cairo, was a doubling of unskilled workers' wages; in Florence, however, they appear to have almost quadrupled (Pamuk 2007, 298–299).

that a third of the population had perished, "Most things cost two times or more what they cost before the epidemic. And labor, and the manufacturers of every art and profession increased in disorderly fashion to double the price ..." (quoted in Herlihy 1997, 46–47). More recent historical analysis suggests that Villani exaggerated only slightly: By 1360, nominal prices in Florence had increased by about 70 percent; but by the early 1400s, they had indeed doubled (Pamuk 2007, 295).

Up to about 1300, the growing purchasing power of bullion, whose supply had remained constant even as population grew, had set off an orgy of silver prospecting and mining throughout Europe (Spufford 1988, chap. 5), increasing the money supply sufficiently to set off an earlier slight inflation, most notably in England in 1305–1310 (Fischer 1996, 32). As bullion lost purchasing power after the Black Death, mining was sharply curtailed and the minting of new coins virtually ceased (Fischer 1996, 48): The money supply stabilized, and may even have contracted, as suddenly less valuable silver and gold were more widely used for ornamental purposes.

Rates of return on land in England, which had peaked at around 12 percent annually in the thirteenth century, fell after the Black Death to 5–6 percent (G. Clark 2007, 168–169). The rent of capital followed suit. In England, interest rates between 1150 and 1350 had hovered between 9.5 and 11 percent; they fell to 7 percent between 1350 and 1400 and, by the late 1400s, to 4.5 percent (Epstein 2000, 61). Similarly, "Rates of interest fell by 50 percent in France and the Low Countries in the century from 1370 to 1470" (Fischer 1996, 55), and the trend seems to have been replicated throughout western Europe (Epstein 2000, fig. 3.1; Pamuk 2007, 308). If the estimates for rents and wages are both accurate, the rent-wage ratio must have fallen to between one-fourth and one-fifth of pre-plague levels.[6] While some surviving landlords simply annexed the holdings of deceased neighbors or of abandoned villages, thus concentrating this form of wealth (Hagen 2002, 34; H. Scott and Melton 2015, n. 42), the share of total income accruing to the elite indeed appears to have fallen: In the Low Countries, the share of the top 5 percent fell from about half of all income before the plague to about a third

[6] As noted above, Clark finds that real rents fell to less than half of former levels, while helpers' real wages increased by a factor of 2.5. This implies that the r/w ratio dropped to about a fifth of its earlier level. If Pamuk is correct that real wages only doubled, the r/w ratio would have fallen to a quarter of pre-plague levels.

afterward (Alfani 2017a, 340); and the share accruing to the top decile in Italy dropped from about two-thirds to less than half (Alfani 2017b).[7]

Landowners of course resisted these changes, attempting both by legal enactment and collusion to restrain wages. In England, a royal Ordinance of Laborers in 1349 forbade workers to demand, or employers to pay, more than pre-plague wages. This being widely ignored,[8] Parliament proceeded in 1351 to enact the more detailed Statute of Laborers (https://sourcebooks.fordham.edu/seth/statute-labourers.asp): No employer was to pay wages higher than had prevailed in 1346 ("the twentieth year of our reign"), and specific maxima were laid down for likely times of labor shortage (haying and harvesting).[9] These strictures found little more success; and efforts to enforce them contributed to the Peasants' Revolt of 1381 (Hilton 1977), which was ultimately suppressed but may have frightened elites into abandoning most of their resistance. What likely mattered more than the Revolt was the failure of landowners to collude (especially at harvest time, they had to pay what laborers demanded or lose their crop) and the ability of at least some dissatisfied peasants to migrate to cities. Even more importantly, as detailed below, landlords could and did move rapidly to more land- and capital-intensive production, with far-reaching consequences for the larger society.

Similar efforts to resist market forces, in France, Provence, Aragon, Castile, the Low Countries, and Italian city-states, failed similarly, almost without exception (Cohn 2007).[10] Legal and social leveling ensued: By the early 1400s, serfdom – the strongest political expression of medieval

[7] In early work, Herlihy, followed by some other students of the period, contended that inequality actually increased in some Italian cities, as surviving patricians took over the property and businesses of the deceased. Alfani shows that this belief rested on errors of measurement; indeed, the property of the deceased was likelier to be acquired by newly well-off workers (Alfani 2017a, 331).

[8] As was admitted eloquently in the preamble to the Statute: "the said servants having no regard to the said ordinance, but to their ease and singular covetise [covetousness], do withdraw themselves to serve great men and other, unless they have livery and wages to the double or treble of that they were wont to take . . .".

[9] e.g., "that none pay in the time of sarcling [hoeing] or hay-making but a penny the day; and a mower of meadows for the acre five pence, or by the day five pence; and reapers of corn in the first week of August two pence, and the second three pence, and so till the end of August."

[10] The west European region in which such efforts came closest to success was apparently Catalonia, where repeated conflicts and rebellions were finally resolved with surrender to peasant demands in 1486 (Aston and Philpin 1985, 35–36).

inequality[11] – was dead, or at least a dead letter, virtually everywhere in western Europe;[12] and the last-ditch effort of elites to preserve outward differences of status, sumptuary laws that forbade newly wealthy commoners to dress and consume like their betters, were also widely ignored (Herlihy 1997, 47–48).

How, then, did landowners adjust? Why did they not resist more forcefully and unitedly? First, and perhaps most obviously, they abandoned the least productive land (some of it having been put to the plow only under the population pressures of the last half-century before the plague) and allowed it to return to pasture or woodland.[13] Second, they reduced the acreage devoted to grain and flax and increased their production of meat, milk, butter, cheese, and wool – all demanding less labor (Pamuk 2007, 294). Third, as the relative cost of raising animals decreased and the number of animals increased, they made greater use of animal power (and also of more capital-intensive wind- and water-power) and applied manure – in greater supply because of the turn to animal husbandry – more plentifully to the land that they continued to cultivate, thus raising the yields per acre and per man-hour.[14]

These adjustments were not a matter of choice, but a prerequisite of economic survival. An instructive example is the marked decline, after the Black Death, of the Benedictine abbey of Bury St. Edmunds. While landowners all around the abbey switched to land-intensive farming, the monks "insisted on producing wheat in the old fashion," with "disastrous" results. By the end of the fifteenth century, the abbey had lost most of its endowment and almost all of its political power (Gottfried 1982, 1983, 150).

[11] Serfs, in Moon's concise definition, "were legally bound to a plot of land and to the person of the landowner, were subject to his or her administrative and judicial authority, and ... passed their servile status on to their children" (Moon 1999, 66). Serfs, however, unlike slaves, were not chattel and could not (albeit with some exceptions) be sold separately from the land to which they were bound.

[12] Fischer (1996, 48–49), aptly summarizing a line of work from Postan onwards.

[13] On the widespread abandonment of farms and even rural villages ("Wüstungen") throughout western Europe in this period, see Fischer (1996, 47 and 455).

[14] On this array of changes, and on many of those described in the next paragraphs, see chiefly Herlihy (1997, chap. 2) and North and Thomas (1973, chap. 7). Windmills were known in Europe as early as the twelfth century but were improved in design in the late fourteenth and first came into wide use in the fifteenth century. Similarly, water-powered sawmills had been invented in the early thirteenth century but were widely adopted only after the Black Death (Benedictow 2004, 390).

The knock-on effects of these western European changes, at least in the judgment of many historians, were even more far-reaching and suggest how wrenching a supply-shock induced adaptation to market forces can be:

1. Because the care of animals, and in particular dairying, was traditionally a female preserve, women achieved greater economic independence.[15] They became major sources of credit in the rural economy and/or borrowed more freely to establish other enterprises (Dermineur 2018). They married later in life (on average four years later), or sometimes not at all, lowering the fertility rate and keeping wages high – an effect that can be traced most clearly in England (Voigtländer and Voth 2013).
2. The greater availability of meat and dairy products afforded, especially to the poor, a more protein-rich diet, increasing median height and (likely) average intelligence, since protein is crucial for brain development (Chertoff 2015).[16]
3. Increased wealth likely meant increased trade. As wages rose and the cost of rents and food fell, commoners' budgets incorporated a greater variety and quality of goods, raising demand for imported luxuries and hence for cheaper and more extensive ocean transport (Pamuk 2007, 295), with downstream effects discussed below.
4. Most clearly in England, the erosion of hierarchy (or so it is argued) contributed to major linguistic change. The efforts of the newly prosperous masses to emulate not only the dress but the accents of their "betters" may have produced the Great Vowel Shift (Benson 2000) that differentiates modern from early English (and makes

[15] Employment opportunities for women may have extended more widely, including into urban occupations (Pamuk 2007, 307 and 310).

[16] Our knowledge of post-Black Death dietary changes rests at this point on narrative accounts and fragmentary estate records. The analysis of stable isotopes in skeletal remains, which can date dietary change with amazing precision (Cheung et al. 2019), has barely begun. Analyzing skeletal remains from a dig at Petrikirche in Berlin, however, Mariana Zechini found "statistically significant differences between the pre- and post-plague populations … Both sexes showed an increased consumption of terrestrial protein following the Black Death, which means they were supplementing their diet with more animal meat" (Zechini 2017, 58). Other studies of European skeletal remains, however, have found no equally clear evidence of such a dietary change; nor, crucially, has anyone yet sought to establish whether places east of the Elbe underwent a change similar to the one that Zechini found in Berlin (private communication from Prof. Gundula Müldner, University of Reading, May 24, 2021). I am grateful to Karin Best for pointing me to this entire line of research.

present-day English spelling the nightmare that George Bernard Shaw is supposed to have parodied).[17]

5. Because they often lived in close proximity to each other, monks, priests, and university students and teachers apparently had an even higher-than-average death rate. An acute shortage of priests, teachers, and Latin scholars ensued: in short, a major loss of human capital.
   a. Lay literacy expanded, but in vernacular tongues more than in Latin (McNeill 1976, 183). In England, the aristocracy, finding few tutors conversant in French, raised a generation fluent only in English,[18] which then displaced French as the everyday language of the nobility (Gasquet 1908, 234–235).[19]
   b. High mortality among the clergy led to widespread recruitment of ill-educated priests, since only priests could administer the sacraments believed to be crucial to salvation; and the decline in land rentals reduced Church income, impelling popes and bishops to such inventive new exactions as the sale of indulgences. The ignorance and corruption of the official Church, combined with the growing literacy and erudition of the laity, paved the way for the Reformation (McNeill 1976, 185).
   c. The monastery-based *scriptoria* were especially decimated; as the supply of hand-copied literature fell and demand among the newly literate laity expanded, prices increased sharply (see more extensive discussion in Chapter 8).
   d. The high death rates in existing universities and the increased returns to human capital spurred an expansion of education, including the founding of some twenty-eight new universities (where Latin, however, remained the language of instruction)

[17] How, Shaw supposedly asked, should the word "ghoti" be pronounced? As "fish," he answered: gh as in laugh, o as in women, ti as in nation. Alas, the almost universal attribution to Shaw appears to be erroneous (Zimmer 2010).

[18] As early as 1362, however, Parliament decreed that all judicial proceedings should henceforth be in English, not (as before that date) in Norman French. Statute of Pleading, 36 Edw. III c. 15.

[19] Shakespeare probably portrayed the next generation of the English nobility accurately, when he put into the mouth of Henry V (b. 1386, reigned 1413–1422) the broken French in which he courts Princess Katherine (whose English is even weaker than Henry's French), finally confessing, "It is as easy for me, Kate, to conquer the kingdom as to speak so much more French: I shall never move thee in French, unless it be to laugh at me." (*Henry V*, Act 5, Scene 2). Yet Katherine's extensive speeches in elegant French suggest that Shakespeare's audience (or at least all but the groundlings) still could get the sense of most of it.

and an untold number of new vernacular-based grammar schools, between 1400 and 1500 (Grendler 2004, 2–3; Herlihy 1997, 69–71).

While no radical labor-saving innovation occurred in agriculture,[20] relevant inventions abounded in other fields, again with far-reaching effects:

1. As labor became more valuable, so did the measurement of time worked. As one historian has noted, "The first new technology of the plague years was time-keeping – mechanical clocks and hour-glasses." (Lienhard, John 1988). Cf. (Landes 1983).
2. The sharp decline in interest rates, coupled with the rise in wages, led to "a massive substitution of capital for labor" (Epstein 2000, 61) in manufacturing throughout the western European economies – depending, again, on the elasticity of substitution under prevailing technologies in various sectors.
3. A remarkable array of labor-saving technological and organizational innovations emerged "that would not have been there with plentiful cheap labor" (Benedictow 2004, 390).
4. The demand for exotic goods opened opportunities for huge profits from long-distance trade, while high wages encouraged the invention of less labor-intensive means of shipping. Beginning around 1450, the Portuguese devised faster and more capacious ships (the caravel and the carrack, respectively) that could travel farther with smaller crews (Herlihy 1997, 50; Smith 1993, chap. 2).[21] Coupled with improved methods of navigation (the compass, better maps), these opened not only wider European and African trade but the voyages of discovery, above all da Gama's opening of a direct ocean route to the spices and silks of Asia (Blaydes and Paik 2019) and Columbus's transnavigation of the Atlantic, both occurring near the end of the fifteenth century.
5. The demand for less labor-intensive technology extended also to the realm of combat, contributing to the military revolution (Pamuk 2007, 311; Parker 1996). It is only after 1350, for example, that

[20] I advance reasons for this failure below: p. 67.

[21] Curtin argued that "[t]he European 'maritime revolution' of the fifteenth and sixteenth centuries was not so much a revolution in ship design as the discovery of the world wind system." (Curtin 1984, 136). This seems, however, to have remained a minority judgment.

gunpowder, cannons, and (after 1400) firearms begin to be used extensively in warfare (Herlihy 1997, 51).

6. Most controversially, it even seems possible that the population losses of this period led to global cooling: As millions of square miles of cropland returned to pasture or forest, CO_2 levels in the atmosphere declined, and with them global temperatures (van Hoof 2004).
7. And, most importantly of all, Johannes Gutenberg combined his skills from minting and blacksmithing to overcome the acute shortage of scribes' human capital and the intense demand for reading matter by devising the movable-type printing press, which quickly overshot the initial need and became itself one of history's most powerful exogenous shocks (see Chapter 8).
8. Early publishers quickly discovered that demand was greater for works in the vernacular than in Latin; but satisfying that demand in turn tended to standardize the various European languages, intensify their usage, and perhaps even solidify national identities (Sasaki 2017).
9. Human capital, not only of scribes but of scholars generally, moved from extreme scarcity immediately after the Black Death to relative abundance by the sixteenth century. Scribes were needed only for ceremonial and presentational volumes (e.g., lavishly illustrated prayer books). And no longer was an arduous study of Latin grammar the *sine qua non*[22] for serious intellectual discourse. The priestly and Latinate monopoly of scholarship was broken – or, at least, on its way to rapid breakdown.

To understate the case, the consequences of yielding to the market in the wake of the Black Death were radical and extensive. They revolutionized western European societies, changed their diet, clothing, language, literacy, and military technology; and, if Herlihy is right, set these nascent states on a route to wealth, power, and colonial conquest. It is the moment at which the "great divergence" attained critical mass.

EASTERN EUROPE AND WESTERN RUSSIA[23]

In the century before the Black Death, as western Europe's population outgrew the ability of the land (given current technology) to sustain it,

[22] Yes, the use of Latin here is intentionally ironic.

[23] The canonical, if somewhat overstated, treatment is Blum (1957). An excellent overview of the then-prevailing scholarly consensus is Brenner's introductory essay in Aston and Philpin (1985, chap. 1).

many peasants effectively "homesteaded" in thinly populated eastern Europe.[24] The process was led mostly by "locators" (*Lokatoren*), agents of landlords, or themselves independent entrepreneurs who had acquired tracts of land, who recruited peasants to settle as tenants on the eastern expanses (Rosenberg 1943, 11). The settlers were offered generous terms, including fixed rents (usually in money, sometimes in grain), rather than the labor dues or sharecropping that had prevailed in western Europe, and even rent-free early years of tenancy. Above all, they were free of the traditional obligations of feudalism that, in pre-plague western Europe, were almost universal. Since most of them came from German-speaking regions, the terms that were used to describe the evolving relationships of tenancy are mostly (and sometimes confusingly) German.[25]

When the Black Death created acute shortages of labor throughout Europe, the eastern settlers, like peasants in the West, sought more favorable terms (Hagen 2002, 34–35). Landowners would not, and likely could not, grant them. Indeed, the general inflation diminished the purchasing power of the fixed monetary rents that the landowners received (Rosenberg 1944, 231). As fairly recent arrivals, the settlers would have found it easy to exit: to move back to the higher wages that were coming to prevail in western Europe. Increasingly, starting in Prussia as early as 1427 (Rosenberg 1944, 231), the landowners forbade them to leave, "binding" them to the soil (*Schollenbindung*).[26] Unlike in England, the landlords colluded successfully, enforcing maximum wages, rarely poaching tenants from each other or offering better terms than their neighboring landowners, and returning escaped tenants to their masters.[27] Fixed

[24] H. Scott and Melton (2015, 8–9) provide an excellent and concise overview of the process.

[25] Lucid and helpful efforts to disentangle the terms, which are often used inconsistently, are to be found in Rasmussen (2010, n. 1) and Kaak (1991, 432–435).

[26] In Russia, peasants continued to enjoy unlimited mobility until the late 1450s, when a single monastery was granted the right to prevent its tenants from leaving, and to recover any who fled. Other monasteries soon received similar privileges or were allowed to limit peasant movement to a single two-week period in each year (either side of Autumn St. George's Day, November 26 in the Julian calendar). The St. George's Day limitation was made universal in a decree of 1497. By the 1550s, exit was possible only with payment of an increasingly heavy fee; chapter 11 of the law code (*Ulozhenie*) of 1649 completed the enserfment of the Russian peasantry (Hellie 1971, chap. 4; 1992, 77). In eastern Europe, too, landowners "tightened the screws" most rapidly after 1500 (H. Scott and Melton 2015, 10ff.).

[27] If at first landowners merely demanded exorbitant exit fees, later usage suggests that threats of violence or actual corporal punishment played an important role. In the nineteenth century Russian estate whose detailed records were studied by Steven

rentals yielded fairly quickly to labor dues (*Frondienst*), an obligation to work one or more (usually more) days a week on the owner's land (the demesne or, in German, the *Gut*). Over time, the required labor rose to as many as five days per family per week (H. Scott and Melton 2015, 10–11),[28] and the demesne incorporated increasing parts of what had been peasant property.[29] *Schollenbindung* advanced to *Gutsherrschaft*, the obligation (which soon became hereditary: *Erbuntertänigkeit*) to work on the owner's land (Kaak 1991). In the most extreme cases, the system turned into one of *Leibeigenschaft*, literally "ownership of the body," a serfdom almost indistinguishable from slavery.

As the economies of western Europe slowly revived, newly prosperous cities, chiefly in the Netherlands, offered a lucrative market for imported grain. Owners in eastern Europe in effect found an exit option, not exporting their land, but the grain that their land produced, through Baltic ports (Aston and Philpin 1985, 37). As Barrington Moore may have been the first to note, the resultant system came to resemble the antebellum US South or (in Immanuel Wallerstein's subsequent telling) the sugar plantations of the Caribbean (Bowman 1980) (H. Scott and Melton 2015, 3–4): Servile labor produced agrarian products for export to more urbanized areas. Cities in eastern Europe remained, in this period, small and insignificant; they tended actually to shrink over time, with the exception of the flourishing port city of Danzig (Lindberg 2009, 610) (Raster 2019, fig. C.1). They offered few exit opportunities to peasants, and indeed their elites usually sided with the landowners (Aston and Philpin 1985, 39–40).

Successful resistance to market pressures meant that few if any of the revolutionary western European consequences ensued. Literacy remained low, printing presses were rare (Sasaki 2017, 1038), no labor-saving innovations arose, languages remained a welter of local dialects,[30]

Hoch, a quarter of male serfs were flogged at least once in any given year; the mean number of lashes was 37.4, and the maximum was 80 (Hoch 1986, 163–164).

[28] In the lands east of the Elbe, the stronghold of the Prussian second serfdom, this process commenced in the late 1400s and reached its apogee only in the sixteenth century (Hagen 2002, chap. 1).

[29] In the fifteenth century, the demesne normally occupied about a fifth of the total land of the estate; by the late sixteenth century, two-fifths (Kaak 1991, 436).

[30] German began to become standardized only with the publication of Luther's translation of the Bible in 1522 (New Testament) and 1534 (entire Bible). I owe to my esteemed colleague Iván Berend, now well past his ninetieth birthday, the delicious story that as late as 1867, his grandfather, standing for election to the first Hungarian parliament after the *Ausgleich* that established the Dual Monarchy, had

women were not empowered, no voyages of discovery sallied forth, and seaborne trade was confined to the intra-European export of grain and import of manufactures and luxury goods. Much as slavery's malign legacy survives to the present day in the US South (Acharya, Sen, and Blackwell 2018), serfdom in eastern Germany and eastern Europe (although technically abolished in Prussia in 1807 and in Russia in 1861) continued to undermine nascent democracies and even today inclines eastern Europe (and eastern Germany) to authoritarianism.[31]

Historians have long attempted to explain the stark divergence of outcomes in western and eastern Europe. Perhaps most famously, Evsey Domar, as part of a general explanation of slavery and serfdom, posited that extreme labor scarcity, coupled with rulers' need for a "servitor" class of warrior-landlords, would lead to serfdom, while milder scarcity of labor, absent such a need, would lead to an egalitarian "homesteader" society (Domar 1970). Matranga and Natkhov explain Russian serfdom by a similar mechanism, augmented by peculiarities of southern Russian soil and geography (Matranga and Natkhov 2019). Eric Williams may have been the first to point to the centrality of the lucrative export trade for plantation slavery in the Americas (Williams 1944); the theme is elaborated in Sven Beckert's recent *Empire of Cotton* (Beckert 2014) and in the impressive MA thesis of the Piketty student Tom Raster (Raster 2019).[32] Brenner rejected such economistic explanations, viewing the divergent outcomes as determined chiefly by relative class power:[33] Eastern landlords colluded successfully, western ones did not; while western peasants, with stronger pre-existing village solidarity, resisted successfully and eastern peasants did not. His explanation, however, has more

to give his campaign speeches in Latin, no other tongue being widely understood by the relevant electorate. Earlier, in the eighteenth century, travelers to Hungary noted that, despite widespread multilingualism, Latin was still the common means of mutual communication, even with innkeepers and servants (H. M. Scott and Simms 2007, chap. 10).

[31] To emphasize the lasting legacy of serfdom in these regions is by no means to accept the whole *Sonderweg* thesis about Germany's peculiar path to modernity (Kocka 1988).

[32] Following in part (but only in part) the logic of Acemoglu and Wolitsky (2011), Raster argues that increased profitability of the landowner's product affords her greater resources to meet the costs of coercion (monitoring, preventing escape, enforcing discipline, etc.) (Raster 2019, 9). Hence the expanded Baltic market for grain may have actually intensified serfdom.

[33] Brenner, however, conceded that eastern Europe's grain exports "enhanced the class power" of landlords (Aston and Philpin 1985, 37).

than a whiff of circularity: Our only evidence that landlords had greater "class power" in the East, or that peasants there were weaker, is the outcome we are trying to explain – that landlords succeeded in the East and failed in the West.

My hypothesis, while still tentative, is simpler and, if correct, can account also for landlords' more successful collusion in the East. East European landowners, I suggest, did not adapt to less labor-intensive production because they could not.[34] Neither climate nor soil quality suited their expanses for the kind of wool, meat, and dairy production that came to predominate in England and much of western Europe.[35] Nor was there much chance of a technological solution,[36] for example, the kind of mechanization of cotton harvesting that Southern US landowners adopted when the Great Migration of African Americans out of the region deprived them of their still semi-servile workforce (Boustan 2017). And, while owners indeed began to export some of their grain to the lucrative markets of Amsterdam and other cities of western Europe, that market had to await the post-plague urban revival: Significant shipments began only in the 1490s (Unger 1997, VIII, 5–6), more than a century after wages had shot up in the West and when the East's "second serfdom" was already well on its way to becoming entrenched. Even more tellingly, some 80 percent of grain exports from the port of Danzig came from the region of West Prussia, which "was dominated by capital-intensive forms of agriculture based primarily on wage labor," not by *Gutsherrschaft* (H. Scott and Melton 2015, 4).

If, indeed, substitution was highly inelastic, there was at first no realistic chance of exit, and no technological solution appeared on the horizon,

[34] This is not to suggest that East Elbia had no animal husbandry or was totally unsuitable for it. Peasants clearly grazed pigs on forest land, and there was some wool and dairy production (Hagen 2002, chap. 1). The output seems however to have been almost entirely for local use. (Cf. Blum on animal husbandry in Russia, on page 70 below).

[35] Another possibility, suggested by the Harvard undergraduate research assistant Can Yesildire, is that east European landowners may have lacked western Europe's urban markets for milk and meat. Most of the land-intensive products, however, notably wool, cheese, and salted meats, could be transported over greater distances; nor is it easy to see how market considerations alone would have given rise to the sharp geographical divide that we see between regions of free and servile labor (see below).

[36] Chiefly because the technological leap would have been too great. The introduction even of horse-drawn labor-saving equipment – mechanical reapers, binders, threshers, and seed-drills – required prior advances in metalworking, chains or belts, and precision parts that were centuries away from appearing.

landowners faced a simple choice: raise wages, and lose money on every unit they produced;[37] watch the peasants exit and abandon production for want of labor; or compel the peasants to remain and to accept compensation that was less than their marginal product. That the owners unanimously chose the third option cannot surprise us, since it also had the effect of sustaining land values, which otherwise were sure to plummet even more than in the West.

Neither can the landlords' ability to collude, and to refrain from poaching others' tenants, remain a mystery. If paying higher wages would be economical for only the few exceptionally efficient landowners (Hagen 2002, 35), none would have had any great incentive to defect.[38]

A first test of this hypothesis, of course, asks whether soil quality or climate obstructed any effort in the East to move from labor- to more land-intensive production.[39] Fortunately Beck and Sieber have compiled a comprehensive Old World data set that, based on soil and climate alone, gauges the suitability, on a continuous scale from total non-suitability (0) to complete suitability (1), of each unit of approximately 5 × 5 km for one of four kinds of food production:[40] agriculture, pastoralism, hunting and gathering, or "sedentary animal husbandry" (Beck and Sieber 2010).[41] A resultant map of the western Eurasian continent's suitability for animal husbandry (Map 4.1) suggests a pronounced and precipitous change

[37] This will have been true of the representative landowner under conventional zero-profit assumptions. Obviously, more efficient estates would have been able to continue production, albeit at a reduced profit.

[38] Peters, in contrast, assumes substantial differences in productivity among landlords, and indeed some motivation of more productive owners to expand their holdings by driving the less productive into bankruptcy; hence collusion could be maintained only with the assistance of rulers (Margaret Peters 2022, 12–13). Rulers in this period, however, were weak compared to landowners (H. Scott and Melton 2015, 10); and large differences in productivity, if the Coase Theorem is correct, could not have prevailed in equilibrium. The less productive owners would find it more profitable to sell their lands to the more productive ones.

[39] A pioneering effort to use soil and climate to predict economic and political outcomes was Easterly (2007). There, the ratio, in any given area, of land suitable for wheat to land suitable for sugar cane proved to have a strong statistical association with present-day equality; i.e., wheat was conducive to equality, sugar cane to inequality.

[40] The categories are not mutually exclusive. Some regions are well-suited to two or more kinds of food production.

[41] As they put it, "Suitability of animal husbandry is very low at minimum temperatures below −15°C., whereas it follows a unimodal function with a peak at ca. 5°C above that. Gleyosols, planosols, andosols, cambisols, and luvisols were among the soil types associated with high suitability for animal husbandry in the model."

Map 4.1 Areas suited by climate and soil for sedentary animal husbandry. (darker = more suited; lightest = least suited).
Source: Data from Beck and Sieber (2010); maps prepared by Jacob Morrier.

between eastern and western Europe:[42] Almost everything west of the present-day western Polish border and the Carpathian Mountains is at least moderately suited to animal husbandry, while everything east of that line is completely unsuited. As it happens, almost all of the areas characterized by the "second serfdom" lay east of this line.

The leading twentieth-century German historian of *Gutsherrschaft*, Heinrich Kaak, has noted the sharp geographical division between areas of free and servile labor and has sought to demarcate it.

> The area of *Gutsherrschaft* was, at least in part, precisely demarcated. The boundary is clear in the West and South. Beginning in East Elbian Schleswig-Holstein, the boundary proceeded to the Southeast, roughly following the Elbe [River], but including the Altmark as part of the East Elbian [i.e., servile] realm and excluding the parts of Electoral Saxony east of the Elbe. Then the area of Lausitz and Silesia lay on the servile [*gutsherrlich*] side, and the boundary then continued to the Southeast, counting Galicia, Ukraine, and some neighboring districts like Podolia, as part of the servile area. (Kaak 1991, 432)

[42] The authors note in their supplementary online commentary that one of the sharpest changes in soil and climate, and one of the few in which a change in suitability coincides with a political boundary, is "the western borders of [present-day] Poland," i.e., today the Oder and Neisse rivers (File S2 Details and interpretation of some patterns. Found at: doi:10.1371/journal.pone.0010416.s003).

Additionally, Kaak emphasizes that serfdom was uniquely linked to grain-growing:[43]

> The area of *Gutsherrschaft* is the region in which grain production formed the focus of the agrarian economy... The share of *specialized crops on the one hand, and of pastoral economy on the other* [my emphasis], was relatively slight here. Binding to the soil [i.e., forbidding peasants to leave] and an economy based on labor dues [*Fronwirtschaft*] could hardly have formed such a close tie to any other branch of agriculture as it did to grain production in the extensive, relatively thinly populated regions of East-Central and eastern Europe. (Kaak 1991, 435)

The association between suitability for animal husbandry and serfdom is perhaps clearest in Prussia. In Map 4.2, maps of Prussia of similar scale and perspective display the Beck–Sieber "suitability" index (Map 4.2b) and (Map 4.2a) a frequently invoked proxy for historical serfdom: the share of large estates (of more than 300 *Morgen*, i.e., some 77 hectares or 190 acres) in total estates in each Prussian county at the time of the census of 1816, only nine years after the formal abolition of serfdom.[44] The census-takers apparently regarded that acreage, as have subsequent scholars (Cinnirella and Hornung 2016) (Raster 2019), as the minimum estate size that would have employed servile labor.[45]

Moving beyond simple inspection, I calculate for each of the 272 Prussian counties in 1816 for which I have data:[46] (a) the total area of the county in hectares; (b) the total number of farms it contained; (c) the

[43] Blum similarly notes the relative unimportance of animal husbandry in the Russian agrarian economy: "it seems to have been subordinate to tillage just about everywhere." (Blum 1971, 166) A partial exception is the serf-based dairy farming known as *Koppelwirtschaft*, which arose in parts of Schleswig-Holstein in the seventeenth and eighteenth centuries (Rasmussen 2010). As Rasmussen emphasizes, however, these estates were "integrated dairy and grain farms. Grain production was not abandoned as dairies spread, but expanded" (Rasmussen 2010, 184).

[44] Census data are from IPEHD, https://www.ifo.de/en/iPEHD (Becker et al. 2014). The map is from Raster (2019, 92) and is reproduced by kind permission of Tom Raster. The four dark lines running northwest to southeast depict rivers; the Elbe is the second from the left.

[45] Despite its frequent use by previous scholars, this remains an imperfect proxy for previous serfdom. In only a few areas of Europe, all much smaller than Prussia, do we appear to have more precise information on, e.g., the extent of peasants' labor dues; and even fewer of those display anything like the sharp contrasts in soil and climate that characterized Prussia.

[46] There were roughly 300 counties at that time; but the Prussian boundaries had shifted at the Congress of Vienna (1815), and a comprehensive reorganization of counties was begun in 1818. This leads to occasional confusion of the names and extent of counties. I restrict myself here to the counties whose names and boundaries can be unambiguously identified.

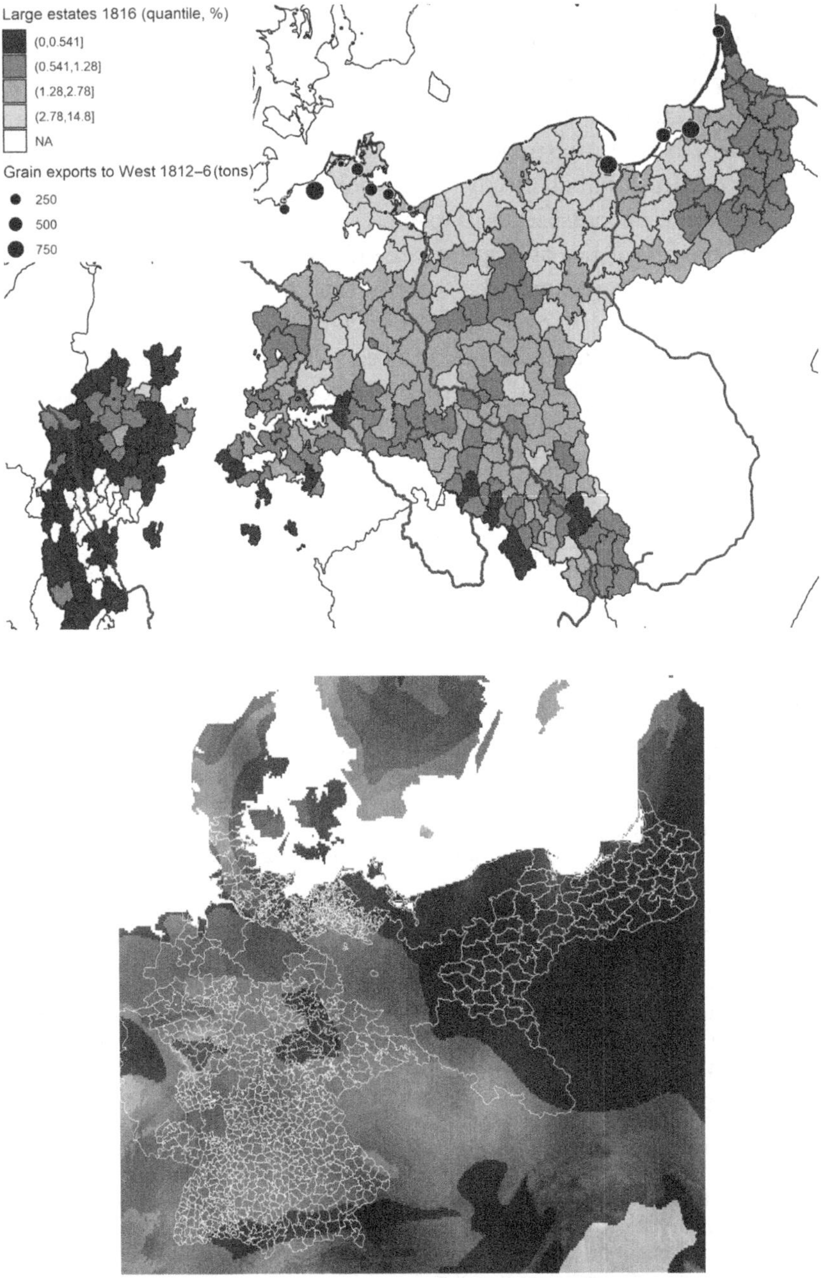

Map 4.2 Large estates in Prussia (4.2a; lighter = greater share of large estates) vs. non-suitability for sedentary animal husbandry (4.2b; darker = less suitable)

number of farms of greater than 300 *Morgen* (likely to have used servile labor);[47] and (d) the county's mean Beck–Sieber score of "suitability for sedentary animal husbandry," that is, the mean of all Beck–Sieber 5 × 5 km rasters whose centroids fell within the given county.[48] For reasons that will shortly become apparent, I also classify each county as to whether it does, or does not, adjoin directly on (e) a port city or (f) a navigable river.[49] My hypothesis of course leads us to expect a strongly negative relationship between the prevalence of large estates and the Beck–Sieber score.[50]

First, simply regressing[51] the share of total farms in each county that consisted of farms of over 300 *Morgen* (i.e., in terms of the above variables, c/b) on the mean Beck–Sieber score (d) yields the following scatterplot (Figure 4.1) and estimated coefficients (Table 4.1). Figure 4.1 also depicts the estimated curve and 95 percent confidence interval from a normal logistic regression.[52]

The Beck–Sieber index appears to display a negative and well-specified association with the share of large, and putatively formerly servile, estates. But what else might be at work, that is, what possible confounders might vitiate the apparent link between serfdom and soil/climate? Two

[47] Unfortunately, the census provides us with no data on the exact size of each farm; they are classified simply as "15 *Morgen* or less;" "15–300 *Morgen*;" and "greater than 300 *Morgen*." Hence, we cannot accurately assess the share of a given county's area that was included in these large estates.

[48] Summary statistics for all variables, as well as their intercorrelations, are presented in Appendix Tables A4.1 and A4.2.

[49] Eight counties in our set adjoin directly on one of the three main port cities: Danzig is touched by Preussisch Stargard, Neustadt, Marienburg, and of course the county of Danzig; Königsberg is bounded by Kreuzburg, Heiligenbeil, and the county of Königsberg; Memel, by the county of Memel and a county on which unfortunately we lack information on share of large estates, Heydekrug. Between 1520 and 1814, according to some accounts, Memel had been largely closed off by sabotage from its rival, Danzig (Geschichte des Memellandes von 1525 bis 1722 2021). The findings here are robust to the exclusion of the county of Memel from the set of port-bounded counties. My source for navigable rivers is European Environment Agency (2020).

[50] In what follows, I am extremely grateful to Caleb Ziolkowski, PhD UCLA 2021, for wise statistical and presentational advice.

[51] Because the dependent variable is left- and right-censored – the share of large farms must lie between zero and one – I employ quasi-binomial logistic regression rather than ordinary least squares (OLS). Results are robust to the alternative specification, but (as might be expected) OLS produces predicted shares of less than zero in counties with high Beck–Sieber scores.

[52] The small values of the scale parameter in Tables 4.1 and 4.2 allay the usual concern that a standard logit estimation might fail to capture the greater variance of the dependent variable.

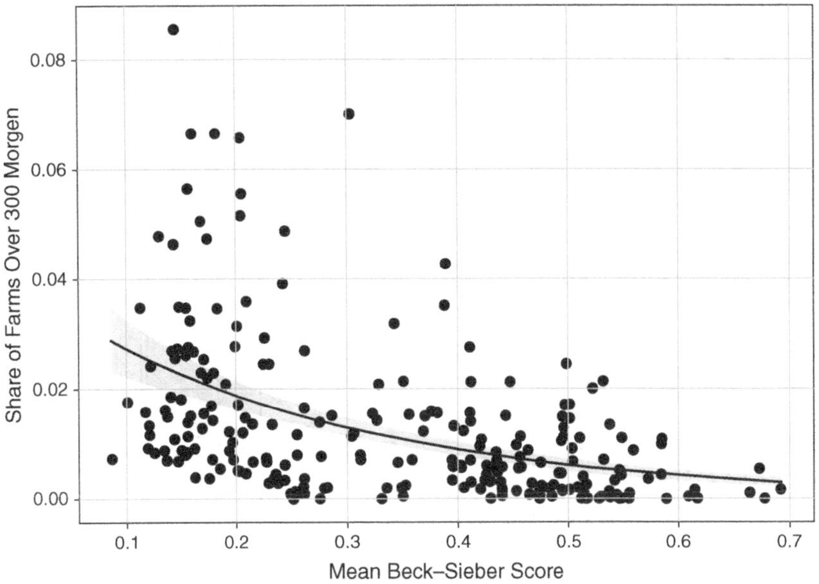

Figure 4.1 Prussian counties, 1816
Large farms as share of total farms vs. mean Beck–Sieber score
(standard logistic estimation)

possibilities suggest themselves at once. (1) Geographically large counties appear to have a greater share of large estates, possibly because county boundaries were drawn not to include more than some maximum number of estates.[53] (2) We know that serfdom became entrenched – or, as many argue, arose – as export markets for grain became available. The demand came from the reviving economies of western Europe, and the only practicable means of transport was by sea. Overland transport being almost prohibitively expensive, those markets were readily open only to counties that lay directly next to a port city or a navigable river.[54] Because

[53] My conjecture here is that Berlin wanted a *Landrat* (county magistrate) to be responsible for only some maximum number of landowners; he would otherwise be overburdened. A county at the 25th percentile had an area of 44,600 hectares; at the 50th percentile, 65,220 ha.; at the 75th percentile, 96,000 ha. The largest county had an area of 270,000 ha., or just over 1000 square miles (1 square mile = 259 ha.); the smallest, 738 ha., or less than 3 square miles.

[54] Estimations that include a Euclidian, or "as the crow flies," distance from a given county to the nearest port or river implicitly assume that the cost of overland transport varies linearly with distance, independent of topography. A county's distance so calculated also turns out to be highly collinear with its surface area (r = –.63), which bears a more plausible relation to share of large estates (see below).

Table 4.1 *Prussian counties, 1816 Large farms as share of total farms vs. Beck–Sieber score*

Binomial logit regression table:

Generalized Linear Model Regression Results

Dep. Variable:	PERCENTOV300	No. Observations:	237
Model:	GLM	Df Residuals:	235
Model Family:	Binomial	Df Model:	1
Link Function:	logit	Scale:	0.011526
Method:	IRLS	Log-Likelihood:	−13.067
Date:	Sun, 08 Nov 2020	Deviance:	2.3742
Time:	17:38:42	Pearson chi2:	2.71
No. Iterations:	10		
Covariance Type:	nonrobust		

	coef	std err	Z	P > |z|	[0.025	0.975]
Intercept	−3.2150	0.136	−23.593	0.000	−3.482	−2.948
MEAN_BS	−3.6924	0.459	−8.042	0.000	−4.592	−2.793

any effect of soil and climate might manifest differently in such readily accessible counties, it seems advisable to control not only for adjacency to a port or river, but to the interaction of such adjacency with the Beck–Sieber index.

Standardizing all non-indicator variables (mean = 0, s.d. = 1) for ease of interpretation, and regressing share of large estates on: (a) the Beck–Sieber index, (b) adjacency to a port, (c) adjacency to a river, (d) the interaction of those terms, and (e) the total area of the country, yields the estimates displayed in Table 4.2.

County area clearly matters: It has a strong and well-specified association with the share of large estates. The relation between a county's Beck–Sieber index and its share of large estates, however, is equally well specified and substantively stronger: Its estimated coefficient is more than 1.5 times that for area (and recall, both area and Beck–Sieber are standardized). By way of contrast, the positive association between share of large estates and market access, whether through a neighboring port or through adjacency to a navigable river, is imprecisely estimated; and, controlling for those possible confounders, the association of large estates with county area and soil and climate remains strong.

The relationship emerges clearly in graphical form. Figure 4.2 displays the relationship (based on the regression in Table 4.2) between county area and prevalence of large estates, holding all other variables at their medians; Figure 4.3 shows the similar relationship between Beck–Sieber suitability scores and prevalence of large estates, in each case with 95 percent confidence intervals.[55]

The strength of the two relationships can perhaps be seen even more vividly when, in Figures 4.4 and 4.5, we plot the predicted share of large estates, together with the 95 percent confidence intervals around those estimates, holding all other variables at their medians, when (1) county area and (2) Beck–Sieber score are (a) at their respective means, (b) one standard deviation (s.d.) above the mean, (c) one s.d. below the mean, and (d) the difference between the two predicted values (b–c). Note that in both cases, (d) differs from zero at conventional levels of significance; and that, in the case of the Beck–Sieber index, (b) differs significantly from (a). Moreover, the point estimate of the effect of a two standard deviation change (from one s.d. below to one s.d. above the mean) in soil and climate is larger than that for county area (.09 vs. .07). Indeed, a two

[55] Confidence intervals in all cases are calculated by bootstrapping with 500 iterations.

Table 4.2 *Prussian counties, 1816 Large farms as share of total farms vs. county's Beck–Sieber score,*[1] *port and river adjacency, interactions, and total area of county (all non-indicator variables standardized)*[2]

Multi quasi-binomial logit regression table (w/ area):

Generalized Linear Model Regression Results

Dep. Variable :	PERCENTOV 300	No. Observations:	235
Model:	GLM	Df Residuals:	228
Model Family:	Binomial	Df Model:	6
Link Function:	logit	Scale:	0.0093932
Method:	IRLS	Log-Likelihood:	−12.714
Date:	Fri, 05 Mar 2021	Deviance:	1.9782
Time:	13:40:16	Pearson chi2:	2.14
No. Iterations:	10		
Covariance Type:	Nonrobust		

	coef	std err	z	P > |z|	[0.025	0.975]
Intercept	−4.5627	0.078	−58.439	0.000	−4.716	−4.410
MEAN_BS_STD	−0.4559	0.081	−5.648	0.000	−0.614	−0.298
BY_PORT_M	0.3771	0.404	0.933	0.351	−0.415	1.169
BY_RIVER	0.1777	0.147	1.212	0.226	−0.110	0.465
PORT_INT_M_STD	0.7003	0.573	1.222	0.222	−0.423	1.823
RIVER_INT_STD	0.1468	0.154	0.955	0.339	−0.154	0.448
AREA_STD	0.2873	0.052	5.547	0.000	0.186	0.389

[1] Recall that a county's Beck–Sieber score is calculated as the mean of all 5 × 5 km rasters whose centroids fall within that county.

[2] Key to variable names: MEAN_BS_STD = mean Beck–Sieber score (-100), standardized; BY_PORT_MEMEL = county is adjacent to the ports of Danzig, Königsberg, or Memel (1) or not adjacent (0); BY_RIVER = county is adjacent to a navigable river (1) or not adjacent (0); PORT_INT_M_STD = interaction between MEAN_BS_STD and BY_PORT_MEMEL; RIVER_INT_STD = interaction between MEAN_BS_STD and BY_RIVER; AREA_STD = area of county, in square kilometers, standardized.

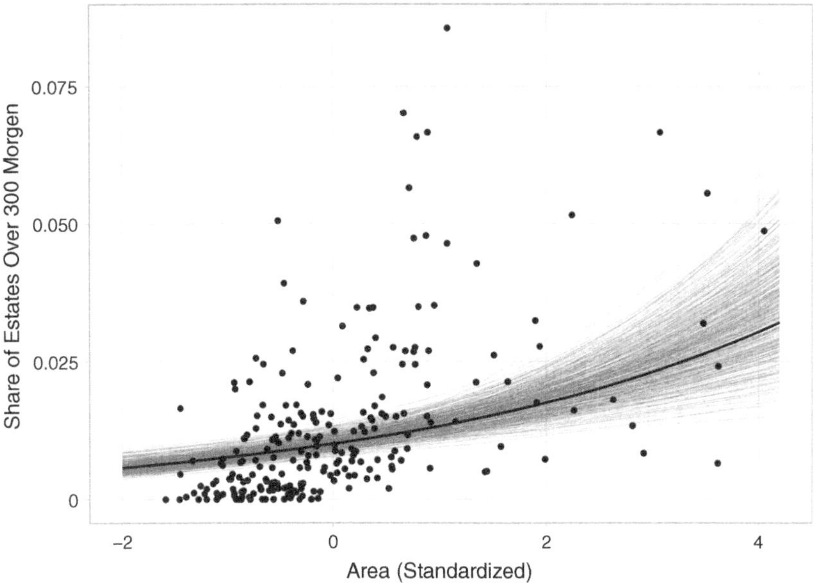

Figure 4.2 Prussian counties, 1816
Relationship between a county's total area and its share of estates of >300 *Morgen* / total estates, controlling for soil, climate, and port or river access

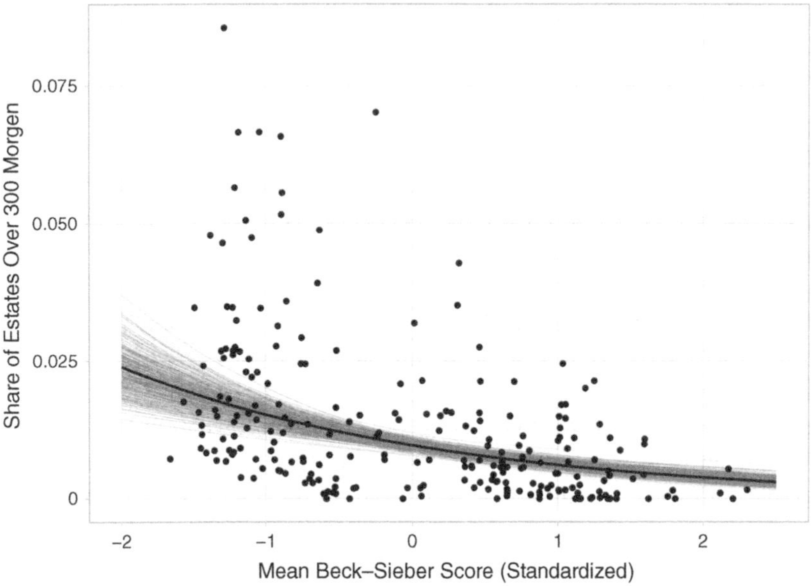

Figure 4.3 Prussian counties, 1816
Relationship between a county's Beck–Sieber score and share of estates of >300 *Morgen* / total estates, controlling for county area and port or river access

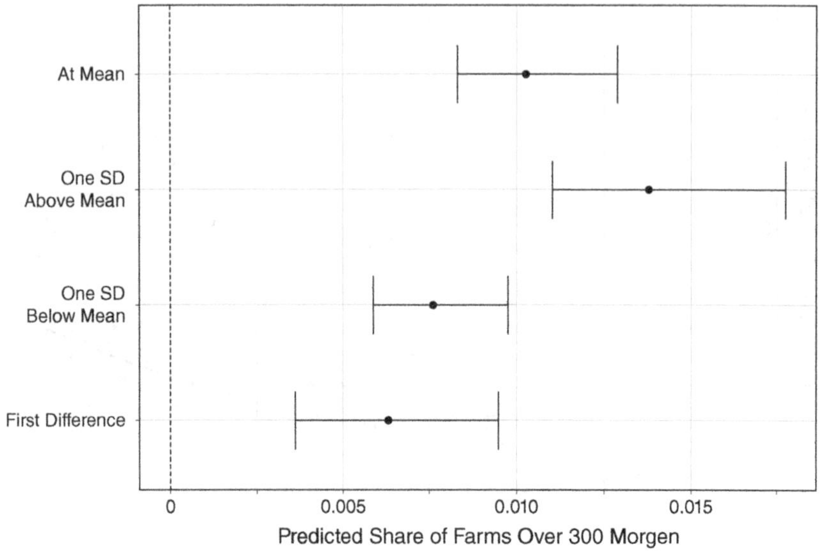

Figure 4.4 Prussian counties, 1816
Predicted share of farms of >300 *Morgen* at mean county area, one s.d. above, and one s.d. below the mean, holding all other variables at their median values[56]

s.d. increase in the Beck–Sieber index roughly halves a county's predicted share of large estates, from 0.015 to 0.007.

While the share of large estates is an admittedly imperfect proxy for historical serfdom (see above, p. 70), it is likely the least imperfect that we now have to test the relationship – if, indeed, there is one – between serfdom on the one hand and soil and climate on the other. And it is almost certainly the best we have to test that relationship against the more conventional view that links East European serfdom chiefly to the export market in grain.

While doubtless the availability of export possibilities intensified serfdom, just as it later intensified slavery in the New World, soil and climate appear to have played at least as important a role. The export trade in grain, which began after the advent of the second serfdom, indeed multiplied the power and wealth of the landowners. Yet it seems unlikely that a second serfdom would have emerged at all, had East European soil and climate allowed as smooth a transition from labor- to land-intensive

[56] Whiskers display 95 percent confidence intervals, again obtained by bootstrapping with 500 iterations.

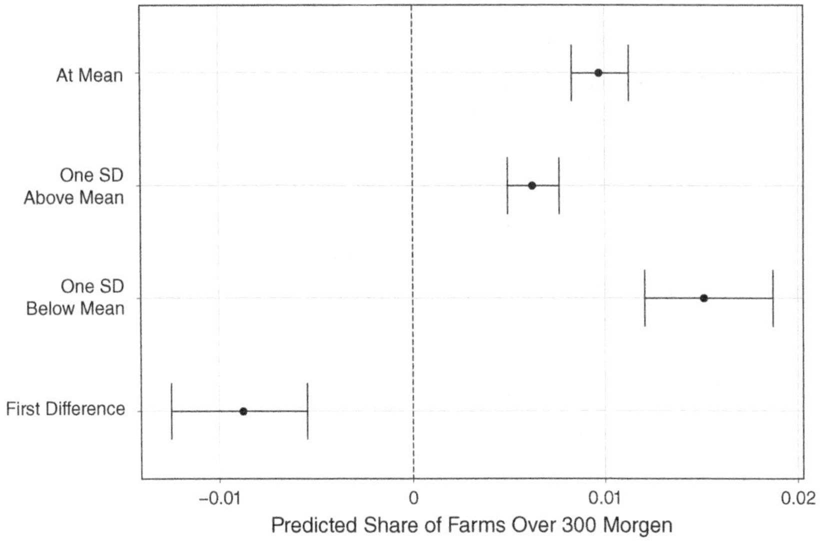

Figure 4.5 Prussian counties, 1816
Predicted share of farms of >300 *Morgen* at mean county Beck–Sieber score, one s.d. above, and one s.d. below the mean, holding all other variables at their median values

agriculture as occurred in England and western Europe.[57] Elastic substitution likely ended serfdom in the West; inelastic substitution may well have precipitated it in the East.

CONCLUSION

The Black Death is generally agreed to have been one of history's most profound and far-reaching supply shocks. Completely unanticipated and almost certainly exogenous, its effects were felt throughout Europe, immediately reducing labor supply by at least half, and ultimately by two-thirds. While it has long been known that the plague's effects differed starkly between western and eastern Europe – ending the remnants of serfdom and reducing inequality in the West, but enserfing formerly free

[57] Other factors, of course, influenced the particular form, and the regional variations, that the "second serfdom" took. Military necessity shaped the subsequent alliance between landowners and rulers, most emphatically in Prussia and Muscovy, and the emergence of absolutism as the dominant form of rule (Beloff 1971, chap. 5) (Anderson 1979) (Peters 2022). The landowners' shared identity as nobles and officers made collusion easier and defection scarcely thinkable (C. M. Clark 2006, chap. 4). These aspects, too, intensified serfdom but seem – to me, at least – unlikely to have been its proximate cause.

peasants and exacerbating inequality in the East – the reasons for those divergent effects have remained contested: Were they military, export-induced, a consequence of state weakness or of inability of eastern European peasants to coordinate (and/or ability of eastern European landowners to collude)?

In accordance with the general theory I advanced earlier, I suggest a simpler possibility that foregrounds elasticity of substitution. As wages rose and land rents fell, western European landowners could moderate their losses by switching from labor- to land-intensive cultivation. Had eastern European landowners been able to do the same, or so I conjecture, all of Europe would likely have experienced the radical changes and the wave of labor-saving innovations that transformed the West, initiated its sustained economic growth and outward expansion, and set it on the path to more participatory governance (Gingerich and Vogler 2020). An equally fortunate outcome might have involved migration of the East European peasantry to the higher wages of the West, and abandonment of grain production east of the Elbe. In the circumstances of the fifteenth and sixteenth centuries, there was no possibility that landowners could adjust in any of the other ways outlined earlier: They could not move their land into some non-agrarian form of production, export it in the short run to an area where land was in shorter supply, or – lacking a time machine – introduce some radically labor-saving technology.

Landowners in the East, if this view is correct, faced a stark choice when labor supply contracted so drastically: abandon production and lose all that they had invested; or bar their tenants from leaving, collude with other landowners and local rulers to mobilize coercion and maintain solidarity, and force peasants to accept lower wages and significantly increased obligations to labor on the lord's demesne. It is the tragedy of the East, and the key to its long delay in modernization, that the owners almost inevitably chose the latter path.

Appendices to Chapter 1

Table A4.1 *Summary statistics*

	MEAN_BS	MEAN_BS_STD	AREA_STD	BY_PORT	PORT_INT	PORT_INT_ STD	BY_RIVER	RIVER_INT	RIVER_INT_ STD	PERCENTOV 300
Count	235.000000	235.000000	235.000000	235.000000	235.000000	235.000000	235.000000	235.000000	235.000000	235.000000
Mean	0.340891	7.482785e–16	–3.911765e-16	0.029787	0.007034	–0.020437	0.268085	0.078837	–0.082201	0.012973
Std	0.153014	1.002134e+00	1.002134e+00	0.170363	0.041688	0.137077	0.443908	0.145877	0.447610	0.014608
Min	0.086403	–1.666713e+00	–1.590388e+00	0.000000	0.000000	–1.215629	0.000000	0.000000	–1.348076	0.000000
25%	0.197175	–9.412349e–01	–6.653244e–01	0.000000	0.000000	0.000000	0.000000	0.000000	0.000000	0.002927
50%	0.349061	5.351029e–02	–2.346678e–01	0.000000	0.000000	0.000000	0.000000	0.000000	0.000000	0.008350
75%	0.474178	8.729340e–01	4.047794e–01	0.000000	0.000000	0.000000	1.000000	0.143858	0.000000	0.015996
Max	0.691965	2.299288e+00	4.051525e+00	1.000000	0.345689	0.031424	1.000000	0.537295	1.286306	0.085586

Table A4.2 *Intercorrelations of variables*

	MEAN_BS	MEAN_BS_ STD	AREA_STD	BY_PORT	PORT_INT	PORT_INT_ STD	BY_RIVER	RIVER_INT	RIVER_INT_ STD	PERCENTOV 300
MEAN_BS	1.000000	1.000000	-0.439152	-0.120216	-0.097264	0.139839	-0.185570	0.023851	0.461785	-0.460069
MEAN_BS_STD	1.000000	1.000000	-0.439152	-0.120216	-0.097264	0.139839	-0.185570	0.023851	0.461785	-0.460069
AREA_STD	-0.439152	-0.439152	1.000000	0.290890	0.314372	-0.180985	0.063144	-0.005001	-0.150484	0.521988
BY_PORT	-0.120216	-0.120216	0.290890	1.000000	0.964989	-0.852689	0.063482	0.034276	-0.067399	0.140537
PORT_INT	-0.097264	-0.097264	0.314372	0.964989	1.000000	-0.685810	0.071140	0.044142	-0.063295	0.164094
PORT_INT_STD	0.139839	0.139839	-0.180985	-0.852689	-0.685810	1.000000	-0.034452	-0.007185	0.060944	-0.063117
BY_RIVER	-0.185570	-0.185570	0.063144	0.063482	0.071140	-0.034452	1.000000	0.894872	-0.304085	0.088634
RIVER_INT	0.023851	0.023851	-0.005001	0.034276	0.044142	-0.007185	0.894872	1.000000	0.153070	0.007257
RIVER_INT_STD	0.461785	0.461785	-0.150484	-0.067399	-0.063295	0.060944	-0.304085	0.153070	1.000000	-0.180757
PERCENTOV300	-0.460069	-0.460069	0.521988	0.140537	0.164094	-0.063117	0.088634	0.007257	-0.180757	1.000000

5

Exogenous Gain of Labor: Railroads, Reproduction, and Revolution

The Russian Population Explosion, 1850–1914

> the extraordinary occurrences of the past two years [1917–1919] in Russia, ... may owe more to the deep influences of expanding numbers than to Lenin or to Nicholas; and the disruptive powers of excessive national fecundity may have played a greater part ... than either the power of ideas or the errors of autocracy.
>
> John Maynard Keynes, *Economic Consequences of the Peace*

Between 1850 and 1914, the population of the Russian Empire almost tripled, growing by approximately 1.5 percent per year.[1] This expansion constituted a rare case of a largely *exogenous* population explosion; and the same change that precipitated the rapid population growth helped the country as a whole to accommodate it but, at a regional level, contributed significantly to Russian unrest and rebellion, albeit by a route opposite to the one that Keynes likely postulated. Not immiseration – for Russian living standards in these years were actually improving dramatically – but uneven economic growth, incited discontent and resistance, especially in the areas left behind.

To prefigure the larger argument, the rapid expansion of Russia's railway system after 1850, motivated by quite different (chiefly military) considerations:

a) principally caused Russia's population explosion, by alleviating previously deadly local famines;
b) allowed that growing population to be fed, and indeed to enjoy a rising standard of living, by opening new lands to cultivation and linking Russian agriculture to wider domestic and world markets;

[1] Poll tax data show a total male population of 18.3 million in 1850 and 53.3 million in 1914–1917 (Moon 1999, 21), equivalent to an annual growth rate of 1.7 percent. Falkus, more conservatively, estimates a total population of 74.1 million in 1860 and 170.1 million in 1913, implying a growth rate of 1.3 percent annually (Falkus 1972, 17).

c) enabled nascent industry to employ Russia's increasingly abundant labor supply, by seasonal migration of peasants to urban work sites;
d) during times of discontent, lowered the propensity to rebel of the regions that were best connected to railways, probably because of their growing prosperity and their access to wider markets;
e) when grain prices fell on world markets, decreased the frequency of unrest in the better-connected regions but increased it in more isolated regions.

Part of the story, of course, will involve the Imperial government's action (or inaction) in the face of rapid population growth. We shall see, however, that those decisions were rarely voluntary; rather, they were motivated, and almost compelled, by military necessity.

RUSSIA AS A CASE OF EXOGENOUS POPULATION GROWTH

Examples of exogenous and unanticipated *diminutions* in labor supply are legion. Epidemics, earthquakes, hurricanes can decimate – and, as we saw in the extreme case of the Black Death,[2] have decimated – the populations of countries and whole continents (Walter Scheidel 2017). Episodes of exogenous *expansions* of labor supply are far rarer. Mass immigrations are usually precipitated by foreseeable "push" and "pull" factors: Famines or accelerating persecutions drive people to more hospitable environments, or rising wages and more immigrant-friendly policies attract floods of new arrivals.

Even entirely domestic population surges, demographers have shown, are usually endogenous[3] – indeed, follow a predictable path now known as the "demographic transition." Improvements in public health or medical care – cleaner water, better sewage disposal, vaccinations, purer foodstuffs – almost always driven by public policy, drastically lower infant and childhood mortality. Parents, traditionally seeking some "target" number of surviving children (typically two or three), and hence accustomed by high infant mortality to give birth to double or triple that target number, adjust only gradually to the newly lowered childhood

[2] It is not by accident that I have chosen a case in which population triples to contrast with one (the Black Death) that reduced population to one-third of its previous level.

[3] To clarify the distinction: Changes that are intended to achieve their result, or that are adaptations to an ongoing trend, are endogenous; changes that are externally caused, or are motivated by entirely unrelated concerns, are exogenous.

mortality.[4] That temporary combination of much higher infant survival and persistent high fecundity produces a population "bulge" that persists for two or three generations but slowly settles at a new, higher but stable (or even declining) equilibrium (Deaton 2013, 155). Here, the endogeneity is evident: The public authorities (or, in some cases, international humanitarian intervention) take measures that reliably increase the share of children who survive into adulthood. As those measures take effect, population "explodes," but does so only temporarily.

This is not what happened in late Imperial Russia. Indeed, the birth rate remained high and may even have increased somewhat. Births continued to average 40 to 50 per thousand of population, or seven to nine children over the average woman's lifetime, with at most a slight increase between the first and second half of the century (Moon 1999, 23–24). Mortality also fell: Life expectancy at birth rose from about twenty-four years before 1850 to over thirty by 1897 (Moon 1999, 25–26 and 32), and the crude death rate fell from 37 per thousand in the late 1860s to 28 per thousand in 1913, a drop of over 27 percent (Natkhov and Vasilenok 2019, 8).

What did *not* decline was that most central cause of the demographic transformation, infant mortality. By 1911, just as in the 1860s, a quarter of all infants died before their first birthday (Natkhov and Vasilenok 2019, 8) and half before they reached the age of five (Moon 1999, 25). Despite improvements in other aspects of public health, Russian childcare and feeding practices remained backward and exposed infants unnecessarily to preventable infections, particularly of the gastro-intestinal tract (Natkhov and Vasilenok 2019, 9–11). Hence improvements in public health, while not completely absent, were not chiefly responsible for the rapid growth of population.

Instead, mortality declined among those who *survived* their first five years of life; and the reason is not far to seek: Nutrition improved and became more reliable. Russia's previously recurrent "demographic crises," chief among them famine and famine-facilitated illnesses, became much rarer – so much so that the last of these before 1914, the famine and cholera epidemic of 1891–1892, seemed to contemporaries a shocking exception (Moon 1999, 33). In short, Russia's population had previously been held back by that most horrible of the Rev. Dr. Malthus's "positive

[4] "Russian peasants were anxious to make sure they had large numbers of children so that sufficient would survive to adulthood to provide new generations of peasants to work on their households' land." (Moon 1997, 869–870).

checks," namely famine; but somehow, in that last half of the nineteenth century, famines almost ceased. Why? And why should famine have previously prevailed so frequently, given that Russia had long been a significant exporter of grain?

The first answer lies in one universal fact. Famine, in most of the world for most of its history, was predominantly local: Rarely was there an overall shortage of food, but rather an inability to bring food to areas of dearth.[5] As one student of Russia in this period has noted succinctly, "... a bad harvest in one province could rarely be compensated by grain shipments from a more fortunate region; hence the frequency in Russia of localized but deadly famines" (Westwood 1964, 26). And why could such interregional shipments not occur? The answer, according to Moon, was equally simple: "Russia's endemic transport problems," which made it "difficult and expensive to move food to areas where crops had failed." (Moon 1999, 28).

Consistent with these facts, David Moon conjectured two decades ago that local famines had abated in Russia after about 1857 because the growing railroad network permitted cheaper and easier interregional transportation of food (Moon 1999, 34). In nineteenth-century India, Burgess and Donaldson have shown, newly constructed railroads sharply curtailed famine and, along their routes, almost eliminated previously large interregional disparities in commodity prices (Burgess and Donaldson 2012). Moreover, in Russia, as in India, a substantial portion of the railroads was laid mostly for military purposes:[6] to be able, in the event of war or rebellion, to deploy troops rapidly.[7] Hence in neither the Indian nor the Russian case is reverse causation likely: Railroads were likelier to have brought about population growth than to have been laid in anticipation of it, or with the intent to stimulate it.[8]

[5] This point has been stated most forcefully by Amartya Sen (1982, chaps. 4 and 10). Some of Sen's empirical work has been questioned, but his general point remains valid. Cases of near-universal famine, e.g., in Ireland in 1847, remain exceptional.

[6] "Although railroad construction stimulated economic growth, strategic considerations were initially more important to railroad building than profitability. Close links were early established between railroading and the military." (Reichman 1987, 18–19) Cf. (Ames 1947, 64).

[7] The earliest line of any significance, that from Warsaw to Vienna, which extended in Russia to the Austro-Hungarian frontier, opened in 1848. Almost its first use was to convey troops to crush the Hungarian uprising of that year (Westwood 1964, 25).

[8] A significant early exception was the route from Riga to Tsaritsyn (Volgograd), built to allow grain to be brought from the Volga to the Baltic (Ames 1947, 65).

Beyond simply relieving local shortages, the railroads in Russia, hardly less than in the Americas, opened *new lands* to cultivation: They both brought settlers in and conveyed their produce out (Moon 1999, 58). To be sure, Russia had developed over the eighteenth century an extensive system of waterborne transport, including many canals, to compensate for its notoriously bad roads; but waterways inevitably froze over in winter and often became too shallow in summer (Starns 2012, 29). To bring grain by water from the Volga region to St. Petersburg took seven months, which – given a frost-free season of only five months – normally meant two navigation seasons (Westwood 1964, 26). The railroad reduced transport time from months to days.

Not surprisingly, regional population growth accelerated with the arrival of the railroad. The area that experienced the most rapid growth in the second half of the nineteenth century was that characterized as "unforested steppe," "open steppe," or often simply "steppe" (see Map 5.1). The South Urals more than tripled in population between 1857 and 1897, while the Lower Volga and Don more than doubled. By way of contrast, the regions of older settlement, the so-called Forest Heartland, experienced a population growth of 50 percent. Siberia, which the railroad had reached only in the late 1890s,[9] grew over the same period by about 70 percent (Moon 1999, 53 and 55). In all, the area under cultivation expanded in the last half of the nineteenth century by at least 12 percent [(Gatrell 1994, 88) in (Eklof et al. 1994, chap. 5)], much of it in the fertile Black Earth (*chernozem*) region, the northern Caucasus, or, later, the almost equally fertile soils of Siberia.

THE ATYPICAL CONSEQUENCES OF POPULATION GROWTH IN NINETEENTH-CENTURY RUSSIA

Absent other changes, population growth of this magnitude would have led to a serious decline in wages – just as the sudden loss of population during the Black Death sharply increased wages. In the standard economic model outlined in Chapter 1, wages are equivalent to the marginal product of labor and hence decline with the ratio of labor to other factors of production. If only land, for example, is the other factor, and total product is given by

[9] The Trans-Siberian Railway was completed only in 1904, but – as with the US transcontinental railway – gradually opened access as the lines were extended from west and east.

$$Y = AT^{\alpha}L^{1-\alpha},$$

then the wage is

$$w = MPL = A(1-\alpha)(T/L)^{\alpha},$$

which must fall as L rises, if we assume that the supply of land (or, in a multi-factor model, all factors other than labor) remains constant and

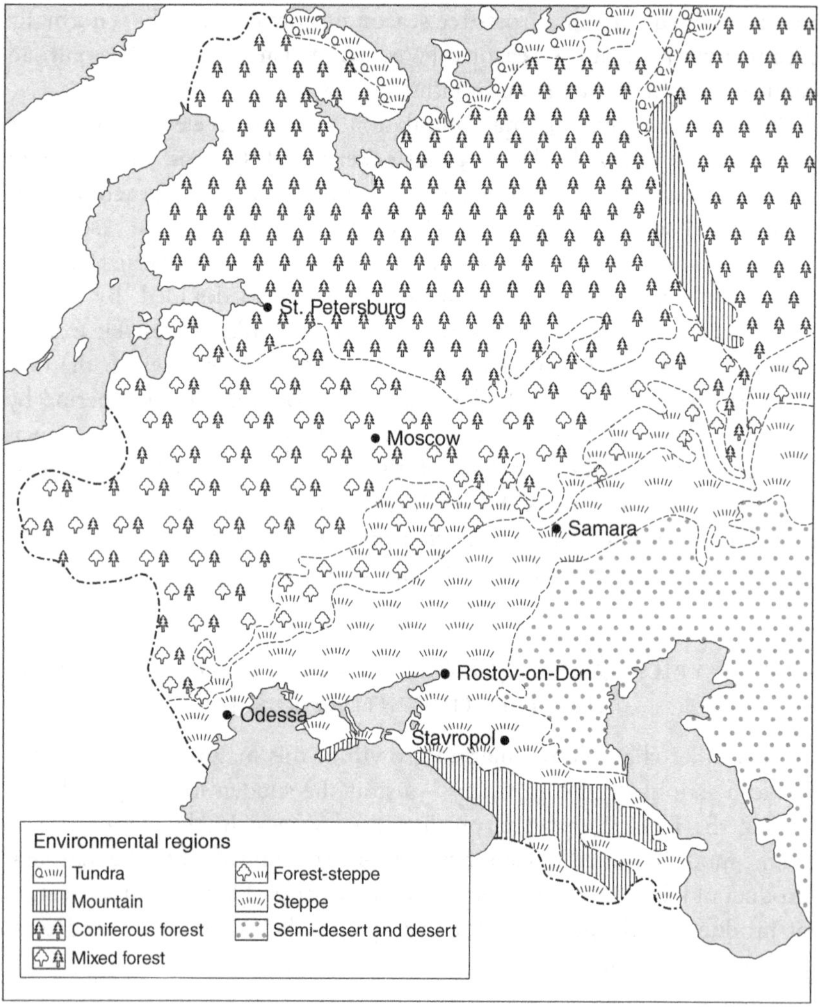

Map 5.1 Environmental and agricultural regions of Russia
Source: (Moon 2013, 9). Reproduced by permission of Oxford University Press, PLSclear Ref No: 54556.

that technology (i.e., total factor productivity, represented by the term A) does not progress.[10] Population explosions, just as in Malthus's analysis, should lead to immiseration.

Russia's population explosion, however, had no such effect. Little doubt by now remains that Russian living standards rose significantly between 1850 and 1910. Perhaps the strongest evidence is anthropometric: Between the 1850s and the period just before World War I, the average height of conscripts to the Russian army rose by about 3 cm., from 165 to 168 cm (Mironov 2012, 119).[11] The increase seems to have been especially pronounced among peasants (Mironov 2012, 122). Per capita national income, according to the best estimates, rose throughout the period by about 1.6 percent annually; during the period of most rapid advance, the 1890s, it rose by 3.4 percent per year (Gregory 1994, 24). Real wages also rose, more in agriculture than in industry; and urban and rural wages converged.[12] Urban skilled wages, if one can generalize from data for St. Petersburg carpenters (Mironov 2012, 310), had peaked around 1850, fell between then and the 1880s by over a quarter, but then grew rapidly to return to 1850 levels by 1913. Real wages in agriculture, however, increased by 50 percent in the decade after emancipation, and "overall, ... during the post-reform period [i.e., after 1861] almost doubled" (Mironov 2012, 319).

This remarkable achievement resulted chiefly from the expansion of the railway system. Government policy, halting and inconsistent as it was, played a lesser but still significant role. Given that, as late as 1900, "Agriculture accounted for 85 percent of the Russian population and for 75 percent of the Russian labor force," and for just over half of national income (Gregory 1994, 30 and 42), the main answer to the apparent riddle of increasing living standards must lie in the countryside. We have already seen that the land under cultivation expanded significantly,[13] chiefly due to

[10] The model implicitly assumes an autarkic economy. Consumption can also increase, in standard trade models, from cross-border trade and specialization.

[11] There is some left-censoring in the data, which may therefore understate the change. In the 1850s, the minimum height for recruits was 155.6 cm.; beginning in 1876, the minimum was lowered to 153.4 cm. Values below that (i.e., for rejected recruits) were not recorded. The situation is even slightly more complicated, as required minimum chest sizes were also changed (Markevich and Zhuravskaya 2018, 1110).

[12] One important study, albeit confined to the St. Petersburg *gubernia*, demonstrates the convergence precisely and in detail: (Borodkin, Granville, and Leonard 2008).

[13] The share of land owned or rented by peasants, individually or communally, also grew – probably because (if the Coase Theorem is correct) they produced more efficiently.

the easier access provided by rail connections. Government policy mattered in one notable way: As the rail network extended into Russia's Central Asian regions, the Imperial government, no less than the US government on the American Great Plains during the same years, worked to displace nomadic peoples in favor of peasant settlers.[14]

Trade, too, raised incomes and living standards. New access to world markets, as railroads connected farmsteads to the ports of Odessa and the Baltic, raised Russia's grain exports to a new level: Shipments of wheat roughly quintupled between 1860 and 1912 (from about 50 million to 250 million *poodi*[15] annually), accounting for between a quarter and a third of total world exports (M. E. Falkus 1966, 416–417). The reduced transportation costs brought prices at the farmstead closer to those on the world market, which in response to growing European demand were rising in any event.[16] Rising commodity prices of course increased the value of farmland (Gregory 1994, 53). As that land became more valuable, peasants presumably sought it more eagerly and, perhaps, more violently.[17] Cropping patterns shifted also. Reliable interregional rail connection allowed regions to specialize in their areas of comparative advantage, confident that they could rely on other regions to supply goods that they no longer produced. The combination of burgeoning export markets and changing domestic demand induced specialization in higher-value crops: Barley and wheat replaced rye; meat, dairy, and sugar beet production expanded; and Russian agriculture became markedly more commercialized (Klebnikov 1991, 359–360).

Agricultural technology also improved, and production became more capital-intensive. Here government policy mattered in two important

[14] "The Russian authorities pursued a deliberate policy of sedentarisation (or 'denomadisation') which was motivated, at least in part, by the aim of transforming the nomads' pastureland into arable land for crop cultivation and to free land for the peasant migrants." (Moon 1996, 149).

[15] In standard US agricultural measure, this translates to an increase from about 35 million bushels in 1860 to 130 million in 1913. One *pood* ≅ 36 lb., so that two *poodi* (72 lb.) are equivalent to 1.2 bushels (one bushel of wheat = 60 lb.).

[16] Wheat prices in Amsterdam rose between 1850 and 1900 by over 85 percent, from .624 grams to 1.17 grams of silver per liter. Even by 1880, they had risen by over 60 percent (1880 price = 1.017 grams per liter). Allen-Unger Commodity Price Dataset, International Institute of Social History, http://webstore.iisg.nl/hpw/allen-unger-commodities/Wheat/, tab "Amsterdam." Accessed 1 June 2020.

[17] Finkel, Gehlbach, and Kofanov find that the areas of most fertile soil were precisely those of greatest peasant unrest in 1917 (Finkel, Gehlbach, and Kofanov 2017). The empirical analysis below does not sustain that putative link, but that may be because of collinearity (see below, p. 100).

ways. The emancipation of the serfs in 1861, although partially counteracted by the communal land settlement that followed it, contributed importantly to the growth of agricultural (and industrial) productivity (Markevich and Zhuravskaya 2018);[18] so, most accounts hold, did Stolypin's reforms of land tenure after 1905. Government-supplied agronomists imparted better techniques and often made modern machinery (reapers, threshers, seed drills) available for rent (Klebnikov 1991, 56 and 157).

In short, and for reasons related substantially but not exclusively to changes in transportation, Russian agriculture became more productive. Between 1870 and the mid-1880s, agricultural output increased by over 1 percent annually; from then until 1900, by about 2.5 percent annually; and in the last decade before World War I, by 3 percent annually (Gregory 1994, 44).[19] At the same time, without access to wider markets, to the higher grain prices they offered, and to the industrializing world's seemingly bottomless demand, there would have been little incentive to invest or to advance technically.

Russia's "railroadization" in the second half of the nineteenth century (Gregory 1994, 16), in short, both spurred rapid population growth and, by increasing available land, granting Russian agriculture access to world markets, and stimulating technical advance, allowed that growing population to be better fed. As Crisp put it succinctly in her magisterial study of the pre-1914 Russian economy, "the effect of the railways was truly revolutionary" and, even more than the abolition of serfdom, demarcated a new age in Russian economic development (Crisp 1976, 17).

INDUSTRIALIZATION: THE RISING RATIO OF CAPITAL TO LABOR AND THE MOBILIZATION OF SURPLUS LABOR

The Russian leadership might have taken no action to increase investment, but Russia's dismal showing in the Crimean War had exposed the country's military inferiority; and it was plain that, in an industrializing age, military prowess was achievable only with economic success (Blum 1971, 577). The overwhelming advantages in manpower and territory

[18] Serfdom, like slavery, simply keeps labor artificially cheap; that in turn subsidizes labor-intensive production and discourages labor-saving technical innovation.

[19] Gregory relies on Goldsmith's estimates for the initial period; between 1870–1874 and 1883–1887, total growth in output was 17 percent; that implies an annual growth rate of at least $(1.17)^{1/15} = 1.01$.

that had given Russia victory in the Napoleonic Wars no longer sufficed. The same motive that led the Czarist government, after much initial resistance, to build railroads now led it increasingly to pursue industrialization (Gerschenkron 1962, 17).[20] That motive was simple and irresistible: survival. If Russia did not develop rapidly, it could – and likely would – be defeated in some future war. Industrialization was not a matter of choice, but of the country's continued existence.

With that goal firmly in mind, the Imperial government sought to attract foreign investment – not least, as the reforming Count Sergei Witte (Finance Minister 1892–1903) had argued, because Russia lacked sufficient domestic savings (Gregory 1994, 59). Given adequate guarantees that their investments would be secure, such investment would have entered in any event, given the inevitably higher marginal productivity of capital in a land where capital was scarce. As currency risk abated with Russia's move toward the gold standard (1895–1897[21]), indeed the return on capital in Russia approached 2.5 times that prevailing in western Europe (Gregory 1994, 75). Foreign investment in Russia boomed; by 1900, annual gross capital imports were equivalent to 2.7 percent of gross national product (Swetzer 1996, 37).

State-directed investment was less important than Alexander Gerschenkron had argued, but a state policy that did stimulate investment was *high tariff barriers*: Duties on manufactured goods varied from 25 to 28 percent; averaged over all categories of goods, from 30 to 40 percent (Crisp 1976, 30). Although the motivation for these exorbitant duties was chiefly fiscal – the Russian state had few other sources of revenue – they provided a guaranteed domestic market, and licensing provisions often granted foreign investors a monopoly in that market. Capital poured in from abroad, such that by 1914 Russia was the world's largest international debtor, regarded throughout western Europe as "a land of unlimited economic opportunity" (Gregory 1994, 67, 61).

As in other cases of industrialization, the problem was not so much bringing capital to labor, as labor to capital: Peasants had to move off the farm and into the industrial workforce.[22] The land reform that accompanied emancipation in 1861 retarded industrial development by incentivizing

[20] Gerschenkron saw a clear link between the two policies: "[T]he railroad building of the state assumed unprecedented proportions and became the main lever of a rapid industrialization policy" (Gerschenkron 1962, 19).

[21] In 1897 the ruble became completely convertible to gold.

[22] In some cases, capital moved to labor, as industry sprang up in rural areas.

peasants to stay "down on the farm."[23] First, a peasant who left the village for good, that is, by changing his legal place of residence to a city, forfeited his claim to a share in the communal property at the next redistribution – and did so without compensation. Second, the departed member's tax and redemption burdens[24] would then fall on all remaining members of the village – something they understandably might not welcome (Burds 1998, 15; Gregory 1994, 50–53; Gerschenkron 1962, 120–121).

What nonetheless permitted rapid growth of an industrial workforce was seasonal migration (Burds 1998): During rural "down times," when farm labor might otherwise be idle, the peasant could claim an internal passport, move temporarily to the city, and take a job in industry.[25] Such a temporary move neither absolved the peasant from his tax obligations in the village nor stripped him of his claim to communal property. As industrial demand for labor grew along with the supply of villagers seeking urban work, so did the issuance of internal passports: Some 1.2 million were issued annually between 1861 and 1870; between 1906 and 1910, almost 8.8 million annually (Burds 1998, 22). Predictably, the demand for passports was highest in the regions nearest to industrial centers: As Burds has put it, "the percentage of issued passports declin[ed] in definite concentric rings as one moved away from Moscow" (Burds 1998, 21). By 1896, in the regions closest to Moscow, some 40 percent of adult peasant males received internal passports (Burds 1998, 21). Thus, despite peasants' sentimental and legal ties to the land, there was a "vast internal migration of the Russian population after 1861" (Gregory 1994, 51). The 1897 Census showed some 12 million peasants living outside their native provinces (Brooks 1985, 11).

Without the cheap and rapid transportation that railroads provided, however, these temporary moves would have been impossible for all but the few peasants who lived in closest proximity to industry. Perhaps the clearest evidence of railways' importance is the extent to which railroad

[23] This was by design. Preventing rapid urban migration or the emergence of a landless rural proletariat were among the aims that informed the emancipation decrees (McCaffray 2005, esp. 12–14).

[24] "The peasants ... were saddled with redemption payments that were to amortize the land over nearly a half century." (Gregory 1994, 58).

[25] An older tradition, which also expanded, involved seasonal migration for rural work during times of high demand (Burds 1998, 110). Workers were especially in demand on large commercial tobacco and sugar beet farms in southern Russia; on the eve of World War I, migrant agricultural laborers numbered some four million in European Russia (Brooks 1985, 12).

strikes, increasingly common after 1900, "had a powerful ripple effect on job opportunities for peasants in surrounding regions" (Burds 1998, 123).

Human capital also grew. Literacy had been of little value in the countryside, but as peasants discovered its value in urban work and life, they rushed to acquire it. In the 1860s, only some 6 percent of male peasants had been literate (Mironov 1991, 234). The 1897 Census counted 21 percent of Russia's adult population (but almost half of those aged ten to nineteen) as literate, a share that roughly doubled by 1914. In the rural areas closest to industrial centers, however, over two-thirds of males were literate (Brooks 1985, 4; Mironov 1991, 237). Newspaper circulation also expanded, both in cities and in the countryside, to an extent that alarmed local authorities, who feared the spread of dangerous ideas (Burds 1998, 178).

Just as the railroads had effectively expanded Russia's ratio of land to labor, so too did they facilitate a rising ratio of physical and human capital to labor. Hence the country's staggering population growth was accompanied by rising, rather than falling, wages and living standards.

THE PERILS OF UNEVEN DEVELOPMENT: THE AREAS LEFT BEHIND

Even as life improved overall, some regions and sectors fared less well. Much as in the contemporary USA, the same high tariffs that stimulated industrialization were a yoke around the neck of Russian agriculture:[26] They taxed farm implements and farmers' objects of consumption; and exports, although booming, would have expanded even more without the tariff-imposed constriction of trade.

Regions that lay far from any urban center, or that poor transportation left isolated, also fell behind. As Mironov notes, "The ... lowest rate of growth [in wages] occurred in those districts that were isolated from cities and roads" (Mironov 2012, 324). Rural areas with poor railway access were especially disadvantaged: Their peasants could not easily engage in seasonal migration, they remained less literate, and even their postal service was poor. Perhaps most problematic of all: High transportation costs meant that their produce sold for less, and the price at the farmstead was inevitably lower, the more distant the nearest rail connection. These

[26] "If [the government's policies] had been deliberately contrived as a yoke to fit the necks of men who sold the products of agriculture and bought those of industry, the design could hardly have been more perfect." (Robinson 1949, 246, originally published 1932).

"cut off" areas were thus especially vulnerable to fluctuations in the world grain price. Such fluctuations are almost always passed along linearly – for example, a rise or fall of twenty kopecks per *pood* in Odessa would mean the same change of twenty kopecks in even the most distant village – and hence would be a higher percentage increase or decrease, the lower was a region's pre-existing price.[27]

Their isolation, however, in no way prevented peasants in those disadvantaged regions from developing a passionate interest in the wider world, and in politics. Where literacy was low, the arrival of a newspaper (in remote areas, at best once a week) was followed immediately by the gathering of a crowd, either in the village store or tea room, or in good weather outdoors, who listened attentively as one of their literate fellows read the news aloud (Burds 1998, 176–177). Moreover, the newspaper then "passed through countless hands, and read aloud, reached the ears of countless more peasants, literate and illiterate." (Burds 1998, 176)

Newspaper subscriptions were surprisingly common – in Moscow Province, the average village subscribed to 2.5 newspapers – but, paradoxically, achieved their highest numbers (as Burds puts it) "in areas most cut off from railway and communication routes" (Burds 1998, 177). The reason, on reflection, is simple: Those living near such a route could buy at a newsstand or train station and saw less need to subscribe; also, they had ready access to less formal means of communication.

The combination of low literacy, frequent communal reading, and the heated discussions that usually followed each reading combined to make these more isolated villages hotbeds of political interest. As one peasant wrote, after each communal reading, the community would "passionately discuss what was read, usually divided into two parties, the Progressives and the Black Hundreds" (Burds 1998, 177). Thus the isolated regions had both stronger economic reasons for discontent and considerable experience with collective deliberation and discussion – likely even more such experience than regions that were better connected to the larger world.

A CONNECTION TO REGIONAL UNREST?

Perhaps counterintuitively, then, we might expect to see *less* unrest in localities with good railroad connections. We would also expect grain

[27] E.g., if the Odessa price were two rubles per *pood*, a change of twenty kopecks would be 10 percent; if in some remote village the pre-existing price were one ruble, the same absolute change would mean a 20 percent rise or decline.

prices to affect unrest, but – again, it seems surprising to ask – in which direction? Those who see rebellion as a response to deprivation, either absolute or relative, would take an inverse correlation for granted: Falling grain prices induce greater unrest; rising ones, more contentment. If, as others argue, peasants are often discontented but lack the resources to mobilize – therefore, if rebellion is something of a "luxury good" – the association will be positive: High grain prices conduce to greater unrest, lower ones to grumbling but stolid acquiescence. I incline to the latter view but regard this as an empirical question. If, however, grain prices are in general associated with greater unrest, then, given the greater vulnerability to grain price fluctuations of regions with poorer rail connections, we should also expect that high grain prices will be associated with yet *greater* unrest in areas remote from railways. If we take as our measure of railroad connectivity "track density," that is, the kilometers of track per square kilometer of territory, then we would expect the estimated coefficient on the interaction of Odessa grain prices and railway density to be *negative*: In regions with good railway connections, high grain prices will be associated with unrest, but with *less* unrest than in more remote regions.

Why should better railway connections be associated with less unrest, all else being equal? Such regions, I suggest, will have remained on average more prosperous, better able to withstand temporary price shocks, and more mobile and individualistic; and, with less experience of communal reading and response, will have had less fully developed "forms of horizontal political organization" (Burds 1998, 179). They will therefore have been *less* likely to engage in collective protest or resistance. It may of course also be the case that troops could be sent more readily to suppress revolts in better-connected regions – and that, anticipating such a response, peasants were more hesitant to rebel.

Admittedly, this view runs much against the prevailing wisdom, which regards railroads as a radicalizing, indeed revolutionary, force (Reichman 1987). No less a figure than Trotsky called them "the channels along which the strike epidemic spreads" (Reichman 1987, 6); and their most eminent recent student has seen them (and their accompanying telegraph lines) as an important transmission belt for political news and radically democratizing ideas – albeit perhaps more from the provinces to the center, than the other way around (Reichman 1987, 144). But this view focuses on railway *workers* rather than those whom the railways served. Railway workers – who by 1905 numbered some 750,000 – were indeed radicalized and powerful; they had "the highest strike propensity of any industrial group" (Reichman 1987, 17, 5). They played a crucial role in the events of 1905 and 1917, able especially in wartime to "produce incalculable social effects merely by a stoppage of rail traffic for a few days" (Augustine 1965, 666). It is easy to jump from those facts to the conclusion that railways also radicalized the districts through which they ran. As we shall see, the opposite is closer to the truth.

To summarize, we expect in any statistical analysis to find three relationships, all of them to some degree counterintuitive. The occurrence of peasant unrest in a district (*uyezd*), we anticipate, will correlate:

a) *negatively* with the district's access to railroads, that is, with its track density;
b) *positively* or *negatively* with grain prices (measured as the price of wheat at Odessa), depending on whether rebellion is a "luxury good" or a result of deprivation;
c) *negatively* with the interaction of track density and grain prices if rebellion is a luxury good, *positively* if unrest arises from deprivation.

In other words, we suppose that, where U_{ij} represents the likelihood of at least one unrest event in *uyezd* j at time i,

$$U_{ij} = f(G_i, RR_{ij}, G_i * RR_{ij}, \mathbb{X}_j),$$

where G_i, is the Odessa grain (wheat) price at time i, RR_{ij} is the track density in *uyezd* j at time i, $G_i * RR_{ij}$ is the interaction of wheat price and track density, and $\mathbb{X}_j$ is a vector of *uyezd*-specific control variables, including population, soil quality, intensity of previous serfdom (Finkel, Gehlbach, and Kofanov 2017) (Dower et al. 2018), and the percentage of total peasant arable[28] sown to wheat in 1881.[29] We should expect the coefficient on RR_{ij} to be negative but regard those on G_i, and $G_i * RR_{ij}$ as an open question, to be decided empirically. Following Finkel et al., we expect the coefficients on soil quality and previous serfdom to be positive, therefore, to be associated with a greater likelihood of unrest.

For later Imperial Russia, we have data on track density[30] and peasant unrest over time and on time-invariant soil quality and previous serfdom

[28] More specifically, peasant allotments, i.e., the lands received by village communities under the terms of the emancipation settlement.

[29] The area sown to wheat in any given year will vary with anticipated grain prices. I take 1881 as the base year to avoid this possible source of endogeneity. The 1881 data are from Central Statistical Committee 1901 and were supplied by Brendan McElroy.

[30] I employ log-transformed track density to compensate for the extreme skew of the data.

at the *uyezd* level.[31] Monthly wheat prices are those reported at Amsterdam for wheat from Odessa;[32] these are available only for the years from 1885 through 1901, and the unrest data also terminate in 1901, so the analysis is confined to that timespan. Given this information, we can estimate empirically the model specified above.[33] We do so using a standard logit model (given that 92 percent of district-years have no unrest events) that employs a three-knot cubic spline to account for time trends.[34] We also interact the three-knot spline with fixed effects for each of the thirteen main regions noted standardly by Kopsidis, Bruisch, and Bromley (2015).[35] This allows time to have a unique – highly

[31] Track density (kilometers of track divided by square kilometers of area) is from the geocoded version of a railway map included in vol. 4 of the National Atlas of Russia, History and Culture (Natsionalnyi atlas Rossii). See: https://национальныйатлас.рф/cd4/129/129.html . List of unrest events was compiled by Brendan McElroy from vols. 7 and 8 of the series *The Peasant Movement in Russia*, respectively: A. S. Nifontov and B. V. Zlatoustovskii, eds., *Krestianskoe dvizhenie v Rossii v 1881–1889 gg.: Sbornik dokumentov* (Moscow: Izdatelstvo sotsialno-ekonomicheskoi literatury, 1960) and A. V. Shapkarin, B. V. Zlatoustovskii and N. I. Pishvanova, eds., *Krestianskoe dvizhenie v Rossii v 1890–1900 gg.: Sbornik dokumentov* (Moscow: Izdatelstvo sotsialno-ekonomicheskoi literatury, 1959). Share of population that were serfs before 1861 and soil quality are from Castañeda Dower et al. (2017).

[32] Any missing monthly prices were imputed from other series, based on their average covariation with the Amsterdam/Odessa prices.

[33] The following analysis incorporates the findings of joint research with Caleb Ziolkowski (Princeton) and Brendan McElroy (Michigan), with expert and unflagging research assistance from Can Yesildire (Harvard undergraduate). Our analysis will be presented in much more extensive form in a joint paper, on which we are now working.

[34] Cubic splines are piecewise cubic functions that interpolate data and guarantee smoothness at the points chosen for the knots – including the boundary points. A three-knot spline is a flexible function, allowing for a time trend that "bends" up to three times. There are effectively five degrees of freedom, making it roughly equivalent to a four-degree polynomial term. But, unlike a polynomial term, the cubic spline spreads out the knots in a more even manner, making it much more flexible than a polynomial term (Hastie and Tibshirani 2017). Further, splines, unlike polynomial terms, avoid overfitting the data (including at the extreme ends of the range of the data).

[35] Baltic region (Estland, Livland, Kurland), Lake region (St. Petersburg, Pskov, Novgorod, Olonets), Far North (Arkhangelsk, Vologda), Urals (Viatka, Perm), Central Industrial region (Kostroma, Vladimir, Iaroslavl, Tver, Moscow, Kaluga, Nizhnii Novgorod), Bielorussia (Smolensk, Mogilev, Minsk, Vitebsk), Lithuania (Kovno, Vilna, Grodno), Southwest region (Volyn, Kiev, Podolia), Malorossiia (Chernigov, Poltava, Kharkov), Novorossiia/Southern Steppe region (Bessarabia, Kherson, Taurida, Ekaterinoslav, Don Cossacks Oblast), Central Agricultural region (Orel, Tula, Riazan, Tambov, Voronezh, Kursk), Middle Volga (Kazan,

flexible – effect in each region. We thus account for any dynamic relationship between region and time – and unobserved variables that change with time. Further, the regional fixed effects allow for varying baselines of unrest at the level of the region. The results of that procedure appear as Table 5.1.

It appears that, in any given *uyezd* in any given year, the likelihood of peasant unrest was significantly lower, the better its railway connection; and that, where railway connection was good, but not otherwise, unrest tended to increase with the price of wheat. Moving from the first to the third quartile of log-transformed railway density is associated with a statistically significant *decrease* in predicted probability of unrest by about 3.2 percentage points, therefore, from the baseline of 8.0 percent to 4.8 percent, or about 40 percent of the baseline probability of unrest. On the other hand, the price of wheat has no general association with unrest, but rather is linked to increased unrest only in regions with better transport (see estimated coefficient on interaction term, density x wheat price). In an *uyezd* with good railway connections (in the third quartile of log-transformed track density), high wheat prices were associated with a somewhat *higher* probability of unrest (an increase of 1.0 percent) than in districts whose railway connections were in the first quartile (a decrease of 0.6 percent). The estimated difference – 1.6 percentage points – while substantively small, attains conventional levels of statistical significance. I conclude from this, at least tentatively, that in well-connected (and, presumably, more prosperous) regions, rebellion was indeed a luxury good;[36] while in the "cut off" regions, unrest was likelier associated with deprivation: At the very least, it was unaffected by grain prices and may well have risen when the price of wheat fell. Similarly, although the effect is smaller and estimated with less precision, the greater the share of arable land planted to wheat, the higher is the likelihood of unrest when railroad density is higher (see estimated coefficient on the interaction term, density x area sown to wheat).

As regards the control variables: Unrest was indeed somewhat associated with the extent of prior serfdom, as Finkel et al. found; but, in our more articulated model, good soil is basically unrelated to the probability

Simbirsk, Penza, Saratov), and Lower Volga (Astrakhan, Samara, Ufa, Orenburg). The present analysis treats the Baltic as the baseline region.

36 If the areas with high railway density were less likely to rebel simply because they were more accessible to Imperial troops, the price of wheat should have had no effect.

Table 5.1 *Logistic regression of peasant unrest over time on* uyezd-*level railroad density, percentage of former serfs, percentage of area planted to wheat, and soil quality; and on monthly Odessa wheat prices*[37]

	Logistic Model
(Intercept)	-14.483 ***
	(1.828)
Wheat Percent	0.072
	(0.069)
Wheat Price	0.074
	(0.058)
Log Railroad Density	-0.529 ***
	(0.100)
Serf Percentage	0.115 *
	(0.067)
Good Soil	-0.038
	(0.079)
Log Population	0.985 ***
	(0.115)
Wheat Percent × Wheat Price	-0.011
	(0.048)
Wheat Percent × Log Railroad Density	0.189 *
	(0.098)
Wheat Price × Log Railroad Density	0.302 ***
	(0.101)
Wheat Percent × Wheat Price × Log Railroad Density	-0.089
	(0.102)
N	8194
logLik	-2033.973
AIC	4191.946

*** $p < 0.01$; ** $p < 0.05$; * $p < 0.1$.

of unrest. It seems likeliest that, given the strong correlation between soil quality and area sown to wheat (rye, as every farm child knows, can be grown on poorer soil), this is merely a symptom of collinearity: "Area sown to wheat" (wheat percent) correlates with "good soil" at $r = .46$ (see Appendix Table A5.1) and hence likely picks up most of the effect of soil quality. Unsurprisingly, a larger population is associated with a higher probability of at least one episode of unrest.

The crucial finding here is that, controlling for other factors, the best connected – and presumably economically most advanced – parts of

[37] Model includes regional fixed effects; see text.

Russia were less likely to rebel; it was peasants in the "cut off" regions, economically left behind, who were more likely to do so. Fully in accord with conventional wisdom, however, peasants in those more isolated areas grew more content, or at the very least no more discontent, when grain prices were high; much against conventional wisdom, peasants in the prosperous areas grew *more* rebellious when wheat commanded a higher price. They appear to have regarded rebellion as a luxury good.

CONCLUSION

Czarist Russia's population almost tripled between 1850 and 1914. That rapid growth turns out to have been a largely exogenous positive shock to the country's supply of labor, owing little to improvements in public health – since infant mortality declined not at all – but almost everything to the rapid extension of Russia's railways, which afforded a growing and less regionally insecure food supply and thus sharply diminished the previously frequent regional famines. One can regard that shock as exogenous, since the railroads were built chiefly to serve military needs and, from the 1880s on, to accelerate industrialization. There appears to have been no conscious goal of alleviating famine, although a few lines were built to facilitate grain exports, which grew enormously.

Not only was the skyrocketing Russian population better fed, it enjoyed a markedly higher standard of living overall. This could only have been possible if the supplies of land and capital grew, or technology advanced, even more rapidly than the population. They did, again for exogenous reasons intimately connected to railway expansion. The supply of land, and especially of more fertile land, grew only because – just as on the Great Plains of North America or the pampas of Argentina – railroads brought settlers in and carried their produce out. Those early railroads were built, as we have seen, chiefly for military purposes, not to facilitate settlement. Later railroads were indeed built to facilitate industrialization; but industrialization was pursued (against considerable resistance[38]) only because it had shown itself to be a military necessity.

What led to unrest in a generally improving environment, I suggest, was not development per se, but *uneven* development – proxied, again, and almost certainly conditioned, by access to railroads. Where connections were good, peasants had access to wider markets, both domestic and

[38] See inter alia Emmons (1968, chap. 6).

global; and, when their labor was not needed on the farm, they could join the army of seasonal migrants and take up work in the growing cities, usually in industry, or (less often, but still significantly) in labor-intensive agriculture in other regions. In more isolated regions, opportunities were fewer, produce prices were lower (to incorporate higher transport costs), and – paradoxically – what Burds has called "horizontal mobilization" was easier, facilitated by the collective reading of newspapers and ensuing vigorous political discussion.

It is therefore not surprising that, holding equal such other factors as soil quality, extent of previous serfdom, and any regional peculiarities (fixed effects), one finds unrest to be less frequent, the denser was a region's railway network. Since peasant unrest presumably might have also borne some relationship to wheat prices, or to the share of the region's area that was sown to wheat, the regression also included those variables. The somewhat surprising result was that unrest *increased* with rising wheat prices in the well-connected and more prosperous regions but either remained the same or *decreased* in the more isolated regions when wheat prices were high.

What I have investigated here, I must emphasize, is peasant unrest over a fifteen-year span near the end of the nineteenth century. That of course excludes the stillborn revolution of 1905, let alone the successful revolutions of March and November 1917. *Pace* Lord Keynes, we have no certainty that rapid population growth, or for that matter uneven development, "caused" the Soviet Revolution. These findings may be suggestive, but we can only plausibly link the exogenous and related shocks of rapid population growth, railway construction, and industrialization to episodes of peasant unrest – and chiefly in the regions with less access to railroads and therefore with diminished opportunity.

Alexander Gerschenkron argued that much unrest would have been avoided had peasants found fewer obstacles to moving out of agriculture and into industry. To the extent that the poorly connected regions were populated precisely by peasants who might otherwise have moved to the cities, and whose discontent with their rural life festered, these results support him.

Appendix

Table A5.1 *Summary statistics and intercorrelations of variables*

Summary Statistics for unrest events between 1893 and 1901, uyezd-level data								
	N	Mean	Std	Min	25%	50%	75%	Max
Year	8194	1893	5.00	1885	1889	1893	1897	1901
Railroad density (kms of railroad per unit area of province)	8194	9,81E+09	1,10E +11	0.0	0.0	7,50E+08	1,60E+09	0.00010
# of events in *uyezd* in year	8194	0.107	0.431	0.0	0.0	0.0	0.0	8.0
Population of *uyezd* in 1897	8194	178927	109005	21026	113659.5	156612	218676.5	1375949
Percentage of wheat sown by Peasantry	8194	0.08397	0.13756	0.0	0.00130	0.01708	0.09571	0.63005
Price of Odessa wheat in Amsterdam	8194	132.4	18.96	91.4	125.9	137.9	143.1	169.5
Serf percentage (F&G)	8194	0.39603	0.24464	0.0	0.19183	0.43461	0.60200	0.85212
Soil quality (F&G)	8194	0.45380	0.38915	0.0	0.06372	0.324858	0.86729	1.0

	Year	Railroad density	Event	Population	Wheat percent	Wheat price	Serf percentage	Good soil
Year	1.0	0.14	0.03	0.09	0.0	–0.41	0.0	–0.0
Railroad density	0.14	1.0	–0.0	0.18	–0.07	–0.05	0.14	0.1
Event	0.03	–0.0	1.0	0.11	0.06	0.01	0.05	0.05
Population	0.09	0.18	0.11	1.0	0.34	–0.04	–0.2	0.27
Wheat percent	0.0	–0.07	0.06	0.34	1.0	–0.0	–0.31	0.46
Wheat price	–0.41	–0.05	0.01	–0.04	–0.0	1.0	–0.0	0.0
Serf percentage	0.0	0.14	0.05	–0.2	–0.31	–0.0	1.0	–0.08
Good soil	–0.0	0.1	0.05	0.27	0.46	0.0	–0.08	1.0

6

Exogenous Loss of Land

Blockade, Hunger, and the Nazi Pursuit of *Lebensraum*

The [pre-1914] prosperity of Europe was based on the fact that, owing to the large exportable surplus of foodstuffs in America, she was able to purchase food at a cheap rate measured in terms of the labor required to produce her own exports . . . The war had so shaken this system as to endanger the life of Europe altogether.

Keynes, *Economic Consequences of the Peace*

[Hitler's] genocidal plan commanded such wide-ranging support because it concerned a practical issue, the importance of which, following Germany's experience in World War I, was obvious to all: the need to secure the food supply of the German population, if necessary at the expense of the population of the Soviet Union.

Tooze, *The Wages of Destruction*

We have seen in other chapters that societies, or affected groups within them, will try to adapt to a supply shock – by factor substitution, factor mobility, or factor-saving technological innovation – if it seems at all possible to do so. With rare exceptions, it is only when none of those adjustments seems possible that those affected will bear the costs and risks of a political – which is to say, a coercive – solution. Most coercive efforts, if they are undertaken at all, remain domestic, that is, internal to a given state or jurisdiction. At least in modern times,[1] the costliest and riskiest kind of coercive solution has been the pursuit of foreign conquest[2] – usually

[1] In the ancient world, however, conquest of neighboring territory, slaughter or enslavement of its existing population, and settlement by part of the conqueror's subjects, was commonplace. The Roman Republic provides interesting and less well-known examples (Scheidel 2004).

[2] Colonial conquest, of a society with a much less advanced technology, is more frequent. Often, societies have undertaken conquest opportunistically, in the belief that territory or resources could be won at a relatively low cost.

to remedy some sudden and unanticipated shortage of a crucial natural resource (ores, petroleum), or of land.

It is, however, an astonishing fact of twentieth-century history that, in the 1930s and 1940s, Germany and Japan – and, on a more modest scale, Italy – pursued precisely such a strategy of conquest: Germany, to acquire and settle *Lebensraum*; Japan, to establish client states and colonies that would constitute the "Greater East Asia Co-Prosperity Sphere" and afford "life space" (*seimei kūkan*, 生命空間); Italy, to achieve *spazio vitale*.[3] Each regime claimed to be motivated by a desperate need for secure sources of food and natural resources. Those countries' leaders, certainly supported by powerful groups within their societies and eventually, to all appearances, by the mass of their populations, wagered (and, of course, eventually lost) immense quantities of lives and resources in what Adam Tooze has accurately called colonialism's "last great land-grab" (Tooze 2008, 462) – with the crucial difference that, at least in the case of Germany, the land-grab encompassed in its planning the merciless slaughter of some forty-five million of the conquered territories' native inhabitants.

In other substantive chapters, I have tried to illuminate how and why the response to a common supply shock varied across large regions – for example, eastern vs. western, or southeastern vs. northwestern, Europe. Here, I explore not only why the response to a common shock varied between one country and all its neighbors – Germany, after all, was the only European state that undertook such a genocidal project – but also why the response differed *within* Germany. For only a minority supported the clearly stated Nazi plan of conquest in Germany's last free elections, and we have already strong indications of how that minority differed – in religion, class, and age – from Hitler's opponents. What remains unsatisfactorily illuminated, however, is *why*: What was it about the Nazis' supporters that opened them even to consider such a ghastly project?

Germany, I shall suggest, differed in having experienced the trauma of extensive hunger and starvation in World War I; and, within Germany, early electoral support for National Socialism was strongest in the regions that had experienced the highest rates of starvation-induced mortality.

But I shall try first to elucidate how it could be that supporters of National Socialism saw the path of conquest as necessary – indeed, as the only course that could guarantee their nation's survival. This is not a task

[3] *Lebensraum* is discussed more fully below. On the Japanese quest for autarky, see Dower (1986, 277–279); on Italy, Rodogno (2006, 47–54).

for the squeamish, and I emphasize the ancient adage that "to explain is not to excuse." Millions died as a result of the actions of Germany and its Axis allies, the great majority not from combat or aerial bombardment, but from premeditated slaughter or starvation.[4] We must accept, however, that Adolf Hitler and his minions saw the alternatives to conquest clearly and, despite evidence to the contrary, dismissed each in turn as unworkable. Their madness did not lack method. We must also recognize that millions of Germans, knowing exactly what he had in mind,[5] embraced Hitler's plan of conquest and ethnic cleansing; and that, as we now know, much of Germany's military leadership and bureaucracy was fully complicit in both the conquest of territory and the planned slaughter or starvation of millions of Russians and Poles – and, it goes without saying, in the genocide of the European Jews.[6]

It is necessary preliminarily, however, to survey more generally the developments in Europe during and after World War I.

EUROPE'S FOOD INSECURITY

Keynes, as everybody now remembers, predicted in 1919 that the Treaty of Versailles, if not modified, would lead to economic catastrophe and a new world war. Fewer recall that, in chapter two of *Economic Consequences of the Peace*, "Europe Before the War," Keynes analyzed also the dire straits in which Europe as a whole found itself in 1919. Up to about 1870, Keynes argued, Europe had been "substantially self-sufficient" in food; after that point, largely because of its rapidly growing population, it had come to rely increasingly on imported food – which,

[4] Roughly 85 million people died in the war, including at least 20 million in China and 24 million in the USSR. Roughly half (about 45 million) were civilian deaths (WW II Deaths 2020). Some 2.2 million Soviet prisoners of war were deliberately starved to death (Tooze 2008, 482).

[5] As detailed below, any reader of *Mein Kampf* who missed this message would have to have been extraordinarily dense; nor did Hitler or his acolytes disguise it in their speeches, particularly to peasant audiences.

[6] The *Generalplan Ost*, which explicitly envisioned the killing of some 45 million persons, "was agreed between the Wehrmacht, all the key civilian ministries, and the Nazi leadership ..."; and far from being secret, was communicated "to all German soldiers and occupation administrators in Soviet territory." (Tooze 2008, 467 and 476–480) The claim that the vaunted German armed forces retained clean hands, and that solely the SS and the *Einsatzgruppen* carried out the bloody work of extermination, has repeatedly been exposed as a self-serving lie.

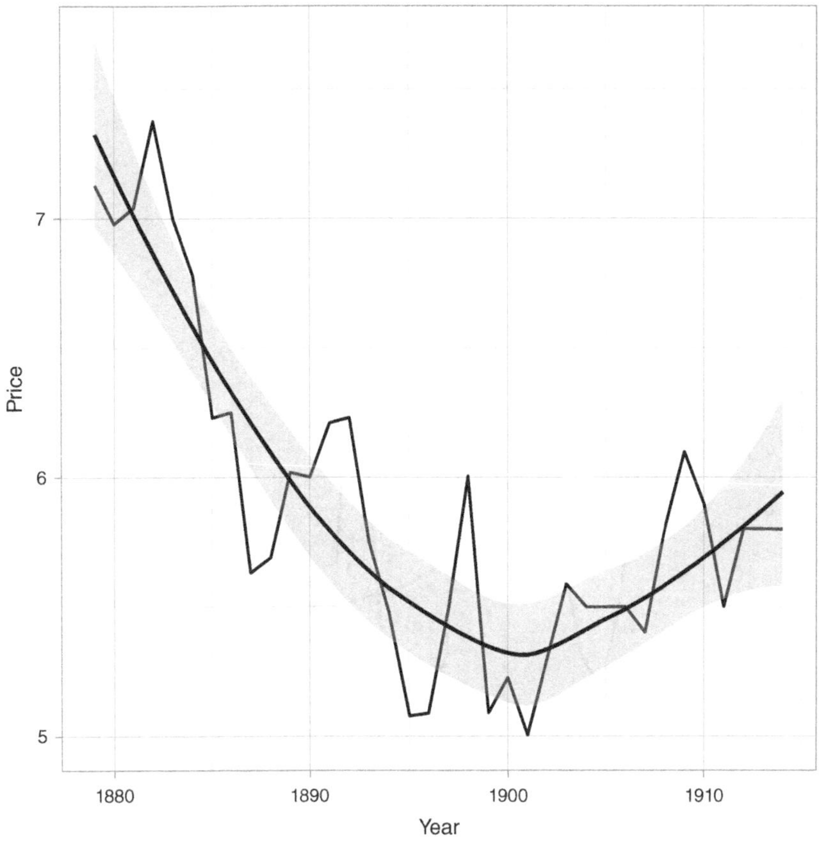

Figure 6.1 London bread prices, 1879–1913

moreover, in real terms had become steadily cheaper for some thirty years (Keynes 1920, 9–10).

Even before the war, Europe's reliance on the lands of the New World had become precarious; the real cost of food, as Keynes noted impressionistically, had begun to rise after 1900 (Figures 6.1 and 6.2). The Great War, however, had interrupted commerce, sunk much of the Atlantic cargo fleet, unsettled previously fixed exchange rates (before 1914, all had been pegged to gold), destroyed physical plant (chiefly in northeastern France), and torn apart Europe's prewar high degree of internal commerce and specialization (Landes 2003, 360–361). These blows, together with rising postwar protectionism, had curtailed the supply of foodstuffs and raw materials from the New World. We have seen in Chapter 1 that trade, no less than direct acquisition, can increase the

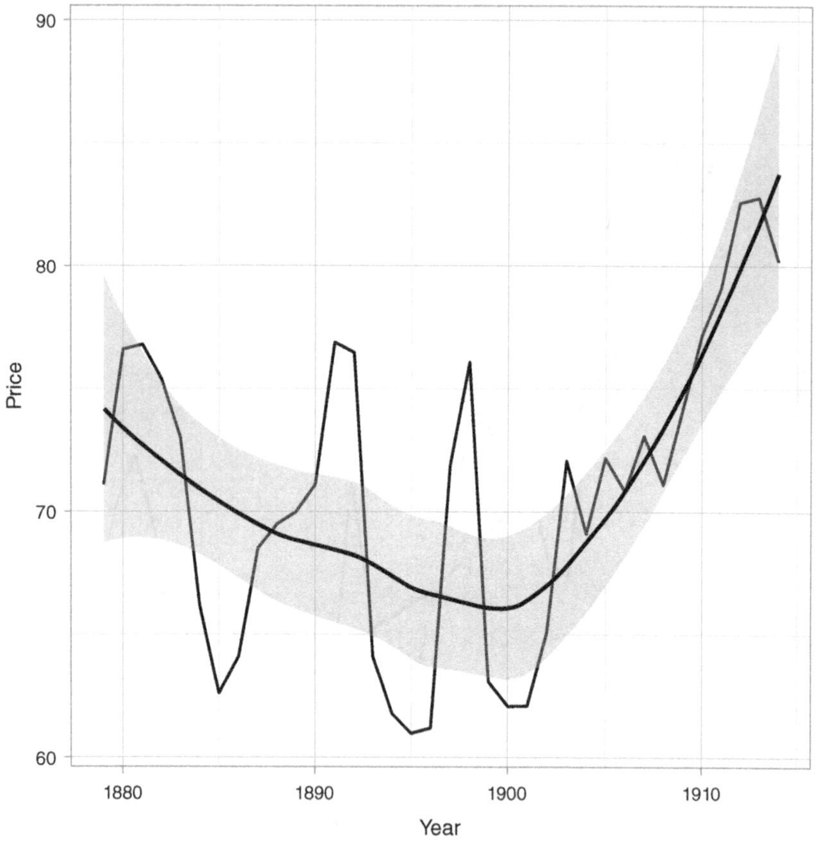

Figure 6.2 Paris bread prices, 1879–1913.
Source for both figures: (Allen 2001). The lowess smoother has a bandwidth of 0.8.

supply of a factor; indeed, beginning in the 1870s, Europe had effectively annexed the lands of the New World: The "imperialism of free trade" (Gallagher and Robinson 1953) guaranteed that their products flowed to Europe as smoothly as if Europe, the Americas, and Oceania had been part of the same state. In the terms used here, then, the war and its aftermath constituted a massive negative shock to Europe's supply of *land* – one that, at a minimum, drastically increased the costs of foodstuffs and raw materials and, at worst, threatened hunger and starvation.

Reality, after 1919, swiftly bore out Keynes's dire prediction. France, on the eve of the war, had exported foodstuffs with a value just under half of the food it imported; by the first half of 1920, food exports were less than a quarter of food imports.[7] Even Britain, which could still count on its Empire (and not least on the luxuriant grain fields of the Punjab in the "jewel" of that Empire's crown, India), could not fully recover; by 1929, its exports had climbed back to not quite 85 percent of prewar levels.[8] Moreover, before the war Britain, and to a lesser extent France, had used substantial earnings from overseas investments to cover the cost of imported food; those holdings had virtually all been liquidated during the war to pay for imported armaments.

The war had, paradoxically, also made Europe relatively more abundant in human and physical capital.[9] Not only did the belligerent powers face a diminished supply of land, but also of low-skill labor. The manpower losses from prolonged trench warfare and futile "human wave" attacks were significant, involving not just the many dead but those who returned too maimed to re-enter the workforce. Of their male population of military age (15–49), both Germany and France experienced combat fatalities of 13 percent and the United Kingdom over 6 percent.[10] The number permanently disabled can only be estimated but may well have raised the total manpower losses in both Germany and France to something approaching 15 percent of all adult males.[11] Moreover, because most governments exempted from conscription the skilled workers, who

[7] Between January and June of 1920, France imported goods worth 15.6 billion (inflated) francs and exported 7.49 billion; it imported foodstuffs worth 3.85 billion and exported .80 billion. In 1913, food imports had amounted to 1.82 billion, exports to .84 billion (Federico and Tena Junguito 2018).

[8] In constant dollars, UK exports in 1913 totaled $2.566 billion; in 1929, the highest level since the war, $2.154 billion (Federico and Tena Junguito 2018).

[9] The fighting in France's industrial northeast had, of course, destroyed perhaps one-third of the country's physical capital (Piketty 2003, 1020); but the voracious wartime demand for steel, munitions, and armaments among all belligerent powers had forced more than offsetting industrial investments – so much so that an intractable issue in postwar Europe was its glut of steel (Maier 1975).

[10] Serbia, the dubious champion in this category, lost 23 percent of all its males between the ages of 15 and 49 (Winter 2001, 5692).

[11] The German census of 1925 counted 101,400 men and 36,200 women as "crippled," and ascribed the higher numbers for males (a difference of roughly 65,000) to wartime injuries. A more detailed census of wartime injuries in 1924 had counted 66,000 men as having lost at least one hand or one foot in the war (Prinzing 1931, 189). Those numbers would have amounted to less than 0.4 percent of Germany's total male working-age population at the time of 18 million (Statistisches Reichsamt 1925, 12). Thousands more, however, suffered facial injuries so severe as to make them unwelcome in most workplaces.

were needed to keep war industries running, losses of human capital were likely less than those among low-skill workers and peasants.[12]

As land and land-intensive products grew scarcer and dearer,[13] and as the wages of low-skill labor also rose, the returns to the now relatively more abundant factors, human and physical capital, inevitably fell. A signal pattern of the 1920s was "wage compression," in which the wage differential between skilled and unskilled workers diminished.

Every European state had to adapt somehow to these radically changed circumstances. Perhaps the most obvious adjustment was somehow to expand one's home market – peacefully, it was understood – to include areas that could supply the necessary imports. This possibility was really open only to the British Empire, which turned increasingly to Imperial Preference and exploitation of the raw materials of its colonies and dominions. Another option was land reform – either breaking up large estates (e.g., in eastern Europe) or consolidating small ones (notably in France) – to achieve supposedly optimal size. Brassley, however, estimates that, while Latvia and Estonia redistributed over half of their agricultural land, and England and Wales roughly a quarter, German land reform affected just over 2 percent of its farmland (Brassley 2010, 151).

Keynes advocated, as at least a partial remedy, a "Free Trade Union" that foreshadowed today's European Union but would have encompassed a rather different area. As Keynes envisioned it, such a Union would initially comprise "Germany, Poland, the new States which formerly composed the Austro-Hungarian and Turkish Empires, and the

12 As early as the November 1913 "munitions crisis," Germany began to pull skilled workers (*Facharbeiter*) back from the front and to exempt such workers from conscription. The low-skilled could be replaced by women and youth, the skilled industrial workers could not. By the summer of 1917, 500,000 had thus been deferred from military service (Sichler and Tiburtius 1925, sec. Appendix 8) (Feldman 1992, 69 and 243).

13 Despite the stock phrase about the "farm depression of the early 1920s," in fact world prices of agricultural products remained considerably higher than they had been in the prewar period. The average price of wheat on US markets between 1909 and 1913, for example, had been 89 cents per bushel; at the close of the war (1918–1919) its price per bushel was 208 cents, a year later 222 cents, 2.5 times its prewar price. At its lowest point in the 1924 farm recession, wheat still remained just above its average prewar price, at 96 cents per bushel; but by August 1924, it had recovered to 117 cents per bushel. Cotton prices, after a sharp dip in 1921, rose steadily, peaking at 2.5 times their prewar level in late 1923 and remaining at twice their prewar level in 1924. (United States Federal Reserve Board 1915, no. October 1924, pp. 790–791) Note that, because the USA remained on the gold standard, real prices increased at least as much as nominal ones; indeed, for gold-scarce Europe, the real prices will likely have been higher.

Mandated States [i.e., former colonies of Germany]."[14] A free trade area so constituted would hardly be self-sufficient but might achieve economies of scale to rival those of the USA[15] In the future, however, Keynes imagined that such a Union might grow to include much of the British Empire, and more: "the United Kingdom, Egypt, and India, ... Belgium, Holland, Scandinavia, and Switzerland ..." and, one day perhaps, "France and Italy" (Keynes 1920, 265). Even the modest beginning that Keynes proposed proved unrealistic; his grander vision was, well, visionary. It had no chance of success.

EUROPE'S THREE MAIN OPTIONS

The countries of the European Continent likely considered the three main kinds of adaptation outlined in Chapter 2, only to perceive quickly that only one – intersectoral factor mobility – held out reasonable prospects of success. Two of the other possible remedies could be eliminated almost at once, namely:

1. *Factor substitution.* In theory, newly abundant human or physical capital could be substituted for land in agriculture. Farming could become more mechanized (at a minimum, substituting tractors for horses) and farmers, better educated. The minuscule acreage of many European farms, however, impeded both mechanization and the deployment of human capital. Of all German farmsteads 74 percent comprised fewer than ten hectares (25 acres), and the average French farmer tilled a risible 2.8 hectares of arable (seven acres, or about three city blocks) (Tooze 2008, 176–177). In the majority of French departments, the average holding was less than half a hectare (Brassley 2010, 153). To be sure, the Coase Theorem would predict rapid consolidation of holdings in the presence of well-functioning markets in land; but those markets did not in fact function speedily or

[14] The first halting steps in this direction centered around the coal, steel, and agricultural low-tariff area negotiated between France and Germany in 1927 (Maier 1975, 516–545).

[15] American intervention in the last months of the war had raised European awareness of US industrial power and, with it, the importance of economies of scale. As we shall see, Hitler, in particular, saw not only abundance of land and natural resources, but its huge and unified domestic market, as the secret of America's industrial prowess.

well in most of interwar Europe.[16] There, as elsewhere, peasants tenaciously resisted leaving the land, and encumbrances to title discouraged land purchases by outsiders. Factor substitution in agriculture, in other words, was at best a longer-term solution; for the present, it was foreclosed.

2. *Factor-saving technological innovation.* Perhaps some new crop or technology, like the potato in an earlier century (Nunn and Qian 2011), could make European land productive enough to overcome the shortfall and permit the Continent to regain self-sufficiency. In food, this would have meant a hybrid-based "green revolution"; or, to dream even more wildly, today's genetically modified crops that triple the production per unit of land.[17] From the perspective of what has already been said about technological innovation (Chapter 3), this was simply too big a leap for the science of the period to achieve. The most elementary knowledge of genetic structure lay decades in the future,[18] and even the high-yielding hybrids and cropping techniques that permitted the actual Green Revolution of the 1960s would have taken years of concentrated effort to achieve. Again, the practical obstacles to this course were insurmountable.
3. *Factor mobility (a) Among jurisdictions*: Before the War, Europe's signally abundant factor, labor, had emigrated to the New World, leaving Europe with fewer mouths to feed.[19] Now, owners of human capital had the strongest incentives to emigrate and owners of physical capital, to invest abroad. Foreign investment was impeded by currency risk and Germany's burden of reparations, and human capital – except in the *annus horribilus* of the 1923 hyperinflation – rarely exited:[20] Transit was more difficult, and parts of the New

[16] This is a case in which institutions do constrain the possibilities of adjustment – a theme to which I return in the concluding chapter.

[17] Both worldwide and in the US, crop yields per hectare roughly tripled between 1961 and 2014, largely due to genetically modified crops (Ritchie and Roser 2013). I can attest from personal experience that Nebraska wheat fields normally yielded thirty bushels per acre, in exceptionally good years forty bushels per acre, in the 1950s; today, yields of over seventy bushels per acre are regarded as normal.

[18] The Crick and Watson paper on the structure of DNA did not appear until 1953.

[19] In the late nineteenth century, European population densities were the highest in the world: forty-one inhabitants per square kilometer, vs. thirty-one per square kilometer in the second highest region, Asia (Goldewijk 2005, 354).

[20] Between 1919 and 1932, a total of just over 600,000 Germans emigrated; of those, the single year of 1923 accounted for 115,000 (Sternberg 2018). In the comparable period 1880–1893, some 1.8 million Germans emigrated to the USA alone (Schmal

World were less welcoming. This option, too, had at best limited practicality.

There remained, it seemed, as the only realistic possibility:

Factor mobility (b) Among sectors: Newly abundant, and therefore cheap, human and physical capital could flow into whole new sectors of the economy, including such high-tech specializations as chemicals, optics, specialty steel, and electronics.[21] Especially if firms coupled these with Taylorist techniques of "scientific management," proponents argued, they would generate more than enough earnings to purchase the needed imports, despite the newly erected barriers and the increased cost of food.

As Tooze has pointed out, the "export powerhouse" strategy was exactly the one advocated, and largely put into practice, in Weimar Germany between 1924 and 1930 by Gustav Stresemann, with the backing of most of German industry (Tooze 2008, chap. 1). Yet even in the most prosperous years of the Weimar period, a significant number of Germans doubted the long-term prospects of that strategy. One reason, assuredly, was German civilians' wartime experience.

GERMANY'S PARTICULAR SENSITIVITY TO THE ISSUE OF FOOD SUPPLY

The general issue that Keynes had outlined resonated with particular force in Germany, not least because during the war its citizens had suffered actual starvation.[22]

2020). The US immigration restrictions enacted in 1924 had a significant effect (Bade and Oltmer 2004, 27).

21 Probably because of the relative abundance of human capital, the interwar period experienced significant technological breakthroughs, which continued even into the Great Depression (Frieden 2006, chap. 7).

22 This is not to suggest that hunger did not arise among the populations of other belligerent powers, only that – with the likely exception of the Ottoman Empire – it did so to a much lesser extent. In Italy, food consumption per capita exceeded 1913 levels in every year of the war (Broadberry and Harrison 2005, 290). In Russia, grain production even in its worst years (1916 for wheat, 1917 for rye) fell by only about 20 percent from prewar levels; and, given that grain exports from Odessa were completely cut off, the national food supply was adequate; shortages were local and arose from mismanagement and breakdowns in transportation (Broadberry and Harrison 2005, 257–258). French agricultural production, stricken by the loss of some of its richest soil, fell by 1918 to three-quarters of 1913 levels; but France was not blockaded, and the wartime shortages could mostly be made up by imports (Broadberry and Harrison 2005, 171–173). In the Ottoman Empire, however, and especially in Lebanon and Syria, bad harvests, government

Even before the war, and despite high tariffs that had been cynically promoted as assuring self-sufficiency in wartime (Gerschenkron 1966, chap. 1), Germany had imported fully a third of its foodstuffs – more than any other country – and half of its livestock feed (Vincent 1985, 124) (Wehler 1987, 58), as well as huge quantities of nitrate fertilizer.[23] The British blockade, which began in earnest in late 1915, interdicted almost all of these imports; and the lack of fertilizer, as well as of manpower and horses (since both had been conscripted into combat), caused domestic production to recede rapidly as well. Between 1916 and 1917, imports of grain fell 85 percent; of vegetable fats and oils, 81 percent; of meat, 69 percent; of butter, 56 percent; of livestock, 34 percent (Broadberry and Harrison 2005, 58).[24] Domestically, the production of livestock fell by 40 percent, of grain and potatoes by 35 percent.[25] By 1918, agricultural production overall had fallen by between 40 and 50 percent (Wehler 1987, 58) (Broadberry and Harrison 2005, 46).

Despite drastic government intervention, including deploying prisoners of war as farm workers, the import of 700,000 conscripted laborers from the occupied territories, and the rapid expansion of the Haber-Bosch process for fixing nitrates from air,[26] much land went fallow and yields on the rest dropped precipitously (Wehler 1987, 58 and 279). Rationing, which began in some locations as early as January of 1915, became severe: By late 1916, the official rations provided only 1000 calories[27] per day per person, at best 60 percent of the necessary daily intake of even a sedentary worker. The available foods, prominent among them potatoes and root vegetables, were deficient in fats and vitamins.[28] To be sure, a

mismanagement, and the Anglo-French blockade occasioned as many as a million deaths (Broadberry and Harrison 2005, 125).

[23] Before the war, 24 percent of Chilean nitrate exports went to Germany (Chancerel 2015, 14).

[24] Percentages are calculated from the tonnage (or, in the case of livestock, head) reported in Broadberry and Harrison (2005, table 2.13). Presumably imports of butter and livestock fell less because they could in part be imported from neutral sources on the Continent.

[25] See also the more detailed statistics for Westphalia in Roerkohl (1991, 346).

[26] The new process was expanded at breakneck speed to provide explosives for combat, and of course the military had first claim on its output. It nonetheless sufficed to cover only about half of Germany's prewar consumption of nitrate fertilizers; but a lack of phosphates – for which no synthetic substitute was found – more severely constrained production (Vincent 1985, 125).

[27] More properly, and almost universally in Continental usage, kilocalories. I hew here to the American usage, which denotes kcal as "calories."

[28] The shortage of fats impeded also the production of soap, with dire consequences for personal hygiene.

lively black market, stimulated by strict price controls and growing inflation, came to account for between 30 and 50 percent of total agricultural production.[29] The better-off survived, the poor became seriously malnourished (Wehler 1987, 61). As we shall see, region also mattered: Rationing was administered equitably and compassionately in some areas, inefficiently or corruptly in others.

Late 1916 and early 1917 became notorious as the "hunger winter" or the "rutabaga winter" (*Steckrübenwinter*), named after the root vegetable that replaced most of that year's failed potato crop and often became the principal source of nourishment. Actual starvation began to set in. Death, as in most famines, rarely came directly from malnourishment, but from diseases that attacked those weakened by hunger (tuberculosis, dysentery, influenza) or that resulted from specific dietary deficits (scurvy, rickets). Starvation led especially to increased deaths from tuberculosis; they increased between 1914 and 1918 by almost 60 percent nationally[30] and more than doubled in five German cities.[31] Indeed, as we shall see, deaths from tuberculosis increased over prewar levels in every urban area except the smaller towns of Bavaria and (understandably) the blockade-silenced port of Bremerhaven.

The overall civilian death toll, from all causes, was shocking, especially in the blockade's worst year, 1917. Judging by the official mortality tables, the losses were greatest among children, those over seventy years of age, and – for all ages between fifteen and sixty – women (Table 6.1). The especially striking gender difference among those between fifteen and thirty years of age, where female mortality rose over four times as much as that among civilian males, may well have arisen from mothers' relinquishing their own nourishment to keep their children alive (Vincent 1985, 137).

[29] Roerkohl (1991, 354) provides a list of black-market prices in Bonn in the Winter of 1917–1918. These ranged from one and one-half to over five times the officially permitted prices: e.g., beef, officially 2.75 marks per (metric) pound (i.e., 0.5 kg), sold on the black market for 4.75; butter, officially 3.40 per pound, went for 14 marks; and bacon (*geräucherter Speck*) was officially 2.75 marks per pound, but its black-market price was 15.50. The price controls of course curtailed farmers' incentives to expand production.

[30] 1914: 92,896; 1919: 147,406. (Internationale Vergleiche 1922, 9*). Among 266 German cities of population 15,000 or more, tuberculosis deaths increased by 63.3 percent, from 34,091 to 55,663 (Reichsgesundheitsamt 1921, 56*).

[31] Essen, Rostock, Krefeld, Halle, and Mülheim an der Ruhr.

Table 6.1 Mortality 1917 vs. 1913, ages 1 and higher[32]

Males

Age	Deaths 1913	Deaths 1917[33]	Percent Change
1–5	41,124	40,732	-1.0
5–15	17,929	26,535	+48.0
15–30	36,268	40,065	+10.5
30–60	110,652	128,663	+16.3
60–70	65,028	83,805	+28.9
70 and over	93,001	124,947	+34.4
Total	364,002	444,747	+22.2

Females

Age	Deaths 1913	Deaths 1917	Percent Change
1–5	38,645	38,607	-0.1
5–15	18,290	26,304	+43.8
15–30	34,060	48,802	+43.3
30–60	93,279	121,442	+30.2
60–70	64,646	79,770	+23.4
70 and over	114,556	153,304	+33.8
Total	363,476	468,229	+28.8

Source: Statistisches Reichsamt (1916, 31; 1921, 33)[34]

What nonetheless leaps off the page is the shocking increase in mortality among children of both sexes between the ages of five and fifteen.[35] Nor was death the only consequence of malnourishment. Even the children who survived often incurred permanent damage – missing teeth, chronic weakness, brittle or misshapen bones, even mental

32 Deaths among infants under one year of age actually fell by 49 percent (from 277,196 in 1913 to 141,244 in 1917), but that was because in that *annus horribilis* births fell by just over 50 percent (1913: 1,894,593; 1917: 939,938. (Statistisches Reichsamt 1916, 24 and 31; 1921, 26 and 33). As noted below, infants and children under five years of age received extra rations. The huge increase in deaths occurred among those five years and older.

33 Includes only civilian deaths.

34 Population statistics in the Imperial period always appeared with a considerable lag, exacerbated by the war; and the volume for a particular year was always published in the succeeding year. Thus the volume that appeared in 1921 was labeled *Statistisches Jahrbuch 1920* and reported statistics for 1917.

35 The *Reichsgesundheitsamt* estimated the increase in this age bracket between 1913 and 1917 to have been even higher, around 55 percent (Reichsgesundheitsamt 1919, 17).

retardation – from prolonged lack of vitamins, fats, or protein (Vincent 1985, 140 and 160–162). The effects of rickets, including "bowed or misshapen bones," were noted as "appearing frequently" in children as early as 1919 in an official report of the Ministry of Health, which added that bones that broke spontaneously or easily were "no rarity." These effects, too, were noted most frequently in children who had been deprived of nourishment between five and fifteen years of age – therefore, given that the hunger peaked in 1917, those born roughly between 1901 and 1914.[36] Apparently infants and toddlers had better odds of survival and suffered less lasting damage because they received higher rations, especially of vitamin D–rich milk; and older adolescents, if they survived, incurred fewer lasting effects, because by age fifteen growth was almost complete (Roerkohl 1991, 310).

One postwar study, limited to children entering elementary school in 1924 in the city of Mannheim, found that the incidence of severe bone damage from rickets ("severe rickets-related deformations of the upper and lower limbs") had quadrupled from its prewar level,[37] almost certainly due to wartime malnourishment. Another local study, in the smaller town of Remscheid, established that 35 percent of schoolchildren showed lasting aftereffects of rickets.[38] That would correspond to the broader measure employed in Mannheim: If one included there, in addition to "deformation of the upper and lower limbs," "pronounced changes in the rib cage," 31.3 percent of boys and 23.1 percent of girls exhibited persistent effects of rickets (Prinzing 1931, 213).

If these figures extend to the broader population – and interregional variation, discussed below, makes that uncertain – some 9 percent of children, who under prewar conditions would have exhibited no symptoms of rickets, manifested "pronounced" effects in the postwar generation. That will have served as a recurrent reminder, not only to the affected but to all around them, of what food insecurity could portend.

[36] The hunger began in 1916 and ended in 1919. Those born in 1901 would have been fifteen years of age at its onset, and the last group of affected five-year-olds would have been born in 1914.

[37] In 1913, 3.1 percent of boys and 2.3 percent of girls had shown that level of damage from rickets; in Mannheim in 1924, the incidence was 13.3 percent among males and 10.4 percent among females (Prinzing 1931, 213–214).

[38] Prinzing notes, however, that a study in Dortmund, using a different classificatory scheme, found no postwar increase in rickets-related deformities (Prinzing 1931, 214). Whether that was due to different criteria or to genuine regional differences remains unclear.

Although deaths from tuberculosis soon returned to prewar levels – in 1924, 93,074 were recorded (International Vergleiche 1927, 15*) – and in Weimar's prosperous period actually decreased (55,672 deaths in 1928) (Internationale Vergleiche 1931, 17*), many of those infected during the war must have continued, in that pre-antibiotic age, to exhibit symptoms. As we shall see below, deaths from tuberculosis may have left a particularly strong imprint on survivors' memories.

The extent of malnourishment varied not only by class (although even among the better-off, many proved unable or unwilling to exploit the black market) and by age, but by *locality*. As no less a figure than Hindenburg noted in a desperate letter to Chancellor Bethmann-Hollweg in November of 1916, hunger prevailed especially in "the coal mining districts of the Ruhr, the Siegerland, and other industrial regions" (Huegel 2003, 220). Roerkohl notes that the symptoms of malnourishment "appeared earlier in the large cities and the industrial districts than in small or mid-sized cities or in the countryside" and, more generally, that there was "a conspicuous discrepancy in the level of supply among individual sections of the country, administrative districts (*Regierungsbezirke*), as well as cities" (Roerkohl 1991, 297, 317). At the other extreme, politically powerful landlords east of the Elbe often shielded their produce from state requisitioning and kept their tenants well-fed (Roerkohl 1991, 317).

The mortality statistics in the yearbooks of the Statistisches Reichsamt tell us with greater precision how much mortality increased, in each of Prussia's provinces and each of the Empire's states other than Prussia, between the last full prewar year of 1913 and the worst year of the famine, 1917.[39] If we simply map that ratio – mortality 1917/mortality 1913 – for each such unit, we obtain the illuminating Map 6.1, which one may compare to the political units of Map 6.2. While indeed the industrial regions of the Ruhr suffered above-average increases in mortality, the most striking increases were in the small states of north central Germany (notably Mecklenburg-Schwerin and Lübeck) and in the Prussian province of Brandenburg, which included hard-hit Berlin, chemical and metalworking industries, and lignite mines. Southern Germany suffered least: Bavarian mortality actually decreased slightly (see Appendix Table A6.1).

[39] Unfortunately, I have located no regional figures that exclude the (much lower) mortality among infants under one year of age. If one includes them, the national increase in mortality is 2 percent, as against the increase of some 25 percent among those one year of age and older. The map and table presented here assume that the regional variation in overall mortality mimics that of mortality among those who had passed their first birthday.

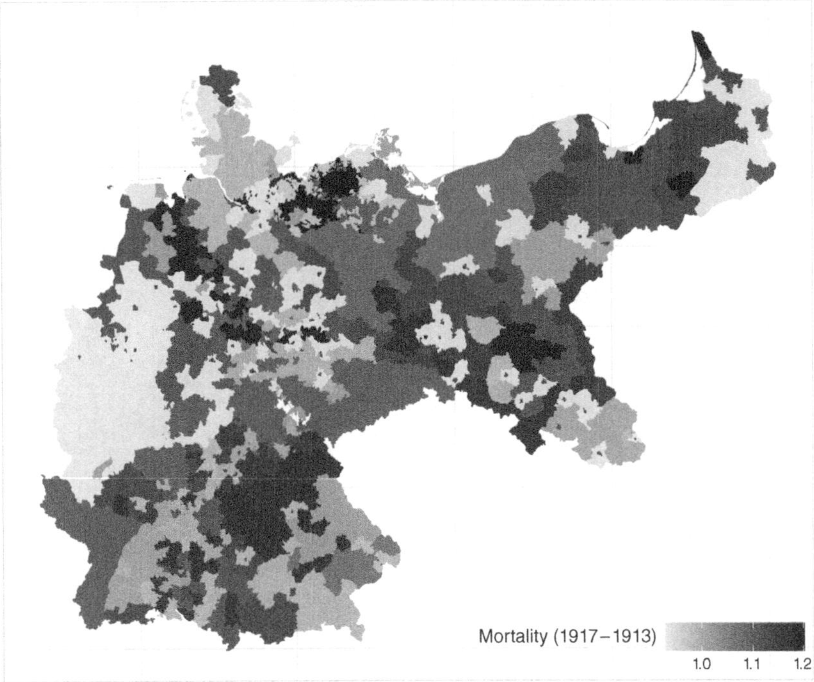

Map 6.1 Regional variation in excess mortality in 1917 (mortality 1917/mortality 1913)
Sources: 1913 mortality (Statistisches Reichsamt 1916, 25); 1917 mortality (Statistisches Reichsamt 1921, 26); https://censusmosaic.demog.berkeley.edu/data/historical-gis-files

Even among cities within the same state or province, the incidence of famine varied.[40] Some municipal governments actually turned to the black market to sustain their citizens (Münkler 2013, 587). While there was movement among regions after the war, it is reasonable to assume that the lasting damage to children of the blockade years would have been most frequent and most visible in the regions and cities that had endured the greatest shortages.

Just after the war ended, in December of 1918, the *Reichsgesundheitsamt* estimated, based on excess (i.e., above-normal) civilian mortality, that at least 763,000 deaths could be attributed to wartime malnutrition (Reichsgesundheitsamt 1919, 15). Since, despite the armistice, the blockade

[40] Cities enjoyed considerable autonomy in how they administered rationing. Industrial workers, for example, could not take time off to stand in line for rations; hence some cities, but by no means all, instituted special evening hours exclusively for workers (Huegel 2003, 182). In cities that failed to institute such measures, workers were presumably even less well nourished.

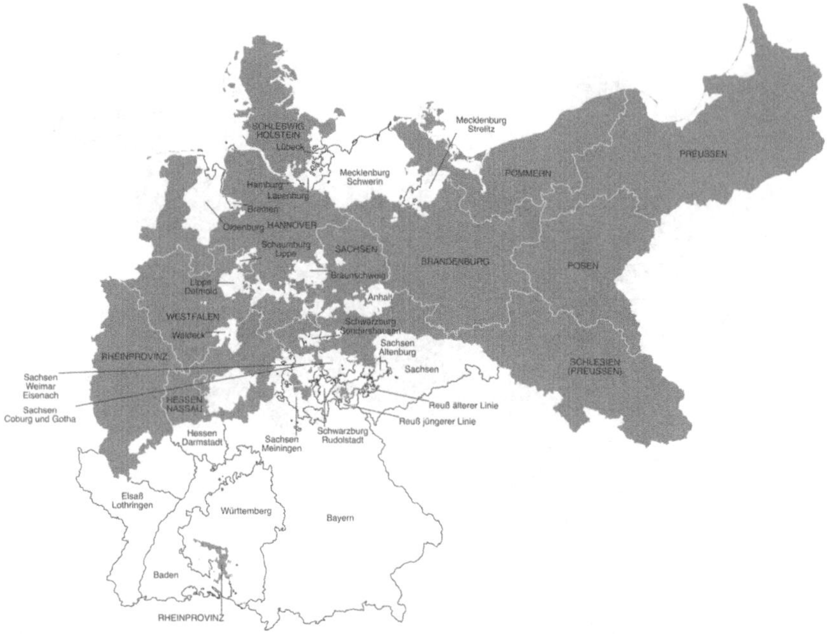

Map 6.2 States of the German Empire and provinces of the state of Prussia

continued until the signing of the Versailles Treaty in June of 1919, deaths presumably did not greatly abate; but the political turmoil prevented any exact keeping of records (Vincent 1985, 132 and 145). Conservatively, then, at least 800,000 Germans died as a result of the blockade, and as many as three million may have survived with lasting effects from rickets, scurvy, or tuberculosis.[41]

THE SEARCH FOR FOOD SECURITY

The experience of blockade and wartime deprivation broadened the appeal of autarky – or, at least, of self-sufficiency in food – and the

[41] The prewar population of Germany had been 65 million, of whom at least 25 million were under the age of twenty; if half of that cohort (or the comparable postwar cohort) were included in the ten-year interval of those aged five to fifteen, at least 12 million children would have been in this vulnerable age group. If even a quarter of those (based on the Mannheim and Remscheid samples) showed "pronounced" effects of malnutrition, the afflicted would have numbered 3 million. Of those, half, or 1.5 million, would have exhibited severe deformities of their arms or legs, as against some 300,000 before the war (2.5 percent of 12 million).

territorial expansion that supposedly would guarantee it, not least among political economists and students of geopolitics (Vincent 1985, 150). Whereas before the war adherents of autarky had advocated accretions of territory in such varied locations as the Baltic, Africa, eastern Europe, or even Belgium and France, after the 1917 Russian collapse and the peace of Brest-Litovsk they came to focus exclusively – not least in the military high command – on the Ukraine and western Russia. Ludendorff, in particular, welcomed the idea of turning "whole Russian provinces ... into settlement colonies for German peasants and war veterans." Some publicly advocated, in addition, the creation of puppet states in Poland and the Ukraine that "could really be nothing but German colonies" (Smith 1986, 193). Left unaddressed in most of these fantasies was the question of what, precisely, was to happen to those areas' current inhabitants;[42] and opponents of such imperialist designs, assuming that the indigenous population would remain largely in place, argued that domination of these areas could be sustained only by massive military force, whose costs would outweigh any conceivable benefit to Germany.

Germany's surrender on November 11, 1918, called a halt to such ambitious designs; but the continuation of the blockade for seven more months, and likely also the deprivations of the hyperinflation of 1923, in which the purchasing power of the *Reichsmark* collapsed even more swiftly on foreign than in domestic markets, allowed the idea of autarky to retain its appeal. One indicator was the impressive sales (by 1933, a total of 220,000 copies) of Hans Grimm's 1926 novel, *Volk ohne Raum*. Comprising two volumes and almost 1400 pages of florid prose, it was likely more displayed and cited than read.[43] As its title conveyed, it was a semi-mystical plea for "living space" – *Lebensraum* – for the German people.[44]

[42] One memorandum from the Pan-German League (*Alldeutscher Verband*) did however advocate "the ethnic cleansing of all annexed territories" (Broadberry and Harrison 2005, 65).

[43] There are eerie parallels to a similarly popular American novel (and subsequent film) that appeared only a decade later: Margaret Mitchell's *Gone with the Wind* (1936). Comparable in length (1037 pages) and style, it similarly attempted to rehabilitate the image of a rural, hierarchical, racist society; and, of course, the memorable utterance of its heroine, Scarlett O'Hara, would have resonated with most survivors of Germany's wartime blockade: "As God is my witness, I'll never be hungry again."

[44] Some argue, although the evidence is unclear, that Hitler first encountered the expression *Lebensraum* in Grimm's work.

Even in the Foreword, Grimm argued that, without sufficient territory, Germany's children were likely to become "sick cripples, furtive thieves, or poor whores" (Grimm 1927, I: 9–10).[45] If indeed the 1920s witnessed an unmistakable upsurge in the number of "sick cripples" among the children who had endured wartime shortages, his plea for autarky would have resonated all the more strongly.

For the reader who made it as far as volume two, Grimm put into the mouth of his didactic protagonist, Cornelius Friebott, an even clearer message. It was a "simple fact," that whenever the number of people in an area exceeded its ability to nourish them, "relations of social dependency" and of "dependence on foreign agriculture" arose. In the extreme case (to return to a formulation in the Foreword), this dependency would culminate in a "slavery of need and deprivation" (Grimm 1927, I: 10 and II: 316–317). Only by drastically expanding its territory – exactly where, Grimm left vague – could Germany avoid this fate.

Whatever the popularity of Grimm's (and others') pleas for the necessity of *Lebensraum*, Weimar Germany after its stabilization in late 1923 resolutely pursued instead Stresemann's policy of "fulfilment," which subsumed the "export powerhouse" strategy mentioned earlier. Germany would first gain some relief from the burden of reparations (achieved in the 1924 Dawes Plan) (Tooze 2008, 5–7), then exploit its technical superiority and its abundance of human and physical capital to achieve the export earnings that would finance imports of foodstuffs and raw materials. A major market for German exports would be the United States, with which Stresemann pursued a close alliance.

That policy enjoyed considerable success and was ratified in the 1928 parliamentary elections. The "Weimar coalition" of Socialists (SPD), Catholics (Z), Progressives (DDP), and Stresemann's Liberals (DVP) achieved together over 55 percent of the total vote and 58 percent of the seats (Statistisches Reichsamt 1931, 4–6) (Tooze 2008, 12–13).[46] The US stock market crash of October 1929, the ensuing world Depression, and not least the passage of

[45] It is further worth noting that during the War prostitution had also become much more widespread, especially at the front; most soldiers would have availed themselves of the services of the rather pathetic women, often driven to prostitution by hunger or poverty, who accommodated scores of enlisted men each day, allowing each only a few minutes. (Officers were entertained in more comfortable quarters at a more leisurely pace.) (Münkler 2013, 381–386). Soldiers would surely have remembered prostitution as another consequence of hunger and impoverishment.

[46] The Weimar Constitution instituted a strict system of proportional representation, with closed party lists: Each party received one seat in the Reichstag for each 60,000 votes, or major fraction thereof, that it received nationally.

the US Smoot-Hawley Tariff[47] in June 1930 rapidly terminated both Weimar's "golden years" of prosperity and its political support for the Stresemann strategy. The crucial US market was effectively closed to those exports that the German "powerhouse" was supposed to provide (Tooze 2008, 29). The Weimar coalition collapsed, and the new elections of September 1930 elevated Hitler's fledgling National Socialists (NSDAP) to the second-largest party (after only the Socialists) in the Reichstag: From the risible 2.6 percent of the vote that they had garnered in 1928, the Nazis entered the new parliament with 18 percent of the vote and almost 19 percent of the seats (Falter 1986, 41–45). No small part of their appeal was Hitler's insistent demand for autarky: a Germany that would not depend on what were now evidently insecure international markets.

Hitler had been clear from the beginning about his aims. The first volume of *Mein Kampf* had appeared, to decidedly modest sales (an initial press run of 10,000 copies), in 1925 and the second volume, which summarized his goals of territorial expansion, in late 1926. Practically contemporaneous with Grimm's *Volk ohne Raum*, Hitler's screed argued even more vehemently for the necessity of self-sufficiency;[48] and, unlike Grimm, Hitler left no doubt about where *Lebensraum* should be sought: to Germany's east, in Poland and Russia (Hitler 2016, chap. II: 14).[49] A return to Germany's boundaries of 1914, advocated by many nationalists, would be wholly inadequate (Hitler 2016, II: 736). Moreover, territorial expansion would almost certainly have to be achieved by armed conquest: The National Socialist movement, Hitler held,

> must, without regard to "traditions" or prejudices, find the courage to gather our people and their strength to march out along that road which leads them out of today's paucity of *Lebensraum* toward new soil and territory ... (Hitler 2016, II: 732)

[47] Blaming the Smoot-Hawley Tariff for the rise of Hitler – in other words, entertaining the counterfactual that without the Tariff the Nazis would never have come to power – seems untenable. It did, however, lend credibility to Hitler's argument that important markets for German exports were unreliable.

[48] The only "healthy relationship" between a people and its territory is one that "secures a people's sustenance [*Ernährung*] on its own soil and territory." Anything less "will lead, sooner or later, to the detriment, if not to the annihilation, of such a people" (Hitler 2016, II: 728).

[49] "The National Socialist movement must attempt to eliminate the misalignment between our population and our territory, ... [which is] the source of our sustenance." "We shall halt the eternal Germanic drive toward the South and the West of Europe and cast our view toward the land in the East." "The future goal of our foreign policy" must be "an Eastern policy" that seeks "the acquisition of the necessary arable (*Scholle*) for our German people" (Hitler 2016, II: 732, 742, 757).

At first, Hitler's more extreme argument found a far smaller audience than Grimm's. Sales of *Mein Kampf* remained modest – in 1927 a total of 5,607 copies of both volumes; in 1928, 3,015 (Plöckinger 2006, 181) – and critical attention, even in right-wing publications, was meager. Demand first began to grow in 1929 (total sales of 7664) and skyrocketed in the spring of 1930, when the Depression began in earnest.[50] The Nazi Party press (Fritz-Eher-Verlag) responded in early May of 1930 with a new "people's edition" of the book (two volumes in one, more portable but no cheaper), which quickly went through multiple press runs of 10,000 copies each. In all of the year 1930, spurred on only in part by the Nazis' surprise parliamentary victory in September, the book sold a total of over 54,000 copies (Plöckinger 2006, 182).[51]

No one who read the book, or who attended to the party's press or its leaders' many stump speeches, could have failed to understand that eastern expansion and settlement were among the Nazis' chief goals; or that they were prepared to win that additional territory by force of arms.

Hitler's aims, and his reasons for adopting those aims, were laid out at greater length and more starkly in his unpublished "Second Book," composed in 1928 (Hitler 1961). Far from being the "secret" book that Gerhard Weinberg (who first brought it to light) believed it to be, its existence and content were widely known among the Nazi elite; and Hitler fully intended it for publication, even commissioning one of his associates to correct the proofs – and promising to give the manuscript to Winifried Wagner[52] as a birthday present (Plöckinger 2006, 161–164). Moreover, many of the passages in the Second Book merely reproduce,

[50] Unemployment in Germany had always been seasonal, and statistics were not seasonally adjusted. In January and February of 1930, the percentage of union members who were unemployed remained about what it had been in the same months of 1929. But unemployment in March of 1930 was 28 percent higher than it had been in March of 1929 (21.7 versus 16.9 percent); in April, almost double (20.3 vs. 11.1 percent); in May, more than double (19.5 vs. 9.1 percent); in June and July, on average 2.4 times what it had been in the comparable months of pre-Crash 1929 (Petzina 1987, 240).

[51] By way of comparison, among other late Weimar books, Thomas Mann's *Zauberberg* sold 50,000 copies in its first year; Döblin's *Berlin Alexanderplatz*, 40,000 copies in its first eight months; and Remarque's *Im Westen Nichts Neues*, by far the best seller of the Weimar period, an astonishing 800,000 copies in its first eight months (Vogt-Praclik 1987, 31, 39, 49).

[52] The daughter-in-law of the composer Richard Wagner, she ran the Bayreuth Festival (beginning in 1930) with an iron hand, was a fanatical devotée of Hitler, and provided the Nazis with considerable financial support.

sometimes word for word, Hitler's stump speeches (Tooze 2008, 6).[53] That the book did not see print had nothing to do with any shyness about its content, but much to do with the emptiness of the party's coffers in 1928. Its poor electoral showing that year had left it too impoverished even to hold a party congress (Tooze 2008, 13); and the head of the Fritz-Eher-Verlag, Amann, feared that a second Hitler book would destroy any remaining sales of *Mein Kampf*. [See Weinberg's introduction to *Hitler* (1961, 36).]

We may therefore take the Second Book as reflecting how Hitler's views had evolved since the writing of *Mein Kampf* – or how he was becoming bolder in expressing them. Here, at any rate – and we must remember, this reflected the views of the entire Nazi leadership – he stated with utter frankness his plans for eastern aggression and ethnic cleansing: The Slavic inhabitants of the regions that Germany was to seize and settle would either be confined to reservations or expelled.[54] He left unsaid, but implied clearly by the parallel he frequently drew with the European conquest and settlement of North America (Snyder 2015, 14–18), that his plan countenanced the annihilation of the great majority of these areas' native inhabitants.[55]

What appalling logic led Hitler to this conclusion? In the Second Book, and presumably in the speeches it summarizes, he purports to consider carefully each of the major options that Germany faced, after its vulnerability had manifested itself so starkly in the World War. His analysis is suffused with his racial and anti-Semitic thinking, but he was reasonably clear-eyed about the possible courses that Germany might follow.

[53] In his introduction to the German edition of the Second Book, Weinberg advances as proof a long excerpt from one of Hitler's 1928 speeches on foreign policy (Hitler 1961, 27–29).

[54] I refer any doubters to Hitler's exact words: "The racial (*völkisch*) state ... must reach the decision, either to cordon off (*abzukapseln*) these racially alien elements ... or simply to remove them without further ado and to transfer the territory and soil that are thereby freed up to its own racial comrades (*Volksgenossen*)" (Hitler 1961, 81).

[55] The former head of the German Colonial Office, Bernhard Dernburg – a *Liberal* politician, credited with reforming German colonial policy – apparently believed he was only stating a universally accepted fact when we wrote, "The history of the colonization of the United States ... had as its first act the complete annihilation of its native peoples" (Snyder 2015, 16). Hitler may have genuinely believed that these territories were "thinly settled" (below, p. 127). In any event, he failed to appreciate that, shortly after the arrival of the Europeans, the native population of North America had numbered fewer than two million (Ubelaker 1988); the population of the areas he proposed to conquer was at least 40 million.

Germany's existential problem, according to Hitler, was that its territory did not suffice to feed its population, let alone to offer them the rising standard of consumption that comparison with other countries – above all, with the USA.[56] – would lead Germans to demand (Hitler 1961, 120). To this dilemma, he contended, there were only five possible solutions.

- The most obvious was to *improve and expand German agriculture*: to achieve an "increase in the yield of its soil" or "the cultivation of its last remaining wastelands." That held out some promise, he conceded, but would never suffice to make Germany self-sufficient in food – even at the current standard of consumption, never mind that of the future (Hitler 1961, 120–121).
- A second method, advocated by some in Germany, echoed Keynes's 1919 suggestion: form a *European* (or "Pan-European") *Union*, and thus become a state as rich and powerful as the United States (Hitler 1961, 127–129). Although the idea had a certain attraction – Hitler fully appreciated the advantage conferred by economies of scale and a large domestic market (Hitler 1961, 123) – it drew a false parallel. The brilliant success of the American Union rested not just on the size of its population, but on the fact that its millions of people "inhabited [...][57] millions of square kilometers of the richest and most fertile soil."[58] Europe, even if united – something that its linguistic divisions and ancient enmities made unlikely (Hitler 1961, 130) – would have nothing like the same abundance of food and natural resources.
- Germany could also restore the balance between its population and its soil, as it had tried to do throughout the later nineteenth century, by *emigration* (Hitler 1961, 124).[59] Emigration, however, would only deprive Germany of its ablest and most ambitious citizens (who, in addition, would mostly wind up augmenting the talent pool of the

[56] As others have noted, Hitler's envy of the USA, whose citizens in his view enjoyed both "enormous" wages and cheap consumer goods (Hitler 1961, 123), informed much of his analysis – as did, also, his admiration for America's system of racial segregation.

[57] Hitler left a blank here, apparently planning to fill in the exact number of square kilometers later.

[58] Hitler added that the US population was "of the highest racial value," by virtue of its being a nation of mostly European immigrants.

[59] He also considered, and opposed, birth control, arguing as a coldly calculating eugenicist. Rarely, he asserted, were the first one or two of any litter the best specimens. Only if every couple had many children could the "racial value" of the German population be maintained and augmented (Hitler 1961, 125–126).

USA), leaving behind a populace of "lower racial value." Moreover, to continue to assert herself as a great power, and to achieve economies of scale, Germany needed an even larger population.

- As a fourth possibility, Hitler took up the Stresemann strategy of turning Germany into an "*export powerhouse*," able to use the "foreign earnings [from its exports] to acquire the foodstuffs and raw materials that it lacks" (Hitler 1961, 59). What this strategy overlooked, Hitler argued, was that exports needed to find markets. As the number of exporting nations increased, these markets were becoming steadily more limited and more bitterly contested (Hitler 1961, 60–61).[60] The pressure of competition would force Germany to lower wages, offshore production to places like China (*sic*), and dismantle its welfare state (Hitler 1961, 60, 122). Worse, to the extent that Germany penetrated the international market, it would inevitably attract the fatal enmity of Great Britain. To checkmate Britain would require a formidable navy; and the attempt to build such a navy was exactly what had led to an arms race with Britain, and consequently to Germany's encirclement, in the years before 1914 (Hitler 1961, 122, 163).

It seems almost superfluous to point out Hitler's two fundamental errors here: International trade is not zero-sum, but – except in rare circumstances – welfare-improving for all countries; and, if international markets become insecure, the obvious answer is international cooperation to keep them open. Moreover, the costs of autarky to all countries are severe enough to make such cooperation almost certain. Any deprivation will be short-term, and – as the Nazis' subsequent early policies showed (Frieden 2006, 202ff.) – can be met by appropriately large short-term fiscal stimulus.

Having shown, however, at least to his own satisfaction, that none of these four options could realistically solve Germany's fundamental problem – or, at best, could do so only temporarily – Hitler turned again to the difficult and risky path of conquest. Only more land could make Germany self-sufficient; the only available land lay to Germany's east, in the "thinly settled" territories of Poland and western Russia (Hitler 1961, 102);[61]

60 Hitler, in the tradition of mercantilism, viewed the world market as zero-sum. He regarded the USA and Japan as particularly dangerous commercial rivals (Hitler 1961, 60).

61 It was Hitler who described these territories as "thinly settled" (*dünnbesiedelt*). In fact, in 1920 Poland had roughly 90 persons per square kilometer, Germany

these territories, if they were to become a secure part of Germany, would have to be colonized by ethnic Germans; and settlement would only be possible through conquest and – as we have already seen – expulsion or confinement of the existing population. As Hitler put it in what he presumably regarded as a poetic phrase: "Before the plow must go the sword, and ahead of the economy, an army" (Hitler 1961, 124).

Why imagine that this was even possible? Fortunately, Hitler argued, the most formidable opponent, Russia, was now in an advanced state of decomposition. Russia, he held, had been strong only so long as it was ruled not by ethnic Russians, but by a thin elite of Germanic blood. Because this Germanic stock had constituted the majority of the Russian officer corps, repeated wars had successively reduced its numbers. The rise of Slavs to leadership positions in the army and the bureaucracy had already weakened the Czarist empire; but with the Bolshevik Revolution, "Jewry" (*Judentum*) had taken over. This insured the further dissolution of the Russian state; and this development was "a blessing for the future" (*ein Glück für die Zukunft*) for it had "broken the spell that would have held us back from seeking the goal of German foreign policy where it solely and alone can lie: territory in the East" (Hitler 1961, 159).

Consider what Hitler was arguing here. In the terms I outlined earlier, Germany could never remedy its loss of access to land (and hence its food insecurity) through

- *technological innovations* in agriculture; nor
- *factor substitution* (moving to a kind of agriculture that used land less intensively and newly abundant human or physical capital more intensively); nor
- *movement* of the newly abundant factors of human and physical capital
    - to *other jurisdictions* (emigration); or
    - to *other sectors* (optics, electronics; the "export powerhouse" strategy); nor
- achieving somewhat better access to land and resources within Europe, and greater economies of scale, by *joining a European Union*.

He was asserting precisely that, all of the peaceful options outlined earlier being foreclosed, Germany must either accept a sharply reduced

135 per square kilometer. The USA, by way of comparison, had a density in 1920 of 14 persons per square kilometer (36 per square mile) (Stoops and Hobbs 2002, 15).

standard of living (an idea he rejected out of hand) or resort to the political solution of coercion – in this case, not of some domestic group, but of people outside Germany's borders. However dangerous, costly, and inhumane it might be, Germany must pursue the path of conquest, ethnic cleansing, and genocide.

WHICH GERMANS MOST READILY ACCEPTED HITLER'S LOGIC?

As late as 1928, as we have seen, only a tiny minority of Germans embraced the Nazi strategy; the great majority, at least to judge by their votes, treated Hitler's ghastly proposal with contempt and revulsion. All of that changed, with remarkable speed, after the 1929 financial crash. Suddenly, a substantial minority[62] of the German electorate – the 18 percent that had endorsed the NSDAP in 1930 grew to 37 percent by July of 1932 – endorsed, or at least accepted, the Nazi strategy.

Beginning at the latest with chapter five of Seymour Martin Lipset's *Political Man* (Lipset 1960), a cottage industry has developed around the question of precisely which Germans supported Hitler, either by voting for the Nazis or (more rarely) by becoming a card-carrying member – in Nazi terms, a *Parteigenosse* or "party comrade" (often abbreviated "Pg.") – of the NSDAP. Excellent scholars have invoked as partial explanations such variables as social class, religion, unemployment, age, gender, regional characteristics (rural vs. urban, small town vs. metropolis), combat experience, or even – with reference to Freud – growing up male in a fatherless household (Loewenberg 1971).

Without questioning any of these findings, I want to suggest another possible source of variation, which I think has not previously been examined: Not only did the wartime experience of the blockade incline Germans, far more than other Europeans, to search desperately for food security, but it likely conditioned *some* Germans more than others. Controlling for other relevant factors, I conjecture that the National Socialists will have won their greatest support among the groups and regions that had felt the greatest impact of food shortages during the

[62] It is important to remember, cold comfort though it may be, that a majority of Germans continued to the last to reject the National Socialists. They never exceeded, so long as elections remained free, the 37 percent that they achieved in the first elections of 1932 and indeed receded to 33 percent in the November elections of that same year.

blockade.[63] Indeed, for the most severely affected groups, hunger may have been so universal as to allow support for food security – and thus for the Nazis – to override more traditional loyalties of religion and class.[64] As we have seen earlier, mortality statistics indicate (a) that the single most sorely malnourished group were those born between 1901 and 1911, therefore, who had been between the ages of five and fifteen during the worst of the war (above, p. 116) and (b) that mortality varied strongly by region, so that in some provinces, states, and cities the hunger must have extended well beyond that most vulnerable age-cohort. What light, if any, can the available evidence shed on these two conjectures?

Electoral and membership data. Three relevant sources of information on Nazi support have now been extensively explored: (a) electoral support for the National Socialists, most notably (King et al. 2008) and (Falter 2020b); (b) the party's membership rolls, culminating in the authoritative work of Jürgen Falter (Falter 2020a); and (c) a multi-authored study, also led by Falter, to analyze the so-called surviving Abel and Gimbel files, in which a small sample of members were asked specifically why they had joined the party (Falter et al. 2022).[65]

a. *Electoral support.* Because neither voter surveys nor exit polls existed in 1930s Germany, we must rely on various techniques of ecological inference: in other words, inferring, from the social characteristics that covaried with Nazi support across constituencies, the bounded likelihood that a given group (industrial workers, the unemployed, Catholics) can have voted in favor of the NSDAP.[66]

[63] The effect may have been strongest among those in whom the deprivations of the Great Depression re-awakened memories of the wartime hunger. Galofré-Vilà et al. (2021) offer convincing evidence that Nazi support was associated regionally with what we would now call "deaths of despair" (e.g., from suicide, alcoholism, etc.), which rose sharply during the Depression.

[64] Thus, in these groups, but only in them, the Nazis may indeed have appeared as the kind of *Volkspartei*, representative of all religions and classes, that some early students had purported to see.

[65] The Abel documents were responses to a 1934 contest for "best essay" on why one had joined. The Gimbel ones arose from an effort by the party leadership, also in the 1930s, to elicit from members of the "old guard," who had joined between 1925 and 1928, their memories of that time – which, in many cases, included their reasons for joining (Falter et al. 2022, 10–11).

[66] The pioneering effort in this regard, which has stood the test of time surprisingly well, was Falter's 1991 book, *Hitlers Wähler.* Falter's introduction to the revised and expanded edition (Falter 2020b) is a magisterial overview of the intervening research.

b. *NSDAP membership*. Applicants for membership in the party had to fill out a form that specified gender, year of birth, place of residence, and occupation (*Stand*). Thus we have accurate individual information, but only on those few characteristics and only for the most committed adherents. We should focus our attention on those who joined between 1925 and 1930: The former date marked the "refounding" of the party, which had dissolved after the disastrous 1923 Putsch attempt; and, after the electoral victory in late 1930, opportunists began to flood in.

To prefigure the results: I find evidence that a region's degree of food shortage and starvation during the war is strongly related to its propensity to vote for the NSDAP in the crucial election of 1930, but we find no such relationship regionally – indeed, perhaps a slightly negative one – between food shortages and the share of the population that joined the NSDAP.

Electoral analysis. In the crucial "breakthrough" election of 1930, Nazi support varied strongly among regions (Map 6.3). Much of the variation was due to religion and social class.

Catholics were concentrated in Bavaria, the Rhineland, and parts of Saxony. Having experienced persecution in Bismarck's *Kulturkampf*, they remained fiercely loyal to the party that had formed then to defend them, the *Zentrum*, or Center. Commentators and editorial cartoonists often invoked the *Zentrumsturm*, the "Center Tower," portraying it as an impregnable fortress. As the merest glance at the evolution of party support (Figure 6.3) will show, electoral support for the *Zentrum* (together with the closely allied Bavarian People's Party, or BVP) scarcely wavered so long as elections remained free, varying after the Republic's consolidation in 1924 only between 14.8 and 15.7 percent. Hence Nazi support remained weak in the traditionally Catholic areas: the south, the Rhineland, and parts of the east.

Industrial workers, having suffered even harsher persecution than the Catholics in the later nineteenth century, remained almost equally loyal to the Socialist (SPD) and Communist (KPD) parties, shifting more to the latter as economic conditions worsened.[67] These parties' regional strongholds were in the Ruhr, the large cities (notably Berlin), and some of the mining districts of Silesia. Their combined vote for SPD and KPD[68] fell

[67] These were the political loyalties of the non-Catholic workers. Most Catholic workers were organized in separate non-Socialist trade unions and supported the *Zentrum*.

[68] I credit votes for the short-lived USPD (Independent Social Democratic Party of Germany) to the KPD, which it soon merged.

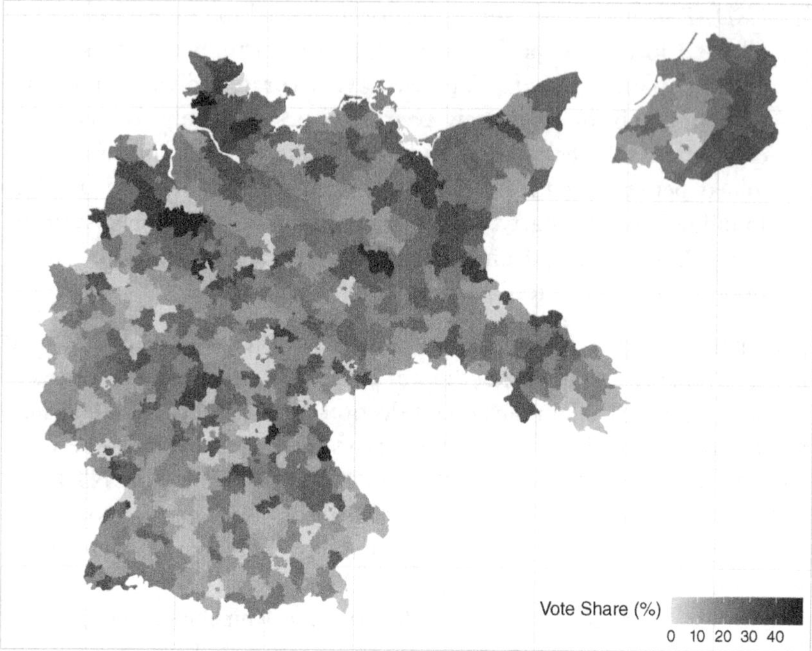

MAP 6.3 National Socialist vote share, 1930[69] (quartiles)

below 35 percent only in the troubled early days of Weimar; even in the last free elections (July 1932), the summed vote for Socialists and Communists held at 37.3 percent. Among both Catholics and workers, party loyalty was buttressed by peer pressure and an extensive array of unions and social support organizations.

In terms of religion and class, then, Nazi support is likely to have come only from the Protestant or secular middle and upper classes. The non-Catholic middle classes traditionally supported either of two liberal parties, the slightly left-of-center German Democratic Party (DDP), which counted Max Weber as one of its founding members, and the slightly right-of-center German People's Party (DVP), led until his death in 1930 by Stresemann.[70] The Protestant upper classes, including prominently the *Junker* owners of great landed estates in East Prussia, found their

[69] Source: (O'Loughlin 2002, fig. 2). Published version was B/W; color version available at https://ibs.colorado.edu/johno/pub/nazi_long/Pnazi_long.htm#_ftn1. Reprinted by permission of Cambridge University Press, license 5097760731385.

[70] The DVP was the direct successor of the Empire's National Liberals; the DDP, of the prewar Progressives (a.k.a. Left Liberals).

home in the conservative and monarchist-leaning German National People's Party (DNVP). And, indeed, between 1924 and 1932 (Figure 6.3), the Nationalists lost over 70 percent of their votes (falling from 20.5 to 5.9 percent of the votes cast) and the two liberal parties, over 85 percent of theirs (from 16.4, they fell to 1.2 percent).[71]

These broad outlines have long been known. King and his associates, working from Falter's data, deployed innovative techniques of ecological inference to provide somewhat greater precision, for example, highlighting the importance, within the Protestant middle class, of the self-employed (*Selbständige*) in providing the nationwide "swing" to the Nazis in 1930 (King et al. 2008, esp. 961–963). Their work also shows that, despite the Depression, the unemployed were no important part of the Nazi electorate; rather, in class and confessional terms, it was the Protestant "working poor," including the self-employed, still holding a job or owning a small

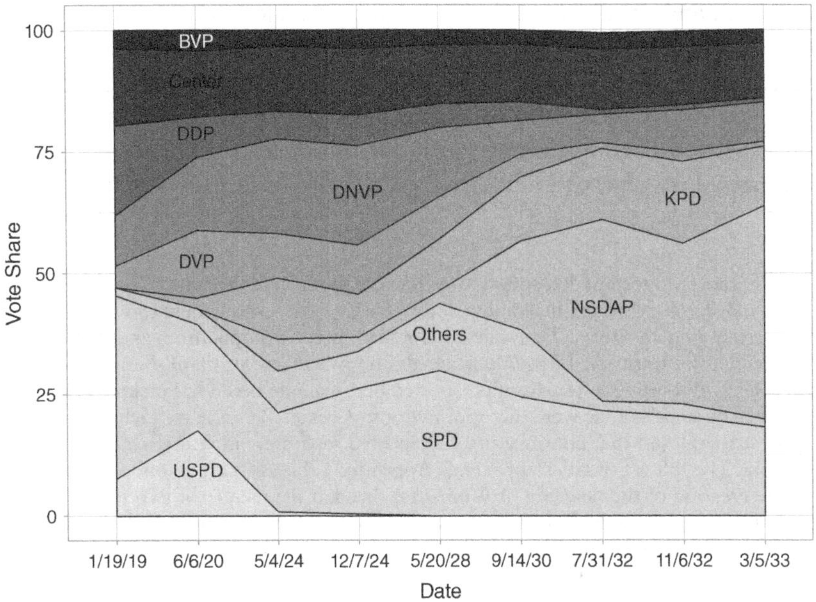

Figure 6.3 Evolution of party support in Reichstag elections[72]

[71] It was this massive defection of the liberals to the Nazis that led Lipset to categorize Fascism as an "extremism of the center" (Lipset 1960, chap. 5).

[72] Chart is reproduced from a public-domain publication of the Bundestag (https://www.bundestag.de/resource/blob/190456/f8d637d1039a06a614cff0264f8b5d10/reichstagswahlergebnisse-data.pdf), which in turn relies on data from Falter (1986).

business but suffering decreased income and increased insecurity, who voted for Hitler (King et al. 2008, 960–961). Tilton and Tooze, in addition, have rightly stressed the importance of the farm vote (Dobkowski and Wallimann 1983, chap. 4; Tooze 2008, chap. 6).

Did the Nazi vote, independent of other social characteristics, increase more in regions or age groups that had suffered the greatest deprivation during World War I? Rigorously testing that conjecture on a regional basis confronts considerable obstacles. First, not only did Germany's external boundaries shift after the War (loss of Alsace-Lorraine, cessions to the newly independent Poland), so did many of its internal ones: Member states merged, lines between provinces and *Regierungsbezirken* were redrawn. It would probably not be impossible, but painfully difficult, to associate the wartime mortality statistics, reported mostly by pre-1919 provinces and states, with the administrative or electoral constituencies that the Weimar Republic employed.

Fortunately, the boundaries of Germany's major cities experienced far fewer changes;[73] and for all thirty-two largest cities (population of 100,000 or more), plus some smaller ones (population 15,000 to 100,000),[74] we have from an early postwar report on the blockade's effect (Reichsgesundheitsamt 1921) far more exact numbers of annual mortality between 1914 and 1918, including specific causes of death. Did

[73] The most important exception was the creation, in 1920, of "Greater Berlin" (*Groß-Berlin*), through the annexation of six formerly independent towns and other surrounding territory. That almost doubled Berlin's population and more than doubled its territory. https://de.wikipedia.org/wiki/Gro%C3%9F-Berlin#Das_Gro%C3%9F-Berlin-Gesetz. Results reported here exclude Berlin but include several of the largest cities that were incorporated into Greater Berlin (e.g., Lichtenberg and Kreuzberg) and that continued to be reported separately in voting or membership data. The full list of cities appears as Appendix Table A6.2. A second instance was the creation of the new city of Wuppertal through the merger of two former cities, Barmen and Elberfeld, and a few smaller towns. I treat Wuppertal simply as a merger of Barmen and Elberfeld.

[74] In each state, cities with populations of less than 100,000 were grouped by size category (50,000–100,000, 30,000–50,000, and 15,000–30,000), with mortality reported only as a sum for all cities in the given category in that state. Only where only a single city fell into the given category was that city named. Working with research assistants and using city populations as reported in the 1905 census (https://de.wikipedia.org/wiki/Liste_der_St%C3%A4dte_im_Deutschen_Kaiserreich), on which the 1921 report claimed also to be based, I was able to ascertain which cities in each state fell into the categories 30,000–50,000 and 50,000–100,000 and to match their collective mortality figures with subsequent voting and membership data (see again Table A6.2). Population data for cities in the smallest category (15,000–30,000) were not readily available.

cities that experienced higher blockade-related mortality prove more supportive of the National Socialists and their goal of *Lebensraum*?

How can we identify specifically blockade-related increases in mortality? Increases in voting for the NSDAP do not correlate with increases in overall civilian mortality among those one year of age and older, which as we have seen rose nationally by about 25 percent. The condition more specifically associated with malnutrition was tuberculosis; as noted earlier, mortality from that disease increased nationally by 60 percent. It therefore seems worth exploring whether Nazi votes in the later Weimar Republic related to a locality's surge in wartime deaths specifically from that disease, which I take as a proxy for the extent of wartime food deprivation. The test that I undertake examines whether (a) the increase in Nazi votes in the given city between the party's low point in the 1928 election and its "breakthrough" in 1930 bears any relation to (b) the city's increase in civilian deaths due to tuberculosis between 1914 and 1918.

There are obvious perils in such an approach. Much of the variation in mortality among cities was endogenous: It depended on how the municipal governments responded. Much as with the current COVID pandemic, however, variance also depended on such irreducible factors as population density, proximity to others at one's place of work, or how crowded one's dwelling was. What seems important here is that most people blamed starvation-related deaths on the blockade itself, and on the Reich's inability to feed its population from its own resources. People appeared to seek food security, not security of food administration.

Among the largest cities, where density of population would have increased susceptibility, increase in the Nazi vote share between 1928 and 1930 appears to have been strongly associated with increased tuberculosis mortality 1914–1918 (Table 6.2 and Figure 6.4).[75] More precisely, I here regress (NSDAP vote share 1930/NSDAP vote share 1928) on (civilian TB mortality 1918/civilian TB mortality 1914).[76] I take the ratio of 1930–1928 votes as the left-hand-side variable as a

[75] I exclude Berlin because of its boundary change after the war – although two of the largest cities that merged into Greater Berlin (Neukölln and Lichtenberg) are included. Essen is excluded as an extreme outlier, with a TB mortality ratio of 3.75; the second most severely afflicted city, Rostock, had a ratio of 2.46. Several of the largest cities or boroughs were missing data for voting, for TB mortality, or for both. For the full list of cities used, see Appendix Table A6.2.

[76] The mortality figures used here are those beginning on p. 40* of (Reichsgesundheitsamt 1921) under the rubric "Die Ursachen der Sterbefälle bei der Zivilbevölkerung in 266 deutschen Orten ...," col. 21, "Tuberkulose, zusammen" [i.e., combining male and female deaths].

Table 6.2 *Increase in NSDAP vote share 1928–1930 regressed on increase in civilian mortality from tuberculosis 1914–1918, German cities with population ≥100,000*

Bivariate regression table for total TB mortality and cities over 100,000:

OLS Regression Results

Dep. Variable:	Change votes	R-squared:	0.149
Model:	OLS	Adj. R-squared:	0.116
Method:	Least Squares	F-statistic:	4.553
Date:	Tue, August 16, 2022	Prob (F-statistic):	0.0425
Time:	22:54:54	Log-Likelihood:	–91.676
No. Observations:	28	AIC:	187.4
Df Residuals:	26	BIC:	190.0
Df Model:	1		
Covariance Type:	Nonrobust		

	Coef	Std err	t	P > |t|	[0.025	0.975]
Intercept	–3.3359	7.055	–0.473	0.640	–17.837	11.165
Total TB	9.2210	4.322	2.134	0.042	0.338	18.104

Omnibus:	13.884	Durbin-Watson:	2.418
Prob (Omnibus):	0.001	Jarque-Bera (JB):	13.540
Skew:	1.453	Prob (JB):	0.00115
Kurtosis:	4.779	Cond. No.	12.6

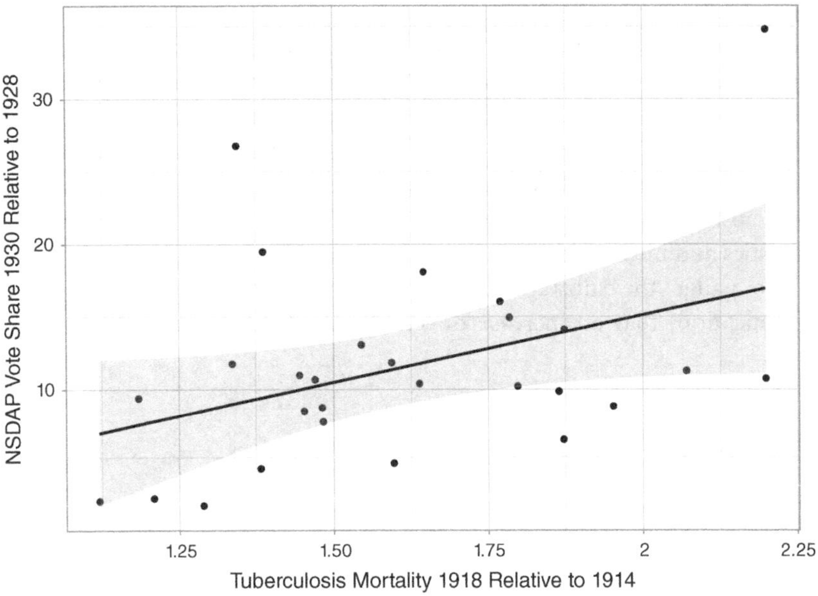

Figure 6.4 Increase in NSDAP vote share 1928–1930 plotted against increase in civilian mortality from tuberculosis 1914–1918, German cities with population ≥100,000

way of controlling for the "bedrock" propensity of a city to support the NSDAP.[77] I use as the numerator 1918 rather than 1917 TB deaths because (a) mortality from tuberculosis was seldom immediate and (b) TB deaths in most cities appear to have peaked in 1918.

Among these largest cities, despite the obvious noisiness of the data (adjusted $R^2 = .12$), we can be reasonably confident ($p = .04$) of a positive relationship between wartime tuberculosis mortality – our proxy for malnutrition – and growth in the Nazi vote between 1928 and 1930.

The association seems to extend beyond the largest cities. It is robust to the inclusion of all cities of population greater than 30,000. The estimated coefficient becomes slightly smaller but is estimated with greater precision. Constrained by the way in which the Health Office reported mortality data, I include five of the eight specifically named smaller cities[78] and eleven

[77] Controls for religion and class (percentage of a city's population classified as Catholic or *Arbeiter*) proved unavailing and, because of missing data for one or both variables in the *Sterblichkeit* source, considerably reduced the number of observations.

[78] TB mortality data are lacking for two, Rüstringen and Schwerin. I exclude Bremerhaven, one of the smaller named cities that did report data (and the only one of its size in the city-state of Bremen), as an extreme outlier. Probably because

groups of two or more smaller cities (of population 50,000–100,000 and 30,000–50,000) in each state (Table 6.3 and Figure 6.5).[79] Note that the median of all these observations is the same as the national average, a 60 percent increase in mortality from tuberculosis (i.e., a ratio of 1.6) and that the range extends (disregarding the special cases of Essen and Bremerhaven) from a decrease of 14 percent (a ratio of 0.86) to an increase of almost 150 percent (a ratio of 2.46). Appendix Table A6.4 lists summary statistics and intercorrelations of relevant variables.

To gauge the substantive effect, we can note (using the all-cities specification) that an increase of one standard deviation in the ratio of

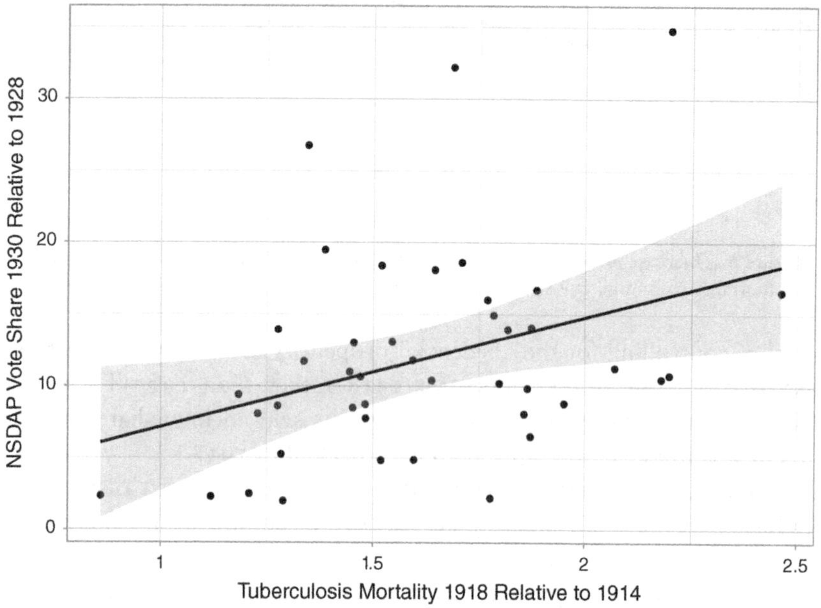

Figure 6.5 Increase in NSDAP vote share 1928–1930 plotted against increase in civilian mortality from tuberculosis 1914–1918, German cities of population >30,000[80]

the blockade halted much of its activity, its mortality from tuberculosis declined (as happened in only one other case), indeed fell more sharply than anywhere else: Deaths in 1918 were 84 percent of those in 1914. At the same time, its vote for the NSDAP in 1930 was twenty-six times what it had been in 1928, the fourth highest ratio among all our observations.

[79] The association, albeit somewhat weakened, is robust to the exclusion of the three obvious outliers in Figure 6.5. These turn out to be Breslau, Mühlheim an der Ruhr, and the Hessian grouped cities with population between 50,000 and 100,000. Removing those, we obtain an estimated coefficient of 5.03 and a t-score of 1.95 ($p = .06$).

[80] Includes groups of smaller cities within states.

Table 6.3 *Increase in NSDAP vote share 1928–1930 regressed on increase in civilian mortality from tuberculosis 1914–1918, German cities of population > 30,000**

Bivariate regression table for total TB mortality and cities over 100,000 plus smaller cities plus grouped:

OLS Regression Results

Dep. Variable:		Change_votes	R-squared:		0.134
Model:		OLS	Adj. R-squared:		0.113
Method:		Least Squares	F-statistic:		6.497
Date:		Tue, 16 Aug 2022	Prob (F-statistic):		0.0145
Time:		22:58:29	Log-Likelihood:		–145.56
No. Observations:		44	AIC:		295.1
Df Residuals:		42	BIC:		298.7
Df Model:		1			
Covariance Type:		Nonrobust			

	Coef	Std err	t	P > |t|	[0.025	0.975]
Intercept	–1.0.839	5.119	–0.212	0.833	–11.415	9.247
total_TB	7.9501	3.119	2.549	0.015	1.656	14.244

Omnibus:	16.273	Durbin-Watson:	2.320
Prob (Omnibus):	0.000	Jarque-Bera (JB):	18.890
Skew:	1.334	Prob (JB):	7.91e-05
Kurtosis:	4.784	Cond. No.	11.2

*Includes groups of smaller cities within states.

1918/1914 TB mortality is associated with an increase of 0.37 standard deviations in the ratio of 1930/1928 Nazi votes. To put it another way, a city at the 60th percentile of mortality would be associated with a 55th percentile increase in Nazi votes; one at the 75th percentile, with a Nazi vote increase at its 61st percentile.

The usual strictures about the ecological fallacy apply but, I suggest, lose some of their force here.[81] The maintained hypothesis is that the shared experience of high wartime malnutrition and mortality, witnessed at the local level, conditioned survivors to be more receptive to Nazi appeals to seize *Lebensraum*. Individual-level experience of hunger or nearby death, or of witnessing the aftereffects in surviving children, would doubtless add to our knowledge but will never be available in more than anecdotal form. For individual-level data, however thin and fragmentary, we must examine who *joined* the NSDAP.

Membership analysis. The invaluable source is Jürgen Falter's analysis of party membership (Falter 2020).[82] I focus here on the roughly 250,000 Germans who joined the NSDAP, presumably out of conviction rather than opportunism, between the "re-founding" of the party in 1925 and the breakthrough election of 1930.[83] Of these, Falter and his colleagues have drawn a representative sample of 17,832 (Falter 2020, 124). Unsurprisingly, the new *Parteigenossen* ("party comrades") from this period were overwhelmingly male (94 percent)[84] and came disproportionately from non-Catholic regions[85]

[81] Concerns could also arise about the use of ratios in a regression (Kronmal 1993). Results here are robust to using a recommended correction, namely inserting on the right-hand side as separate variables the numerator and denominator of the ratio. See Appendix Table A6.3 and estimated effects from that specification.

[82] I am extremely grateful to Professor Falter for his readiness to give me access to his original data and, beyond that, for his friendly advice and keen insight.

[83] By the end of 1930, some 315,000 had joined, but 65,000 of those had joined after the September election. Many of the early joiners had allowed their membership to lapse, or had left the party, with the result that, on the eve of the 1930 election, party membership totaled slightly over 180,000. (Membership at the end of 1930 was 247,000; but, again, 65,000 of those had joined only after the election, many simply jumping on what now seemed a promising bandwagon.) (Falter 2020, 69–70).

[84] Although the Nazis admitted women to party membership, they granted them no role in active politics. In power, they nominated only males to the puppet *Reichstag*. To be sure, the newly enfranchised women were underrepresented in all parties, even the avowedly feminist Communists achieving a membership that was only 20 percent female (Falter 2020, 115–116); but the Nazis made a principle of male dominance and, unsurprisingly, attracted few female members.

[85] The membership application did not inquire about religion; hence Falter can only discern the religious coloration of the applicant's community, not the member's own affiliation.

(76 percent resided in communities that were majority non-Catholic, 60 percent in regions where Catholics constituted less than a quarter of the population) (Falter 2020, 161).[86]

The most distinctive aspect of the membership in that crucial period, however, was its youth: The median age of the new joiners was twenty-eight (Falter 2020, 124). By contrast, among the general population of males over the age of twenty (the pool from which members would most readily be recruited), the median age – likely owing to wartime losses – was between forty-five and fifty (Statistisches Reichsamt 1930, 15). Fully 56 percent of the new joiners came from what Falter defines, somewhat more broadly than I have done here, as *Kriegskinder*, "war babies": those born between 1900 and 1915; in the German population as a whole, roughly 40 percent had been born in that interval (Falter 2020, 133 and 292). The general impression that the card-carrying Nazis were a "young" party (Vincent 1985, 166) is thus confirmed. It is suggestive, at the very least, that this was precisely the cohort that had suffered the greatest increase in mortality during the blockade.

Even more striking was the difference in occupational and confessional makeup between the "war baby" generation and all older cohorts (Table 6.4). Among those who joined between 1925 and 1930 but had been born before 1900, the *Selbständigen*, whom King et al. identify as a core group of the Nazi electorate, were indeed greatly overrepresented (44 percent among the older party "joiners," 18 percent among the workforce generally); so, to a lesser extent, were white-collar and professional workers (*Angestellte und Beamte*). Among the "war babies" (birth years between 1900 and 1915) who joined in that crucial period, the overrepresentation of the *Selbständigen* virtually disappeared. In this age group, the self-employed constituted 13 percent of the party, almost identical to the 11 percent which that group made up of the total workforce of the same ages. Except with regard to gender and religion,[87] this cohort of new party members, if taken alone, would have come close to

[86] This figure excludes joiners from cities with population greater than one million. The predominance of non-Catholics among new joiners grew over time: Between 1925 and 1927, only about half came from communities where Catholics constituted less than a quarter of the population; between 1928 and 1930, closer to two-thirds came from such communities (Falter 2020, 157).

[87] Only in the major cities (population over 100,000) did those who joined the party between 1925 and 1930 accurately represent the confessional makeup of Germany society as a whole: Of the new members from those largest cities, 32 percent were from majority Catholic communities, vs. 29 percent of the electorate as a whole (Falter 2020, 161).

Table 6.4 *Occupation of Nazi Party members by birth cohort*

Birth Year	Occupation[88]	Percentage Among Those Who Joined Party 1925–September 1930	Percentage in Same Cohort among Total Workforce[89]
Before 1900	Self-employed	44	18
	White-collar and professional	27	12
	Blue collar worker	25	27
	Employed in family business	0	13
	No occupation	5	30
1900–1915	Self-employed	13	11
	White-collar and professional	26	19
	Blue collar	50	53
	Employed in family business	6	15
	No occupation	5	2[90]

Source: Falter (2020, 293). Numbers sometimes sum to more than 100 due to rounding.

constituting the kind of catchall *Volkspartei* that some early students believed the NSDAP to have been (Falter 2020, 293).

Here, again, we cannot know the extent to which each potential joiner had personally experienced or witnessed malnutrition or starvation, nor whether any such experiences moved them toward the NSDAP.[91] We can know at best only the extent to which mortality had increased in a new joiner's home city. Moreover, the joiners constituted a tiny fraction of the total population. Nationally, as noted earlier, 250,000 had joined in this period, out of a national population of 62.4 million; thus, joiners made up about four in every thousand German citizens. Falter's sample from these years of just under 18,000 is a yet smaller fraction, fewer than three in every ten thousand citizens. Even in the city with the largest share of

[88] The captions in German, in order, are: *Selbständige; Angestellte und Beamte; Arbeiter; Mithelfende Familienangehörige;* and *Ohne Beruf.*

[89] Total workforce = *Erwerbspersonen.*

[90] This improbably low percentage probably means simply that younger people, faced with unemployment in the Depression, chose not to enter the workforce at all.

[91] For what it may be worth, that small and likely unrepresentative sample, who related specifically why they had joined, and who focused on their experiences in World War I, seems to have mentioned hunger or the blockade with some frequency. This was especially the case among the "war babies" (Rosensprung 2022, 100, 110).

joiners in its population, Augsburg, the Falter sample includes only twelve in every ten thousand of the population. We should therefore expect little from these noisy data.

Nonetheless, if we try regressing (a) the number of 1925–1930 joiners from a given city in the Falter sample as a share of that city's total population on (b) the same proxy for local famine as we used in analyzing voting, namely 1918 TB mortality/1914 TB mortality, we find if anything a *negative* association, both in cities whose population exceeded 100,000 and in our full set of cities (and groups of cities) with population over 30,000 (Tables 6.5 and 6.6; Figures 6.6 and 6.7).

The estimated coefficients are at best marginally significant ($p = .08$. $p = .27$), but the overall tendency is unmistakable. Among Falter's "war baby" generation (those aged 5–15 during the War), which – as we have seen earlier – suffered the overall highest increase in mortality during the blockade, we find also a slight negative association, but one far too imprecisely estimated to be informative (Table 6.7 and Figure 6.8).[92]

Generationally, then, but not regionally, Nazi membership reflected the groups most severely malnourished during the blockade. Those born between 1900 and 1915, and who therefore would have experienced the highest increase in blockade-induced mortality, were overrepresented nationally among those who joined the NSDAP between 1925 and September of 1930, presumably not for merely opportunistic reasons. Cities that experienced the most severe increases in mortality became considerably *more* likely to vote for the NSDAP and its platform of *Lebensraum*; but its citizens may have become *less* likely to enlist as card-carrying members of the NSDAP.

Why these tendencies run in opposite directions will probably remain a mystery, but one possibility is that joining and voting are substitutes for one another: Where the tide was already running strongly in the Nazis' favor, there was less motivation to take the daring step of actually joining the party. Where Nazis appeared to be a disfavored minority, its sympathizers may have been more motivated to join.[93] Or perhaps the experience of deprivation and high mortality could have made people averse to any kind of active participation, willing to express their views only

[92] I have also checked for a possible relationship between a city's TB mortality and the share of its joiners who were "war babies," i.e., (war baby joiners/total joiners). There is no relationship.

[93] I note, as impressionistic supporting evidence, that Trump Republicans in California appear to be more active (e.g., holding weekly rallies) in solidly Blue Los Angeles than in counties where they enjoy strong electoral support.

Table 6.5 *NSDAP joiners 1925–1930 in Falter sample per thousand population vs. 1918 TB mortality/1914 TB mortality among 27 German cities with population >100,000*[1]

Bivariate regression table for TB mortality and cities over 100K:

OLS Regression Results

Dep. Variable:	Total_joiners_per_1000	R-squared:	0.117
Model:	OLS	Adj. R-squared:	0.082
Method:	Least Squares	F-statistic:	3.315
Date:	Wed, 21 Jul 2021	Prob (F-statistic):	0.0806
Time:	09:51:13	Log-Likelihood:	2.2123
No. Observations:	27	AIC:	–0.4245
Df Residuals:	25	BIC:	2.167
Df Model:	1		
Covariance Type:	Nonrobust		

	coef	std err	t	P > |t|	[0.025	0.975]
Intercept	0.9548	0.250	3.813	0.001	0.439	1.471
ratio_mort_TB	–0.2779	0.153	–1.821	0.081	–0.592	0.036

Omnibus:	1.789	Durbin-Watson:	2.082
Prob (Omnibus):	0.409	Jarque-Bera (JB):	0.644
Skew:	0.212	Prob (JB):	0.725
Kurtosis:	3.627	Cond. No.	12.6

[1]Same large cities as in earlier analysis.

Table 6.6 *NSDAP joiners 1925–1930 in Falter sample per thousand population vs. 1918 TB mortality/1914 TB mortality among 43 German cities with population > 30,000*[1]

Bivariate regression table for TB mortality and cities over 100K plus smaller cities plus grouped cities:

OLS Regression Results

Dep. Variable:		Total_joiners_per_1000	R-squared:			0.030
Model:		OLS	Adj. R-squared:			0.006
Method:		Least Squares	F-statistic:			1.260
Date:		Tue, 23 Aug 2022	Prob (F-statistic):			0.268
Time:		12:54:47	Log-Likelihood:			−2.2586
No. Observations:		43	AIC:			8.517
Df Residuals:		41	BIC:			12.04
Df Model:		1				
Covariance Type:		Nonrobust				
	Coef	Std err	t	P > |t|	[0.025	0.975]
Intercept	0.6876	0.188	3.659	0.001	0.308	1.067
ratio_mort_TB	−0.1288	0.115	−1.123	0.268	−0.361	0.103
Omnibus:		1.091	Durbin-Watson:			1.188
Prob (Omnibus):		0.580	Jarque-Bera (JB):			0.803
Skew:		0.333	Prob (JB):			0.669
Kurtosis:		2.929	Cond. No.			10.5

[1]Same set of cities as in earlier analyses of voting patterns. As before, some observations are state-level groups of cities.

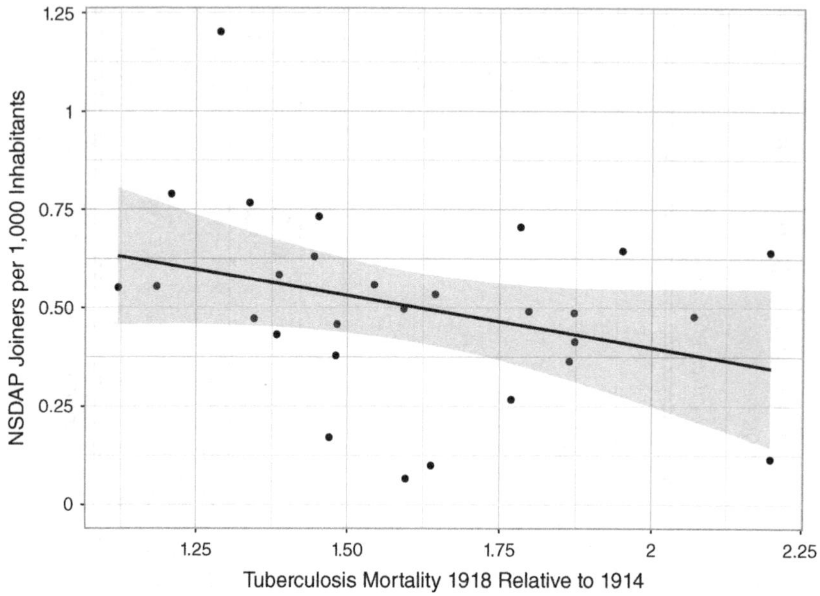

Figure 6.6 NSDAP joiners 1925–1930 in Falter sample per thousand population plotted against 1918 TB mortality/1914 TB mortality among 27 German cities with population >100,000

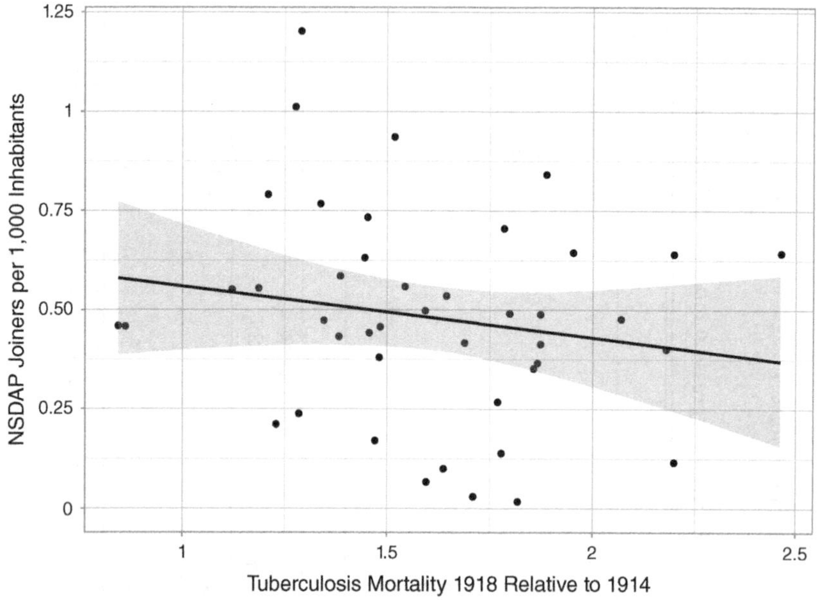

Figure 6.7 NSDAP joiners 1925–1930 in Falter sample per thousand population plotted against 1918 TB mortality/1914 TB mortality among 43 German cities with population >30,000

Table 6.7 *NSDAP "war baby" joiners 1925–1930 in Falter sample per thousand population vs. 1918 TB mortality/1914 TB mortality among 43 German cities with population >30,000*

Bivariate regression table for TB mortality and cities over 100K plus smaller cities plus grouped cities:

OLS Regression Results

Dep. Variable:		War_baby_joiners_per_1000	R-squared:			0.026
Model:		OLS	Adj. R-squared:			0.002
Method:		Least Squares	F-statistic:			1.076
Date:		Tue, 23 Aug 2022	Prob (F-statistic):			0.306
Time:		13:20:54	Log-Likelihood:			53.718
No. Observations:		43	AIC:			−103.4
Df Residuals:		41	BIC:			−99.91
Df Model:		1				
Covariance Type:		Nonrobust				
	Coef	Std err	t	P > |t|	[0.025	0.975]
Intercept	0.1453	0.051	2.842	0.007	0.042	0.249
ratio_mort_tb	−0.0324	0.031	−1.037	0.306	−0.095	0.031
Omnibus:		2.060	Durbin-Watson:			1.221
Prob (Omnibus):		0.357	Jarque-Bera (JB):			1.881
Skew:		0.415	Prob (JB):			0.390
Kurtosis:		2.400	Cond. No.			10.5

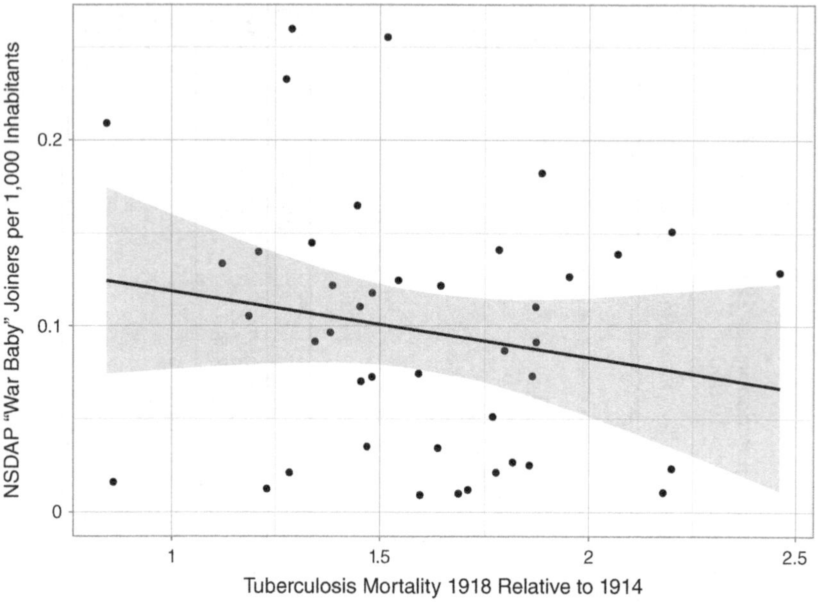

Figure 6.8 NSDAP "war baby" joiners 1925–1930 in Falter sample per thousand population plotted against 1918 TB mortality/1914 TB mortality among 36 German cities with population >30,000

through low-cost voting? Finally, of course, this finding could be only a fluke, unique to Falter's sampling, that masks an absence of any relationship in the overall Nazi membership. One can speculate endlessly; all I can do at this juncture is to report the seemingly contradictory results.

In summary, Europe's negative shock to the supply of land, brought about by the First World War and its aftermath, forced European leaders to choose between adapting economically to a more land-scarce environment, or imposing political coercion. For all countries in the first years after the War, economic adaptation proved the less costly of the two options. Germany in particular adapted with an export powerhouse strategy that allowed it to use export earnings to re-acquire the food it had lost with the land and now had to import at higher prices. However, the success of this strategy collapsed with the closure of markets to German exports following the Great Depression. Without a method of adaptation to land-scarcity, Germany rallied around Hitler's genocidal conquest of *Lebensraum*. Consistent with this story, a regression analysis of electoral support for Nazis shows that the cities most exposed to the horrific implications of the land loss – starvation-induced deaths from tuberculosis – were the most supportive of abandoning the option of adaptation in favor of Hitler's strategy to acquire land by conquest.

CONCLUSION

Taking a longer view of history than that embraced by Keynes in *Economic Consequences*, Tooze has noted that "land hunger" had been, from the seventeenth century onward, among the most important reasons for European colonization and settlement: for the "insatiable European urge to overcome scarcity through the conquest and settlement of vast 'empty' tracts of land, whether in Eurasia, the Americas, or Australia" (Tooze 2008, 166). Having grown to depend vitally on these newly settled lands, Europe found that World War I and its aftermath had again blocked, or at a minimum severely impeded, access to them: Europe experienced, in essence, an exogenous negative shock to its supply of land.

Other European states either fell back on other sources (Britain's Empire), enjoyed already a more favorable land-labor ratio (France's arable per farmer was a third higher than Germany's, Denmark's more than twice as high), or simply accepted a lower standard of living (Tooze 2008, 176). Germany differed in one crucial respect: Many if not most adult Germans in the 1930s "had an acute personal experience of prolonged and insatiable hunger" (Tooze 2008, 168).[94] As we have seen, those who had been between the ages of five and fifteen during World War I, and had emerged alive but possibly disfigured, had witnessed an increase in mortality of over 40 percent (among males, almost 50 percent) among their cohort.

If that horrific experience goes far to explain why Germany's response to the renewed land hunger differed so catastrophically from its neighbors', it also helps us to understand why, *within* Germany, some regions were more drawn to the Nazi appeals than others. In the hardest-hit areas, and especially, within those areas, members of the "war baby" generation, would have seen, or perhaps borne themselves, throughout the 1920s, those starvation-induced "deformations of the upper and lower limbs" or "pronounced changes in the rib cage" that afflicted from

[94] Tooze exaggerates in saying that "almost everyone alive" in Germany in this period had experienced this kind of hunger. As we have seen, those wealthy enough to turn to the black market, or influential enough to prevent requisitioning of produce from their own estates, survived largely unscathed.

a tenth to a third of the surviving members of their cohort. They would surely remember the hunger and would daily face evidence of its lasting consequences.

While such other factors as occupation and religion clearly mattered, the cities that had experienced the highest hunger-related mortality during the war tended, a dozen years after the war's end, to cast their ballots disproportionately in favor of Hitler's vision of autarky. At the same time, fragmentary membership evidence suggests that inhabitants of those most hunger-afflicted cities were no likelier, and perhaps less likely, to join Hitler's party and hence to become (to use one of Hitler's favorite words) "fighters" {*Kämpfer)* for the movement.

Surprisingly, twentieth-century Europe's exogenous loss of land in and after the First World War, and the experience of hunger and starvation occasioned by that loss, propelled one European country (and three-eighths of that country's citizens) onto the atavistic path of conquest. Whether it could still do so today is a matter for conjecture; but surely no one can rule that possibility out.

Appendices to Chapter 6

Table A6.1 *State- and province-level change in mortality, 1913–1917*[95]

State or Province	Mortality 1917/1913
MECKLENBURG-SCHWERIN	1.20276758
PROVINZ BRANDENBURG	1.183915066
ANHALT	1.171310832
LIPPE	1.16585839
STADT BERLIN	1.155453139
RHEINLAND	1.151752316
LÜBECK	1.135746606
HESSEN-NASSAU	1.134555885
BRAUNSCHWEIG	1.134304207
SCHWARZBURG-RUDOLSTADT	1.130286494
SCHAUMBURG-LIPPE	1.119929453
HESSEN	1.115751121

[95] Includes all ages. Because both birth rates and infant deaths were approximately 50 percent lower in 1917 than they had been in 1913, overall mortality was lower than among those one year of age and older.

State or Province	Mortality 1917/1913
HANNOVER	1.115305129
SACHSEN	1.114312754
MECKLENBURG-STRELIK	1.10434322
HAMBURG	1.101903849
OLDENBURG	1.094208265
BREMEN	1.082501663
SACHSEN-ALTENBURG	1.080691643
SACHSEN	1.077661658
WALDECK	1.07266436
PREUSSEN (state average_	1.070883029
SCHLESWIG-HOLSTEIN	1.065837958
SACHSEN-WEIMAR	1.062193855
POMMERN	1.058076225
BAYERN LINKS DES RHEINS	1.028332654
DEUTSCHES REICH (national average)	1.020207429
REUß JÜNGERER LINIE	1.019674936
BADEN	1.01394217
PROVINZ OSTPREUSSEN	1.001912787
SACHSEN-COBURG-GOTHA	1.001254705
WESTFALEN	0.995876763
WESTPREUSSEN	0.985031807
SCHLESIEN	0.97896344
POSEN	0.972444111
SCHWARZBURG-SONDERSHAUSEN	0.967092008
SACHSENMEININGEN	0.965509417
WÜRTTEMBERG	0.957947483
HOHENZOLLERN	0.933549433
BAYERN (state average)	0.928109342
BAYERN RECHTS DES RHEINS	0.914870129
REUß ÄLTERER LINIE	0.905263158

Table A6.2 *Cities included in analyses of voting and party membership population 100,000 or more*[96]

AACHEN
ALTONA
AUGSBURG

(*continued*)

[96] Berlin is excluded because of boundary changes; the cities annexed to it in 1920 are included, wherever data are available.

Table A6.2 (*continued*)

BOCHUM	
BRAUNSCHWEIG	
BREMEN	
BRESLAU	
CHEMNITZ	
DORTMUND	
DÜSSELDORF	
ERFURT	
FRANKFURT	
HALLE	
HAMBURG	
HANNOVER	
KARLSRUHE	
KASSEL	
KIEL	
KÖLN	
KÖNIGSBERG	
KREFELD	
LEIPZIG	
LICHTENBERG	
MAGDEBURG	
MANNHEIM	
MÜLHEIM a. d. RUHR	
MÜNCHEN	
NEUKÖLLN	
NÜRNBERG	
STETTIN	
STUTTGART	
WUPPERTAL	
Population 50,000–100,000 and Specifically Named	
DESSAU	
HEIDELBERG	
ROSTOCK	
GIESSEN	
Population 30,000–50,000 and Specifically Named	
BREMERHAVEN	
WORMS	
SCHWERIN	
RÜSTRINGEN	
Grouped Cities Within States	
Prussia 50, 000–100, 000	Spandau, Frankfurt (Oder), Potsdam, Osnabrück, Linden, Harburg, Stettin,

	Bromberg, Mülheim an der Ruhr, Bonn, Remscheid, München-Gladbach, Koblenz, Oberhausen, Erfurt, Görlitz, Gleiwitz, Liegnitz, Flensburg, Münster, Hagen i. W., Bielefeld, Elbing
Bayern 50,000–100,000	Würzburg, Ludwigshafen am Rhein, Fürth, Kaiserslautern
Sachsen 50,000–100,000	Plauen, Zwickau
Baden 50,000–100,000	Freiburg i. Br., Pforzheim
Hessen 50,000–100,000	Mainz, Darmstadt
Prussia 30,000–50,000	Cottbus, Landsberg an der Warthe, Guben, Forst, Hildesheim, Göttingen, Lehe, Hanau, Tilsit, Stralsund, Stolp, Trier, Solingen, Rheydt, Malstett-Burbach, Neuß, Halberstadt, Mühlhausen i. Th, , Weißenfels, Zeitz, Kattowitz, Ratibor, Oppeln, Schweidnitz, Wandsbek, Neumünster, Recklinghausen, Hamm, Witten a. R., Herne, Graudenz, Thorn, Düren, Nordhausen, Iserlohn, Lüdenscheid, Insterburg
Bayern 30,000–50,000	Regensburg, Bamberg
Sachsen 30,000–50,000	Zittau, Meißen
Württemberg 30,000–50,000	Ulm, Heilbronn, Eßlingen

Table A6.3 *Alternative specification of Table 6.3; robustness check of regression in ratios*[1]

Multivariate regression table for total TB mortality and cities over 100,000 plus smaller cities plus grouped:

OLS Regression Results			
Dep. Variable:	Change_votes	R-squared:	0.130
Model:	OLS	Adj. R-squared:	0.059
Method:	Least Squares	F-statistic:	1.837
Date:	Tue, 17 Aug 2021	Prob (F-statistic):	0.157
Time:	20:37:47	Log-Likelihood:	–135.88
No. Observations:	41	AIC:	279.8
Df Residuals:	37	BIC:	286.6
Df Model:	3		
Covariance Type:	Nonrobust		

	Coef	Std err	t	P > |t|	[0.025	0.975]
Intercept	-1.8041	5.909	–0.305	0.762	–13.777	10.169
Mt	0.0009	0.002	0.565	0.576	–0.002	0.004
overMt1	65.8045	369.354	0.178	0.860	–682.578	814.187
MtxoverMt1	7.6466	3.806	2.009	0.052	–0.064	15.357

Omnibus:	18.698	Durbin-Watson:	2.313
Prob (Omnibus):	0.000	Jarque-Bera (JB):	23.697
Skew:	1.488	Prob (JB):	7.15e–06
Kurtosis:	5.240	Cond. No.	4.11e+05

Mt = TB mortality 1918; overMT1 = 1/TB mortality 1914; MtxoverMt1 = TB mortality 1918 / TB mortality 1914.

Note 1: The large (if insignificant) estimated coefficient on the denominator (overMT1) arises because values of that variable are very small: mean = .00423, s.d. = .00386.

Note 2: The substantive effect of the ratio (MtxoverMt1) in this specification is precisely estimated and large. When all variables in this specification are at their mean, the anticipated ratio of 1930/1928 Nazi votes is 26.1; increasing MtxoverMt1 by 0.5 s.d. above its mean is associated with a ratio of Nazi votes of 40.9; a decrease of the same magnitude leads to an anticipated Nazi vote ratio of 11.5.

[1] Mt = city mortality 1918; overMt1 = 1/city mortality 1914; Mt x overMt1 = city mortality 1918/city mortality 1914.

Table A6.4 *Summary statistics and intercorrelations of main variables*

Table of Intercorrelations:

	Total Joiners Per 1000	War Baby Joiners Per 1000	War Babies out of Total Joiners	Prop Vote 1928	Prop Vote 1930	Change in Votes	Total TB Deaths 1914	Total TB Deaths 1918	Ratio of TB Mortalities
Total Joiners Per 1000	1.00	0.83	–0.22	0.20	0.23	–0.24	–0.18	–0.15	–0.17
War Baby Joiners Per 1000		1.00	0.06	0.12	0.22	–0.19	–0.20	–0.18	–0.16
War Babies out of Total Joiners			1.00	–0.13	0.12	0.12	–0.08	–0.02	0.09
Prop Vote 1928				1.00	0.38	–0.63	0.15	–0.01	–0.37
Prop Vote 1930					1.00	–0.01	–0.13	–0.20	–0.12
Change in Votes						1.00	–0.27	–0.14	0.23
Total TB Deaths 1914							1.00	0.94	–0.12
Total TB Deaths 1918								1.00	0.15
Ratio of TB Mortalities									1.00

Summary Statistics:

Variable	Mean	Median	S.D.	Min.	Max.
Total Joiners Per 1,000	0.50	0.47	0.27	0.02	1.20
War Baby Joiners Per 1,000	0.09	0.09	0.07	0.00	0.26
War Babies out of Total Joiners	0.21	0.19	0.21	0.02	1.54
Prop Vote 1928	0.02	0.01	0.02	0.00	0.07
Prop Vote 1930	0.12	0.12	0.04	0.01	0.22
Change in Votes	11.49	10.42	7.19	2.01	34.79
Total TB Deaths 1914	282.68	241.00	178.07	63.00	696.00
Total TB Deaths 1918	422.73	349.00	253.44	53.00	964.00
Ratio of TB Mortalities	1.59	1.54	0.35	0.84	2.46

7

Exogenous Increase of Human Capital

French Huguenots in German Cities and Principalities, 1685–1715

Few migrations can be regarded as exogenous shocks. Most are either what demographers call "pull" migration, in which people simply move to where their labor or skills command a higher return, or a result of some escalating "push" – persecution, civil war, or economic collapse. "Pull" is always endogenous, and even "pushes" are rarely unanticipated: persecutions typically intensify by steps, economies collapse gradually.

Among the even rarer examples of migration that (a) involved human capital more than low-skill labor and (b) were exogenous and almost entirely unanticipated,[1] was the massive emigration of the Huguenots[2] (Calvinist Protestants) out of France at the end of the seventeenth century, after Louis XIV revoked the toleration supposedly guaranteed by the almost century-old Edict of Nantes.

The Edict had been issued on April 13, 1598, by Henry IV, himself a recent convert to Catholicism.[3] The aim was to end over thirty-five years of religious civil war in France by guaranteeing to the Calvinist Protestant minority "in perpetuity" freedom of worship in their own territories and estates and equality before the law. Nonetheless, on October 18, 1685, Henry's grandson Louis XIV, having on more than one occasion reaffirmed that its guarantees were "perpetual," abruptly and without prior notice revoked the Edict, proclaimed Catholicism the sole legal religion of France, ordered the Protestant churches demolished, forbade

[1] A more recent example is the sudden immigration of Russian Jews to Israel after the collapse of the Soviet Union. See p. 20.

[2] The name is of uncertain origin but had been widely applied, at first in a derogatory sense, to the French Calvinists since about the middle of the sixteenth century.

[3] Raised as a Protestant, Henry had converted to Catholicism only in 1593, after four years on the throne, famously (although unverifiably) explaining, "Paris vaut une messe," "Paris is worth a mass."

Protestant worship, and decreed that the children of Protestants must be raised as Catholics, even if doing so entailed separating them forcibly from their parents[4] (Prestwich 1988, 63–64). Although the Edict's guarantees had been eroded over the previous century, and intermittent persecution had already occurred, the revocation came as a thunderbolt, certainly to the Huguenots and even to most of the Sun King's closest advisers[5] (Hornung 2014, 90).

The Protestants at that point constituted between 4 and 5 percent of the French population of between nineteen and twenty million.[6] At least a fifth of them, or 160,000–170,000 souls, quickly fled the kingdom, perhaps anticipating correctly that the King would soon prohibit their emigration, punishing further attempts to leave with enslavement or death (Scoville 1952a, 297) (Dölemeyer 2006, 26 and 51–52).

That the Huguenots embodied a significant bloc of human capital is scarcely in doubt. They could, indeed, have served as Exhibit A for Max Weber's Protestant Ethic, or at least for the Calvinist variant on which Weber focused.[7] They were highly educated, famously diligent, above average in prosperity, and heavily concentrated in the worlds of business, the professions, technologically advanced agriculture, and even the military.[8] Their prowess in textiles and tailoring was especially renowned; they were among Europe's few breeders of silkworms and weavers of silk.[9] The extent to which the loss of their talents impeded eighteenth-century

[4] Such separations are of course unthinkable in our own more enlightened age.

[5] Supposedly major impetus came from the King's pious former mistress (by then his secret wife) Madame de Maintenon, and prior deliberation was confined largely to the bedroom.

[6] Earlier estimates were considerably higher: as many as two million Huguenots, of whom more than 200,000 emigrated. More recent scholarship has converged on these more realistic figures.

[7] It is also possible, of course, that the Huguenots' precarious position, demonstrated in a bloody civil war and repeated massacres, could have spurred them to acquire that most mobile of resources, human capital. Cf. Becker et al. (2020).

[8] As their most important twentieth-century historian has put it, they "dominated many local industries and branches of trade and [were] among the wealthiest and most industrious of France's middle class." (Scoville 1952a, 296). The *intendant* at Nîmes reported that the Protestants there "have a higher standard of living and are more active and more industrious than the Catholics" (Scoville 1953, 429).

[9] "In Germany [the Huguenots] introduced several kinds of textiles; they made ribbons, gloves, laces, woolen and silk stockings, and fine felt hats; they began the manufacture of blown and cast plate glass; they improved tanning and the hardware trades; and they brought additional land under cultivation and extended the margin of intensive farming" (Scoville 1952b, 410).

French economic growth remains in dispute,[10] but the gain to the jurisdictions to which the Huguenots fled – chiefly England, the Netherlands, Switzerland, Scandinavia, and the parts of Germany that the Peace of Westphalia had confirmed as Protestant – was significant, indeed often transformative.[11]

Not every Protestant part of Europe, however welcomed the refugees. Sectarian differences were part, but only part, of the explanation. The Calvinist provinces and cantons of the Netherlands and Switzerland readily accepted the refugees, as did some (but by no means all) of the few Calvinist parts of Germany. The response of Anglican and Lutheran Europe ranged from enthusiastic welcome to outright rejection. Language also played a role: The Huguenots found the friendliest reception, and certainly perceived themselves as more welcome, where (as in much of Germany, and even in Russia) most of the elites were fluent in French (Lachenicht 2005, 40).

The widest and most interesting variation, however, was to be found in Europe's German-speaking lands, not least because these comprised a patchwork of over 300 jurisdictions (principalities, dukedoms, margraviates, free cities, archbishoprics, etc.),[12] with governance structures that ranged from absolute or limited monarchies to merchant- or guild-dominated, or sometimes even popularly elected, councils.[13]

That some German jurisdictions failed to welcome the Huguenots is at first sight puzzling. Nowhere should their talents have been more welcome than in Germany, which scarcely a generation earlier had lost between a quarter and a third of its population to the Thirty Years War (1618–1648) (Schmidt 2003). That conflict, moreover, at least in the most sorely afflicted regions (chiefly the northeast and southwest: see Map 7.1),

[10] It was long argued that France's loss of human capital contributed significantly to the stultification of its economy in ensuing decades. Scoville's detailed analysis of the sectors in which the Huguenots were most active found little evidence to support that argument (Scoville 1960).

[11] The leading places of refuge (with the number of immigrants in parentheses) were: the Netherlands (50,000), England (40,000), Germany (38,000; of which some 20,000 went to Brandenburg-Prussia), and Switzerland (20,000). Smaller numbers fled even farther, to North America (roughly 3000), to Scandinavia (2000) or even to (Orthodox) Russia (perhaps 300) (Deutsche Hugenotten-Gesellschaft e.V. 2021, sec. Weltweite Ausbreitung) (Dölemeyer 2006, 51–52; Tollin 1886, 240).

[12] In Mark Twain's famous quip, in *A Connecticut Yankee in King Arthur's Court*, this was a period in which it was often impossible at night to "stretch out without a passport."

[13] A useful categorization, albeit for the early eighteenth century and only for the rural jurisdictions, can be found in (McElroy 2020, 146–157).

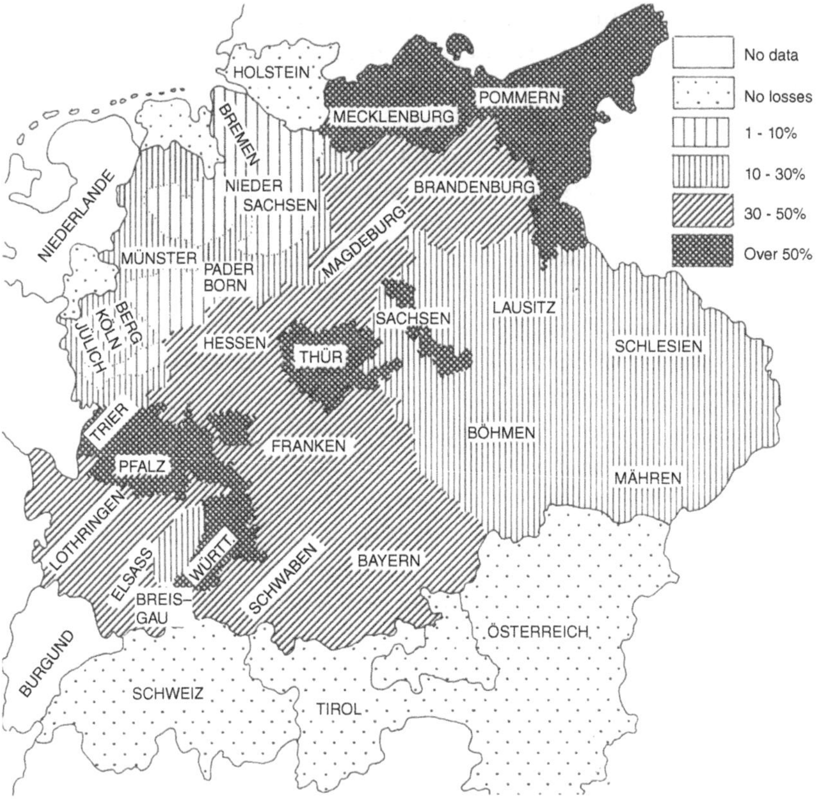

Map 7.1 German population losses in the Thirty Years War (1618–1648)
Source: (Franz 1961, 8). Reprinted by permission of de Gruyter publishers.

had deepened Germany's economic backwardness.[14] Surely there was need of repopulation ("*Peuplierung*"); moreover, an influx of high-skill people would alleviate Germany's backwardness and stimulate economic growth.

Some jurisdictions, most notably the Electoral Palatinate of the Rhine[15] and the Electorate of Brandenburg-Prussia,[16] actively recruited

[14] City-level data on population losses in the conflict, to the extent they are available, appear in Appendix Table A7.1.

[15] The mostly Calvinist-ruled Rhine-Palatinate (Kurpfalz) had begun even in the sixteenth century (and even more generously after Frederic IV's Edict of Mannheim, 1607) to welcome Huguenots who found France uncongenial (Braun and Lachenicht 2007, 17–34; Tollin 1886, 243).

[16] These rulers held the title of "Elector" because of their nominal role in electing the Holy Roman Emperor.

the Huguenots, offering generous incentives and privileges (the example of Brandenburg-Prussia is discussed more extensively below). In other Protestant territories, however, opposition was fierce (Tollin 1886, 264–268): Württemberg, Mecklenburg, Saxony,[17] and most of the Hanseatic city-states[18] either rejected the refugees outright or made their lives painfully difficult; and even in principalities whose rulers sought to welcome the Huguenots, opposition sometimes triumphed (e.g., in the Margravate[19] of Ansbach), surfaced locally (notably in Magdeburg, by then part of Brandenburg-Prussia), or had to be overcome by force (as in the Margravate of Bayreuth) (Tollin 1886, 264–266).

It seems clear that the most progressive and ambitious of Germany's Protestant rulers – informed, as we shall see later, by an important array of new economic ideas – hastened to welcome the refugees, granting them extensive subsidies and privileges. The principality that took in by far the most Huguenots and, not by accident, has been most frequently studied, was Brandenburg-Prussia, soon to become the Kingdom of Prussia.[20] Having lost at least half of its population in the Thirty Years War (C. M. Clark 2006, 66), it also lagged economically and technologically (Dölemeyer 2006, 90; Scoville 1952b, 398–399). Its ruler in 1685, the "Great Elector" Friedrich Wilhelm (ruled 1640–1688), was acutely aware of its disadvantages, not least because he had spent four years of his youth in the Netherlands, then perhaps the most economically advanced area of Europe. There, he had learned shipbuilding, studied at the University of Leiden, and – not least – become a devout Calvinist. Precisely three weeks after Louis had revoked the Edict of Nantes, Friedrich Wilhelm issued the Edict of Potsdam, welcoming the refugees to Brandenburg-Prussia, subsidizing their passage, offering them free housing and subsidized loans,

[17] The Electoral Principality of Saxony and the Free Imperial City of Frankfurt went so far as to forbid Calvinists to own land or become citizens (Braun and Lachenicht 2007, 36; Tollin 1886, 266).

[18] Lübeck opposed their settlement, Hamburg forbade Calvinist preaching (Deutsche Hugenotten-Gesellschaft e.V. 2021, sec. Religiöser Einfluss der Hugenotten in den Aufnahmeländern). Bremen, however, welcomed the Huguenots (Tollin 1886, 267–268).

[19] Margravate is the unlovely English rendering of the German *Markgrafschaft*, more literally (but perhaps no more felicitously) "Earldom of the Marches," "march" having originally meant a border region of the empire.

[20] The Electorate of Brandenburg, whose rulers were "Margraves" but preferred the grander title of "Elector," had merged with the Duchy of Prussia through dynastic marriage in 1618. In 1701 the Elector of Brandenburg-Prussia, Frederick I, proclaimed himself "King in (not 'of') Prussia" and retitled his domains the "Kingdom of Prussia."

promising them complete freedom of worship (and, wherever there was a sizable congregation, state payment of their clergy), granting them the same rights as his native-born subjects, freeing them to practice their trades irrespective of any local guild regulations, and indeed allowing their own judges and courts to adjudicate controversies not only within their community but between them and native-born subjects (Scoville 1952b, 399).[21]

Some 20,000 Huguenots accepted the offer and, assisted by the Great Elector's agents, made their way to Brandenburg-Prussia. Perhaps a quarter of them, or 5000, settled in Berlin, whose pre-migration population was only 20,000 (Hornung 2014, 90). The remainder settled in some forty different towns (90 percent), or on vacant farms (10 percent). The picture of the refugees as highly skilled is borne out by a Prussian census of 1700, which (excluding adults not in the workforce, almost exclusively women) classified them as follows:[22]

Textile workers	37%
Tradespeople[23] (almost all skilled)	20%
Physicians, pharmacists, notaries, teachers	12%
Servants and "workpeople"	11%
Farmers	11%
Clothiers (tailors, hatmakers, etc.)	8%
Landowners	2%.

Folk wisdom and standard histories have long held that the Huguenots could indeed be credited for much of Prussia's subsequent economic growth (Scoville 1952b, 404). Erik Hornung was the first to sustain that view with greater precision. Exploiting the natural experiment that, in fact, the Huguenots were usually not allowed to choose their own place of settlement but were exogenously assigned to specific towns by the governmental authorities, Hornung examines the effect of Huguenot settlement in 1700 on town-level productivity in textile manufacturing – the sector that employed the most Huguenots (see above) and in which they

[21] The full text of the Edict is available at www.potsdamer-toleranzedikt.de/transkription-des-edikt-von-potsdam-1685/.

[22] My calculations, based on data in (Scoville 1952b, 401–402) on a total of 3,204 adults, of whom 710 were "widows, maiden ladies, or wives of officers" and 479 unclassified. Rounding errors make the percentages sum to more than 100.

[23] Includes "bakers, distillers, brewers, confectioners, barbers, wigmakers, and merchants."

allegedly had the greatest impact – a century later.[24] Fitting a simple Cobb-Douglas model,[25] and controlling for such other putatively relevant variables as town size and overall Protestant share of population, Hornung finds that a 1 percentage point increase in a town's share of Huguenot population in 1700 was associated with a 1.5 percentage point higher productivity in its textile manufacturing in 1802 (Hornung 2014, 103).[26] We can be confident that this exogenous infusion of human capital indeed increased productivity.

The Huguenot influx not only augmented, but rapidly multiplied, human capital in Prussia. In an age of slow communication and artisanal production, hands-on instruction was almost the only effective way of acquiring human capital (Hornung 2014, 86). Hence, the fact that the Prussian government encouraged, and often required, the Huguenots to train apprentices (Hornung 2014, 94) soon increased the skills of the native population.

In a pattern that we shall find was more general, native-born artisans within Prussia nonetheless exhibited what one observer called a "prodigious aversion" to the newcomers, and to the generosity with which the government received them. Craft guilds throughout Brandenburg usually admitted the Huguenots only under official duress. Practitioners of the "craft" of divine intermediation were no less hostile: The Lutheran clergy often inveighed against the Calvinist interlopers, until reined in by higher authority (Scoville 1952b, 400). Brandenburg-Prussia, after all, was an unabashedly absolute monarchy. The Elector could override the local artisans' objections and force them to admit the skilled and industrious refugees. Even he, however, could not prevail against the opposition of noble landowners, for example, in the Uckermark region, who feared that

24 Hornung has the advantage that the Prussian authorities were obsessive about record-keeping. The Huguenot share of total population in the early eighteenth century is available for 342 towns; the value of manufactured goods and inputs, the numbers of workers, and the number of working looms, for 637 manufactories in 1802 (Hornung 2014, 96–97 and 103). (The total number of manufactories cataloged was 750, but complete data on inputs were missing for 113 of those.)

25 Log of output is simply regressed on logs of labor (number of workers), capital (number of looms), intermediate inputs (raw materials); and on Huguenot share of town population and a vector of controls (Hornung 2014, 98–99).

26 To guard against endogeneity, Hornung exploits the knowledge that the governmental authorities assigned the immigrants preferentially to the towns that had experienced the greatest population losses in the Thirty Years' War. Using the share of population lost in the War (available for only seventy-one of the towns) as an instrumental variable sustains the finding and yields a coefficient about twice as large (Hornung 2014, 107–109).

nearby settlements of free and prosperous peasants, to whom moreover the Edict of Potsdam had promised freedom from serfdom (*Leibeigenschaft*) "for all eternity" (Klingebiel 1990, 71), would sow discontent among their own serfs (Dölemeyer 2006, 90). The rights that the Huguenots had been promised were disrespected, and most soon abandoned the tracts of land to which they had been assigned (Dölemeyer 2006, 97).

The pattern of support and opposition that manifested itself in Prussia prevailed in most of Germany. Working with research assistants, I have assembled a novel data set of all sixty Protestant German cities for which attitudes toward reception of the Huguenots can readily be ascertained from secondary sources, coding not only the attitude of the city but also that of its territorial ruler (unless a Free Imperial City or a Hanseatic City), as well as a host of other city and territorial attributes described more fully below.[27] These cities (Appendix Table A7.1) are presumably examined in the secondary sources because, despite population sizes that today seem risible, they appear to have been among the most significant in the seventeenth and early eighteenth centuries.

In that data set (for summary statistics and intercorrelations, see Appendix Table A7.2), the great majority of territorial rulers were ready to admit the Huguenots, but the cities were markedly less friendly. Fewer than a quarter of the municipal governments in the sample actively recruited the Huguenots, as against 61 percent of the territorial rulers; seven cities actively rejected the refugees and sixteen showed a mixed reaction or severely limited the numbers they did accept. Perhaps most remarkable, of the thirty-four cities in which rulers were actively recruiting, the municipal governments of 10 (or 30 percent) either hesitated (four cases) or outright rejected (six cases; 18 percent) the refugees (Table 7.1).

Since rulers presumably would have directed the refugees chiefly to cities they regarded as likely to accept them (i.e., exhibited an upward selection bias), these figures suggest that urban resistance must have been even more widespread. What might have inclined most rulers to welcome or even subsidize this importation of human capital (and why did some not do so); and what provoked such "prodigious opposition" in the great majority of cities (and, equally, spurred a minority to accept them)?

[27] For heroic labors in combing the available databases and published sources, I thank particularly Nina Groeneveld, Stephanie Inchaustegui, and Arthur Krön. Jeremiah Dittmar very kindly guided me through his database.

Table 7.1 *Attitude toward Huguenots' settlement of cities vs. attitude of cities' territorial rulers*

		City Attitude				
		Opposed	Mixed Reaction	Welcomed	Actively Recruited	Sum
Ruler Attitude	Mixed Reaction	1	5	0	1	7
	Welcomed	0	7	8	0	15
	Actively Recruited	6	4	12	12	34
	Sum	7	16	20	13	56

Consider first the reasons for urban opposition. Historians seem almost unanimous in regarding the cities' craft guilds as the most embittered opponents (Dölemeyer 2006, 91).[28] Guilds formed the foundation of early modern cities' economies, perhaps more so in Germany than elsewhere (M. Walker 1971, chaps. 2 and 3). Each guild – of bakers, hatters, tailors, butchers, etc. – guaranteed the competence of its members and the quality of their work; but each also extracted monopoly rents and resisted technical innovations. The existing artisans and merchants of Germany's major cities would inevitably see in the potential newcomers unwelcome competition – an unanticipated surge of human capital that, particularly if it proved superior to their own, could only devalue their hard-acquired skills and raise the costs of the newly scarce factors of labor and physical capital.[29] At worst, they rightly feared, this "price scissors" could reduce them to penury. Nor, in the face of this adverse supply shock, did the guilds have any of our usual alternatives to coercive resistance.

That they could engage in *factor substitution* seemed extremely unlikely. Unlike the landlords of post–Black Death western Europe,

[28] A particularly vivid example came from the city of Torgau, one of three Saxon cities that the Electorate's ruler, Friedrich August I, had ordered to accept Huguenots. The Torgau city council protested vehemently against the plan to settle "almost 400 persons, refugee French manufacturers (bey nahe ... vier hundert Persohnen, refugirten französischen Manufacteurs)," including "bakers, shoemakers, tailors, and similar artisans," and – worst of all – brewers of "so-called French beer (so genandtes französisches Bier)," given that the principal economic activity of Torgau was brewing (Middell 2007, 55).

[29] As human capital grew more abundant with the arrival of the Huguenots, in relative terms other factors of production, notably labor and physical capital, grew by definition scarcer and costlier.

who met rising wages by moving to less labor-intensive production, the artisans of the later seventeenth century would have gained little by economizing on the newly scarce inputs of low-skill labor and physical capital. Existing production technologies, for example for fabrics or printing, were unavoidably labor-intensive; printing was, in addition, capital-intensive.[30] The native artisans' plight more closely resembled that of late nineteenth-century European peasants who suddenly faced the competition of cheap imports from the newly opened lands of the New World.

Could the existing artisans instead have moved into a *different sector or jurisdiction* where their human capital would remain more valued? To be sure, the German artisans had the advantage of knowing the local language and might move into sectors that would remain closed to the French-speaking immigrants. Unlike in the decades after the surge of human capital that followed the advent of printing (below, Chapter 8), however, few secular princes now required more administrators; and, if they had, would as before have preferred university graduates. Moreover, the War had so reduced the secular princes' incomes that they often found themselves hard-pressed to pay the *Beamten* they already employed. Nor could the local artisans easily move to other jurisdictions where the Huguenots were unlikely to follow. The only German-speaking lands that would assuredly remain off-limits to the Calvinists were Catholic; artisans from Protestant jurisdictions, unless they converted, would not be readily accepted; and opportunistic conversions – even disregarding the likely social and familial costs – would be suspect.

Finally, could the endangered local artisans find some *technological solution* to their plight? While in theory some breakthrough in the technology of production – perhaps some Industrial Revolution avant la lettre – might, if somehow kept proprietary among the German-speaking artisans, have allowed them to outcompete the Huguenot interlopers, in fact it was the Huguenots who possessed that era's more advanced technologies and hence were better positioned to achieve yet greater progress.

In short, the guild craftspeople would have seen no ready non-coercive way to answer the economic challenge that the Huguenot immigrants presented, let alone the political one – abolition of the guilds – that (as we shall see) they may have rightly feared.

[30] An early printing press, with typefaces and ancillary equipment, cost between four and ten years of a skilled worker's wages (Dittmar 2011, 1155).

Yet not all cities had strong guilds, and to some extent guild strength was endogenous. Guilds tended to be weaker, for example, in the Hanseatic cities, where a "patriciate" of trade-oriented merchants ruled almost unchallenged (Wahl 2016, 72).[31] Larger cities in general – ones of population above 10,000–15,000 – tended also to be ruled by patriciates and to have weak guilds (M. Walker 1971, 27–28).[32] Given that the full-blown guild system depended on local autarky and prohibition of imports (M. Walker 1971, 24–25), we might also expect to find weaker guilds and less resistance in towns that were closer to major trade routes. Finally, guild resistance appears to have been more easily overcome – and hence, in anticipation, weaker – in *Residenzstädten*, that is, cities where a territorial ruler actually resided (Klingebiel 1990, 74).

Apart from guild strength (and its underlying causes), we might expect a town to be readier to accept immigrants the greater the loss of population it had suffered in the Thirty Years' War. Such towns might have lacked crucial skills and hence have welcomed immigrants who could supply them.

The guilds may also have faced opposition from within their respective cities; therefore, some groups may have had reason to welcome the Huguenots, just as the craftspeople in the guilds had reason to reject them. Owners of labor and of physical capital, the two factors that an infusion of new human capital would make relatively scarcer and dearer, might well have found a Huguenot "invasion" to their advantage. To the extent that a town included a proletariat of low-skill workers who were excluded from the guilds, or even more that allowed such workers a degree of political influence, we might expect it to resist the Huguenots less.

Finally, and somewhat paradoxically, owners of "upper-tail human capital" might well have welcomed the additional (and, likely, complementary) human capital that the Huguenots could bring. As we have seen in earlier chapters, such high-end human capital typically becomes more

[31] Only three of the forty-one Hanseatic cities are classified by Wahl as having had a successful guild revolution and hence a "guild constitution": Brunswick, Goslar, and Magdeburg (Wahl 2016, 72). Thomas Mann's great novel *Buddenbrooks*, set in the thinly disguised city of Lübeck, conveys well how patrician rule endured in a typical Hanseatic city well into the nineteenth century, and even through the revolutionary events of 1848.

[32] To the extent that the patricians were also owners of physical capital, which any influx of Huguenot human capital would have made relatively scarcer, they would have benefited directly.

productive the more it agglomerates.[33] Moreover, the talented Huguenots might have increased the quality and variety of goods and services (weaving, tailoring, barbering) that those in the upper tail consumed. Since, as Dittmar and Meisenzahl have established, Protestant towns that adopted "church ordinances" – which secularized the provision of such public services as poor relief and schooling, and usually opened education to all – were likelier to cultivate and attract upper-tail human capital (Dittmar and Meisenzahl 2019), we might expect that early adopters of such ordinances would have been likelier also to accept the Huguenots.

To assess these hypotheses, our sample of the sixty most significant seventeenth-century Protestant German cities includes, to the extent that relevant data were available:

- whether the city's population exceeded approximately 10,000, the threshold posited by Walker (de Vries 1981, 82–83);
- the approximate extent of its population loss in the Thirty Years' War (Franz 1961, 8, 16, and 21);[34]
- its proximity to the nearest major trade route (Yue, Lee, and Wu 2017);
- the extent of guild power, burgher representation, and participative elections[35] in 1700 as coded by Wahl (Wahl 2016), data available for thirty-six of our sixty cities;
- its endowment of upper-tail human capital (Dittmar and Meisenzahl 2019);
- whether it had adopted a church ordinance by 1530 (Dittmar and Meisenzahl 2019); and
- whether it was a "city of residence," that is, one in which the territorial ruler resided (hand-coded from various secondary sources).

EVIDENCE ON CITY ATTITUDE

The small number of cities, in many cases as few as thirty-six, precludes detailed statistical analysis and allows only some partially informative cross-tabulations. What emerges clearly from them, however, is that guild

[33] Recall that, in our own time, most high-skill workers welcome the immigration of more high-skill workers (Hainmueller and Hiscox 2010).

[34] Data on city population and population loss are summarized in Appendix Table A7.1.

[35] Wahl classifies only two cities in our sample as having had participatory elections, so I ignore that aspect here.

strength, at least in this sample, was irrelevant to a city's willingness to accept the Huguenots. The factors that do emerge as moderately important are population loss, city size (albeit in a direction opposite to the one postulated in the literature), status as a *Residenzstadt*, and (with reservations) proximity to a major trade route. Burgher representation, early adoption of a church ordinance, and the presence of upper-tail human capital all appear to be uncorrelated with receptivity to the Huguenots.

Guild Strength

Of the thirty-six cities in our sample for which we have Wahl's codings of municipal governance, only eight had any significant guild influence; of those, precisely half either actively recruited or welcomed the Huguenots (Table 7.2). Among the twenty-eight cities where guilds played no overt role in governance, sixteen, or 57 percent, were similarly welcoming. Indeed, of the three cities in this sample that rejected the Huguenots, none had significant guild participation in governance.

As noted earlier, this finding may result from selection bias: rulers may not even have attempted to settle Huguenots in cities where they

Table 7.2 *Guild power and Huguenot acceptance*

		Guild Participation			
		No Participation	Some Influence	Dominate City's Governing Council	Total
Huguenot Acceptance	Rejected	3 10.71%	0 0.00%	0 0.00%	3 8.33%
	Mixed Reaction	9 32.14%	4 57.14%	0 0.00%	13 36.11%
	Welcomed	11 39.29%	1 14.29%	1 100.00%	13 36.11%
	Actively Recruited	5 17.86%	2 28.57%	0 0.00%	7 19.44%
	Total	28 100.00%	7 100.00%	1 100.00%	36 100.00%

Table 7.3 *Population loss and acceptance of Huguenots among fifty-six German cities*

		Population Loss		
		≤40%	>40%	Total
Attitude of the City	Opposed	3 10.71%	5 17.86%	8 14.29%
	Mixed Reaction	11 39.29%	6 21.43%	17 30.36%
	Welcomed	11 39.29%	8 28.57%	19 33.93%
	Actively Recruited	3 10.71%	9 32.14%	12 21.43%
	Total	28 100.00%	28 100.00%	56 100.00%

anticipated obdurate guild opposition.[36] Our earlier evidence suggests, however (Table 7.1), that rulers may still have underestimated urban opposition.

Population Loss

Cities that had experienced heavy population losses in the Thirty Years War were somewhat more inclined to engage in active recruitment of the Huguenots. Exactly half of the cities on which we have data[37] had lost over 40 percent of their population (Table 7.3). Over a third of these high-loss cities (nine of twenty-eight) actively recruited Huguenots, while barely 10 percent of the less afflicted cities did so – a difference unlikely to be accidental.[38] Overall, however, the difference is less stark: seventeen of the high-loss cities either recruited or welcomed the Huguenots, as did fourteen of the lower-loss cities – 60 vs. 50 percent.

36 In numerous cities where the territorial ruler anticipated strong opposition, he resorted instead to the expedient of creating a new city nearby. See below, p.177.

37 We lack data on city attitude (or have it only for their territorial ruler) in three cases.

38 If we dichotomize into cities that actively recruited vs. all the rest, we obtain a chi-squared of 2.63, $p = .11$.

Table 7.4 *Large vs. small cities: Reception of Huguenots*

		City Size		
		Small	Large	Total
Attitude of the City	Opposed	9 17.65%	0 0.00%	9 15.52%
	Mixed Reaction	13 25.49%	5 71.43%	18 31.03%
	Welcomed	16 31.37%	2 28.57%	18 31.03%
	Actively Recruited	13 25.49%	0 0.00%	13 22.41%
	Total	51 4.55%	7 100.00%	58 100.00%

Chi-sq = 11.61, p = .071
Fisher's exact (two-tailed) = .091

City Size

By the criterion embraced by Walker and de Vries, a minimum population of 10,000, only seven of the fifty-eight cities for which we have data on both population and attitude can be classified as "large." Running directly counter to the prevailing conjecture that large cities would have weaker guilds[39] and hence would be more welcoming, only one of seven large cities actively recruited the Huguenots, while a quarter of the fifty-one smaller cities did so; and only two of the large cities even welcomed the refugees (Table 7.4). To put it another way: fewer than one-third of the large cities readily accepted the Huguenots, while a majority – twenty-nine of fifty-one – of the smaller cities either accepted or recruited them. By conventional measures, the difference is significant. The modal response of the large cities was to dither and temporize, as for example did Frankfurt am Main (Magdelaine 2007, 39ff.).[40] It may be that the larger cities could better resist pressure from territorial rulers (or, in the

[39] Which, in fact, they did not: of the eight large cities, six had politically weak guilds, exactly the same proportion as in the smaller cities.

[40] Frankfurt's *Magistrat* worried first that any acceptance of the Huguenots might attract the dangerous enmity of Louis XIV. After that concern abated, objections arose from the Lutheran clergy and the guilds. The ultimate resolution was to allow the Huguenots to use Frankfurt as a transit hub (*Drehscheibe*), but not to settle there permanently (Magdelaine 2007).

case of Imperial Free Cities, owed allegiance to no territorial ruler save the distant Emperor). Another possibility, equally likely, is that large and flourishing cities were economically often so attractive to the Huguenots that they had no need to offer incentives and/or the Huguenots would settle there even if subjected to some disabilities (Volckart 2002, 205). Finally, smaller towns may have felt particularly threatened by the rulers' efforts to introduce the Huguenots – or by what they saw as the deeper purpose behind their entry (below, p. 179ff.)

Residenzstädte

We have data on this aspect of its status for fifty-four cities, of which nineteen were, and another five had recently been, or soon became, ones in which the territorial ruler resided. Of that total of twenty-four, one-third actively recruited the Huguenots; among the non-residential cities, only one-sixth did so (Table 7.5). Precisely one of the twenty-four *Residenzstädten* rejected the Huguenots, while seven of the thirty cities in which the ruler did not reside turned the refugees away. It seems likely that the ruler could indeed more readily make his writ run in the city from which he exercised power. At a minimum, he could discourage overt opposition.

Table 7.5 *Were* Residenzstädte *more welcoming to Huguenots?*

		City of Residence		
		No	Yes	Total
Attitude of the City	Opposed	7 23.33%	1 4.17%	8 14.82%
	Mixed Reaction	8 26.67%	8 33.33%	16 29.63%
	Welcomed	10 33.33%	7 29.17%	17 31.48%
	Actively Recruited	5 16.67%	8 33.33%	13 24.07%
	Total	30 100.00%	24 100.00%	54 100.00%

Chi-sq = 5.118, p = .1633
Fisher's exact (two-tailed) = .1657

Proximity to a Major Trade Route

Many of a city's characteristics – guild power, population, whether it was the seat of a territorial ruler – were endogenous. One aspect that is largely exogenous was the town's geographical location and its proximity to major trade routes. A city whose location afforded it better trading opportunities, finding it harder to maintain the autarky on which guild rents depended, was less likely to be dominated by guilds and hence – or so it is conjectured – might have been more open to the Huguenots' infusion of human capital. Working from standard sources on major German trade routes in this period [(Yue, Lee, and Wu 2017), and sources there cited], we were able to calculate the distance from each of our sixty cities, in kilometers, to the nearest major trade route.

The cities that actively recruited the refugees appear to have been distinctive. They lay on average within five kilometers of a major trade route (indeed, no city that recruited them lay more than thirteen kilometers from such a route), while the average distance of a non-recruiting city was twice as great (eleven kilometers) (Table 7.6). If we dichotomize city attitude into either "actively recruited" vs. "other" and logistically regress that indicator variable on city distance to the nearest trade route (Table 7.7), we find with reasonable confidence that distance reliably predicts whether the city actively recruited Huguenots or did not: The farther a city lay from a trade route, the less likely it was to engage in active recruitment of the Huguenots.

The cause can hardly have been weaker guilds. In fact, the cities with any degree of guild power lay on average closer to a major trade route than those with weaker guilds: 5.25 vs. 8.65 kilometers. It seems likelier that these were simply flourishing cities that attracted the Huguenots and regarded them as a boon rather than a threat.

Among the cities that did not recruit, the pattern is inconsistent. The cities that were hesitant or inconsistent lay also on average close to a

Table 7.6 *Distance to major trade route vs. Huguenot acceptance*

Huguenot Acceptance	Mean	Median	S.D.	IQR	Min.	Max.	Count
Opposed	12.44	8.16	9.82	7.43	0.14	29.44	9
Mixed Reaction	6.19	0.49	12.35	5.48	0.03	50.55	17
Welcomed	15.65	10.17	15.07	23.16	0.04	51.22	18
Actively Recruited	4.86	3.88	4.24	6.11	0.10	12.90	13

Table 7.7 *Logistic regression of "active recruitment" on distance to nearest trade route*

Dep. Variable:		Actively Recruited		No. Observations		56
Model:		Logit		Df Residuals:		54
Method:		MLE		Df Model:		1
Date :		Sat, 16 Jul 2022		Pseudo R-squ.:		0.05696
Time :		23:07:49		Log-Likelihood :		–27.439
Converged :		True		LL-Null:		–29.096
Covariance Type :		nonrobust		LLR p-value:		0.06866
	coef	std err	z	P > |z|	[0.025	0.975]
Const	–0.7894	0.422	–1.870	0.061	–1.617	0.038
Tr_Distance	–0.0682	0.046	–1.474	0.140	–0.159	0.022

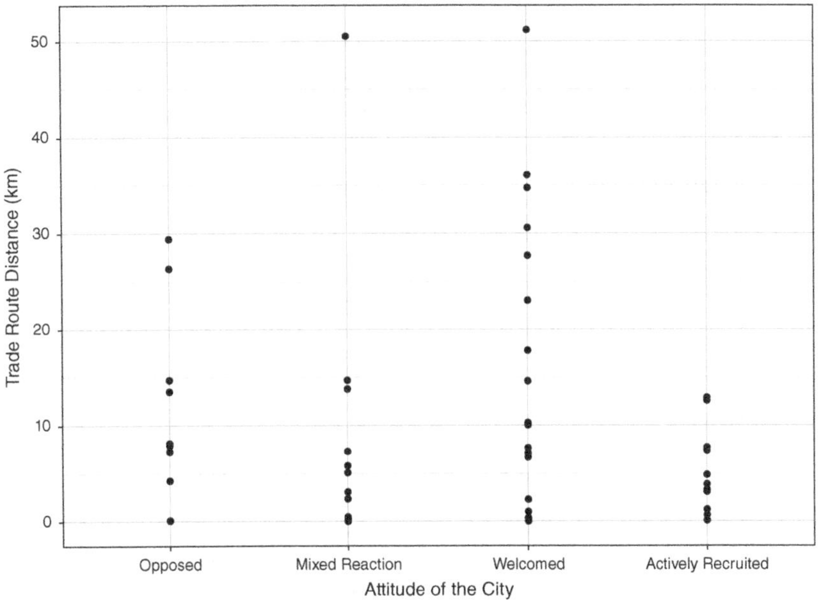

Figure 7.1 Distribution of trade route distance by Huguenot acceptance

trade route, while ones that welcomed without actively recruiting were on average farther from a trade route but exhibited high variation (Figure 7.1). We can say only that cities that eagerly recruited the Huguenots to settle in them tended also to lie very near a major trade route.

Burgher Representation

Wahl defines this aspect of government in late Medieval and early modern European cities as characterized by "a regularly meeting community assembly" that comprised "a comparatively broad cross section of different groups of citizens," including "burghers that were not part of the established ruling elite" (Wahl 2016, 69). These assemblies were not usually elected, but neither were they dominated by guilds or patricians. Might they, therefore, be better able to represent the city's overarching welfare, rather than that of any particular group – in modern parlance, to "internalize the externalities" – and thus to see the arrival of the Huguenots as an asset?

In a word, no. If anything, the cities with this kind of representation were *less* likely to welcome the Huguenots. Of the thirty-six cities in our set for which Wahl specifies values, fourteen, or just under 40 percent, had significant burgher representation. Of those, six (just over 40 percent) either welcomed or actively recruited Huguenots (Table 7.8). Of the twenty-two cities that *lacked* burgher representation, fourteen (64 percent) either welcomed or recruited. While this is hardly a statistically significant difference,[41] it forces us to reject any conjecture that burgher representation would make a city more welcoming.

Table 7.8 *Burgher representation and Huguenot acceptance*

		Burgher Representation		
		Absent	**Present**	**Total**
Attitude of the City	Opposed	**1**	2	3
		8.00%	14.29%	8.33%
	Mixed Reaction	7	6	13
		31.82%	42.86%	36.11%
	Welcomed	10	3	13
		45.45%	21.43%	36.11%
	Actively Recruited	4	3	7
		18.18%	21.43%	19.44%
	Total	22	14	36
		100.00%	100.00%	100.00%

[41] Even if we dichotomize the city's attitude into either "welcomed or actively recruited" vs. "mixed reaction or rejected," we obtain a chi-squared of 1.50, $p = .22$.

Table 7.9 *Early adoption of church ordinance vs. Huguenot acceptance*

		Church Ordinance		
		No	Yes	Total
Huguenot Acceptance	Opposed	7 19.44%	2 8.33%	9 15.00%
	Mixed Reaction	8 22.22%	10 41.67%	18 30.00%
	Welcomed	12 33.33%	8 33.33%	20 33.33%
	Actively Recruited	9 25.00%	4 16.67%	13 21.67%
	Total	36 100.00%	24 100.00%	60 100.00%

Early adoption of a church ordinance, upper-tail human capital

For reasons advanced earlier, one might expect cities that were early adopters of a church ordinance, and in consequence offered wider education and attracted more upper-tail human capital, to have been more open to Huguenot immigration. Twenty-four cities, or 40 percent of our total sample, had adopted a church ordinance by 1530 – a mere thirteen years after Luther had begun the Reformation. Of those twenty-four, precisely half welcomed or actively recruited the Huguenots (Table 7.9). Among the thirty-six cities that adopted an ordinance later, or never adopted one, twenty-one (59 percent) welcomed or actively recruited. That is, to speak colloquially, not a difference to write home about. To be sure, the late or non-adopters were slightly likelier to reject the Huguenots, while the modal response of the early adopters was to temporize; but we find no support for the idea that early adopters, although they did seem to cultivate and attract more human capital (Dittmar and Meisenzahl 2019), also welcomed the Huguenots more warmly.

In our sample, however, a city's endowment of human capital also seems unrelated to its propensity to admit the Huguenots (Table 7.10). Of the eleven cities in which at least one resident was prominent enough to have appeared centuries later in the authoritative biographical dictionary, six either welcomed or actively recruited the Huguenots; of the twenty-four who could boast no such endowment of human capital, thirteen did so. In both categories, in short, almost identical shares (54 percent) were open to Huguenot settlement. Despite the plausibility of the conjecture, there is simply no evidence, at least in this small sample of cities, that the

Table 7.10 *Upper-tail human capital vs. Huguenot acceptance*

		Upper-Tail Human Capital		
		None	Some	Total
Attitude of the City	Opposed	2 8.00%	1 9.09%	3 8.33%
	Mixed Reaction	9 36.00%	4 36.36%	13 36.11%
	Welcomed	9 36.00%	4 36.36%	13 36.11%
	Actively Recruited	5 20.00%	2 18.18%	7 19.44%
	Total	25 100.00%	11 100.00%	36 100.00%

presence of upper-tail human capital inclined a city to favor Huguenot immigration more.

EVIDENCE ON RULER ATTITUDE

The attitudes of the city governments toward the Huguenots varied remarkably and are only partially explained by population loss in the Thirty Years War, proximity to a major trade route, and city size (larger ones being *less* likely to recruit or welcome the refugees). What mattered far more was the posture of the territorial ruler, and here the view was almost unanimously favorable: the territorial rulers of 88 percent of our cities either welcomed or actively recruited the Huguenots; no ruler in our set rejected them.[42] And, as we have observed, one thing that made a city likelier to accept the Huguenots was its being the one in which the ruler resided, and from which he exercised his power: a *Residenzstadt.* We have also seen numerous cases in which the ruler forced a reluctant city to admit the refugees, going so far as to expel the existing inhabitants and settle Huguenots in their houses; or, more commonly, to evade local

[42] Again, selection bias could be at work. The historical accounts, especially by later generations of Huguenots, focus on the rulers who offered them refuge. They may simply ignore, rather than lament, the ones who rejected them.

opposition by creating a new Huguenot town near the German one that had refused to admit them (or that seemed likely to do so).[43]

What, then, so united the rulers in their favorable disposition? To the extent that their enthusiasm varied at all, what made them (even) more favorable?

We can point to two objective factors that clearly mattered, but what likely mattered even more – and this is an interesting and rare case in which it did so – was the power of ideas, or at any rate of a systemic idea about the sources of, and the obstacles to, economic growth: how a state could become prosperous and powerful (or, even more to the point, what in existing arrangements prevented it from doing so).

Population Loss

On the evidence from our sample, the most important objective factor motivating rulers was indeed the share of population that they had lost in the Thirty Years War. That mattered far more among rulers than among cities. We have data on both population loss and ruler's attitude for fifty-nine cities. Of those, as we have already seen, slightly over half (thirty-one cities) had lost over 40 percent of their population. In over 70 percent of those high-loss cities, the territorial ruler not only welcomed, but actively recruited, Huguenots. Among the more fortunate cities that lost 40 percent or fewer of their inhabitants, fewer than 40 percent of territorial rulers (eleven of twenty-eight) actively recruited (Table 7.11). The chance that such a disparity could have arisen by accident is – unless our sample is remarkably biased – less than 2 percent.

There was nothing tender-hearted about rulers' eagerness to repopulate their ravaged states. A smaller population meant a smaller, weaker, and poorer state – and, in turn, undermined the prestige, the external power, and (by no means least) the ruler's revenues.

43 When the residents of the Mannheim district of Seckenheim resisted, for example, the Elector Charles II of Rhine-Palatinate created the new city of Friedrichsfeld (Guillemenot-Ehrmantraut 2007, 26–27). The Count of Hessen-Homburg created the new city of Friedrichsdorf for Huguenots in 1687. There, as in a number of other such cases, non-Huguenots were subsequently forbidden to take up residence, lest they claim the same privileges as the Huguenots had received (Dölemeyer 1997, 308). In a few cases, e.g., Daubhausen, the ruler forcibly relocated the existing inhabitants and replaced them with Huguenots, usually at least compensating the expellees for their lost property (Dölemeyer 2006, 47).

Table 7.11 *Population loss in Thirty Years War vs. active recruitment by territorial ruler*

		City's Share of Population Lost	
		Population loss ≤40 %	Population loss >40 %
Attitude of Territorial Ruler	Ruler actively recruited	11	22
	Ruler did not recruit	17	9
	Total	28	31
	% who actively recruited	39%	71%

chi-sq = 5.99
p = .014
Fisher's exact (two-tailed): p = .019

Revenue Loss

A shrinking population meant shrinking revenues. Even worse, the demands on state treasuries were growing in the late seventeenth century. The Peace of Westphalia had produced at best a pause in the military rivalries that required expensive outlays. Most rulers had little doubt that the talents and productivity of the Huguenots could, at least in part, remedy the shortfall. As Klingebiel has put it with respect to the North German territorial rulers,

> Among the goals of this policy [of welcoming or recruiting Huguenots] was augmentation of the state's financial revenues – all the more, since outlays in the military and prestige [*repräsentativ*] categories persistently grew. An increase of the princely income however could only be lastingly guaranteed by the furtherance of those branches of the economy that seemed both to meet current needs and to promote growth. (Klingebiel 1990, 70)

While we cannot quantify the extent of each ruler's fiscal pressures, there can be no doubt that they weighed heavily.

Ideas

The combined pressures of demography and revenue impelled rulers, and their close advisers, to seek answers: what held their economies back from revival, and what policies could stimulate growth and augment revenues?

The prevailing ideology, or systemic idea, took the guild structure of economic activity as given and assigned no innovative role to rulers – they were, at most, to re-establish a disrupted traditional order, as Edward III had attempted to do when England was ravaged by the Black Death (chapter four).

A radically different systemic picture had recently been offered by the scholar, jurist, and statesman Veit Ludwig von Seckendorff[44] in his influential volume *Der teutsche Fürstenstaat* (Seckendorff 1711). As originally published in 1655, it had urged German rulers to encourage manufacturing and agricultural improvement – and, not least, immigration and full religious toleration – as spurs to economic growth and enhancement of princely revenues.

These ideas were radical enough for a world only seven years removed from the religiously inspired slaughter of the Thirty Years War. It was however in the third edition[45] of his book, which appeared in 1665, that Seckendorff's propounded the ideas that soon became common currency, if not dogma, among territorial rulers. Here, Seckendorff condemned the guild system as a major obstacle to economic growth and called explicitly for the abolition of the guilds (Dölemeyer 2006, 85). Although Seckendorff remained a mercantilist with respect to external trade, he extolled the virtues of vigorous economic competition within the state.

The influence of the third edition was profound. It was known to be, as Leopold von Ranke put it, the Great Elector's "most beloved manual of German policy" (*beliebtestes Handbuch der deutschen Politik*). It was also read approvingly by the rulers, or at least by the rulers' closest advisers, in Hessen-Cassel and Brandenburg-Bayreuth – and, very likely, in many other chancelleries (Dölemeyer 2006, 85). It became – admittedly, to exaggerate somewhat – the "Washington consensus" among that era's territorial rulers. To ones who had been persuaded, by this or similar works, or by experience,[46] that the guild system was a millstone around the necks of their economies, and perhaps even a barrier to repopulation, the entry of the Huguenots must have seemed a golden opportunity: not only to enlarge their populations and gain valuable new human capital,

44 Seckendorff is sometimes regarded as the founder of German economics.

45 It eventually went through eleven editions, the last in 1737. The demand for it appears to have been considerable.

46 The Great Elector had observed during his time there that the vibrant Dutch economy was largely unconstrained by guilds. Cf. Lis and Soly (1995, 230).

but to serve as a kind of solvent to undermine, and ultimately to eliminate, the guilds.[47]

At the same time, the enthusiastic reception that Seckendorff's ideas found among the territorial rulers goes far to explain some of the intense urban opposition to admitting the Huguenots, even in cities that the rulers had expected to be receptive. To the extent that the urban dwellers sensed what in fact was true, that the entry of the Huguenots was part of a larger scheme to abolish guilds, their resistance would be all the stronger. Not only guild craftsmen would be threatened, but – especially, as we have seen, in towns of fewer than 10,000 inhabitants – the whole structure of what Walker apostrophized as "German home towns" (M. Walker 1971).

What paved the way for the Huguenots in Germany, or at least among German territorial rulers, was a systemic idea, a far-reaching explanation of what ailed the economies of German cities and the possibility of a radical remedy. Determined, to the extent they could, to override or circumvent urban opposition to their plans, the rulers saw in the Huguenots not only an influx and multiplier of human capital, but a means to reform their economies fundamentally. The success of the endeavor in Brandenburg-Prussia proved to their satisfaction the validity of Seckendorff's radically new ideas.

CONCLUSION

"Germany" in the seventeenth century was a geographical expression rather than a country. The Peace of Westphalia had settled the boundaries and the religious affiliations of its over 300 separate jurisdictions. When the Huguenots, forced unexpectedly to seek asylum, offered an abundance of human capital to the various Protestant German cities and principalities, those jurisdictions' responses ran the gamut from outright rejection[48] to enthusiastic recruitment. Historians almost unanimously view the injection of human capital, where it was permitted or encouraged, as the source of rapid and enduring economic growth. They diverge, however, in their efforts to explain why not all German rulers and cities welcomed so promising an influx.

[47] On the general tendency of rulers to view the granting of "privileges" to the Huguenots as a means of undermining the guild system, see Dölemeyer (1997, 324–325).

[48] Recall that no territorial ruler in our set rejected them; many cities did.

It is standardly asserted that, on the whole, the territorial rulers welcomed the Huguenots more warmly than the cities – indeed, sometimes had to overcome (or yield to) urban opposition. Yet the response varied even among the territorial rulers, and far more among the cities. Urban opposition, majority judgment also has it, was fueled chiefly by the craft guilds, who saw in the Huguenots dangerously superior competitors in many fields and may well have suspected – with reason – that introducing them was part of a larger plan to undermine and ultimately abolish the guilds.

One conclusion, then, has seemed obvious: the greater the power of its guilds, the stronger will have been the city's resistance; and, to the extent that guild power is endogenous, guilds will have been weaker in larger cities, ones nearer to major trade routes, and (possibly) ones that were better endowed with upper-tail human capital or which, having secularized and expanded education, were on their way to developing and attracting more upper-tail capital. On the other hand, wise and well-informed rulers would shy away from settling Huguenots in cities they knew to be likely centers of opposition; hence, all else equal, they would be able to elicit support (or suppress potential opposition) in the cities from which they exercised power, their *Residenzstädte*.

I bring to this contested issue – why similar German jurisdictions responded so differently to this positive shock to the supply of human capital – at least a modicum of data: coding sixty of the more significant Protestant German cities according to whether they rejected, responded hesitantly or inconsistently, welcomed, or actively recruited the Huguenots; and separately coding the posture of the given city's territorial ruler, if it had one. Then, to the extent data are available, I also specify each city's number of inhabitants in the seventeenth century, how big a share of its population it lost in the Thirty Years War, its proximity to the nearest major trade route, whether it had secularized the supply of public goods, its endowment of upper-tail human capital, and whether it was the city in which the territorial ruler resided.

The first important finding is how overwhelmingly the territorial rulers sought to attract the Huguenots: in thirty-four of the fifty-six cities for which we have data – a clear majority – the territorial ruler actively recruited the Huguenots, often offering them generous inducements and privileges – not least, freedom from guild restrictions. In almost 90 percent of the cities (forty-nine of fifty-six), the ruler either welcomed or actively recruited. In not one of our fifty-six cities – although, again, some selection bias in the historical sources may be at work – did the ruler oppose their entry.

The second finding is how often, and how greatly, the response of a city differed from that of its territorial rulers. Only thirteen of the city governments actively recruited the Huguenots, and seven outright rejected them. Astonishingly, among the thirty-four cities whose territorial ruler actively sought to recruit the Huguenots, six rejected the refugees, and four responded inconsistently or hesitatingly to them. In short, in 30 percent of the cities whose territorial ruler actively recruited the Huguenots to settle, the ruler faced reluctance or outright resistance. Given our presumption that the ruler would seek to settle the exiles only in cities where he anticipated little resistance, the extent of the reluctance is all the more impressive. But which cities resisted, and why?

Surprisingly, guild power, at least among the thirty-six of our cities for which Wahl has coded municipal governance, bears no relation to how the Huguenots were received. While Wahl classifies only eight of our cities as having a significant degree of guild influence, those eight differed hardly at all from the other twenty-eight in their response to the Huguenots: in each case, about half welcomed or actively recruited them, and half rejected or temporized.

We should not be surprised, then, to find that most of the supposed concomitants of guild strength or weakness also had little effect. Larger cities were not likelier to welcome the Huguenots (smaller ones were in fact somewhat more welcoming). Cities with high endowments of upper-tail human capital, or which had secularized the provision of public goods earlier, differed hardly at all in their acceptance of the Huguenots from ones that lacked those features. What was supposed to be a check on guild power, the wide representation of all classes that the concept of "burgher representation" encapsulated, was in fact associated with a slight tendency to be less welcoming to the Huguenots.

Among the few things that did matter (at least for predisposing a city to engage in active recruitment) were proximity to a major trade route and the share of population that a city had lost in the Thirty Years War. An even more consistent, but unsurprising, finding was that cities were likelier to welcome the Huguenots if they were the *Residenzstadt* of the ruler, the one where he resided and from which his power presumably radiated.

All of the thirteen cities that actively recruited Huguenots lay within 13 kilometers, and on average fewer than 5 kilometers (for a heavily laden horse-drawn wagon about 1.5 hours) from a major trade route, while the forty-two cities that did not recruit lay on average over 11 kilometers distant from such a trade route. This had little to do with trade's presumed suppression of guild power – indeed, on average the cities with significant guild influence lay closer to trade routes – but likelier with economic vibrancy and opportunity.

The crucial impetus to acceptance of the Huguenots, then, was the eagerness of the territorial rulers to receive them – and their willingness, if necessary, to crush or circumvent urban opposition. The rulers were motivated by the need to repopulate areas devastated in the Thirty Years War, to revive and expand their revenues, and – as the precondition for achieving the first two goals – to stimulate economic growth. Motivated by a powerful set of new ideas, they sought to undermine and ultimately destroy what they had been brought to see as the chief obstacle to economic growth, the guild system that prevailed (but only occasionally dominated politically) in most cities.

It was likely that broader plan, sensed or known within the German cities, that provoked such "prodigious opposition" in many of them – particularly in the smaller ones. Not just guild craftspeople were threatened; so were townspeople in all but the largest, or most trade-oriented, cities. The strongest rulers, as in Brandenburg-Prussia, overcame the opposition and began the breakthrough to rapid economic growth. The weaker or less assertive ones yielded to the opposition, allowed the cities to exclude the Huguenots, and fell behind economically and militarily.

Appendices to Chapter 7

Table A7.1 *Population, and share of population lost in Thirty Years War, of seventeenth-century German cities*[49]

City	City Size: De Vries Coding	Population Loss During Thirty Years War: No Losses, 1–10%, 10–20%, 20–30%, 30–40%, 40–50%, Over 50%
Hamburg	50–99.9k	No Losses
Danzig	50–99.9k	No Losses
Berlin	50–99.9k	30–40%
Dresden	40–49.9k	No Losses

(*continued*)

[49] Source: de Vries (1981, 82–83).

Table A7.1 (*continued*)

City	City Size: De Vries Coding	Population Loss During Thirty Years War: No Losses, 1–10%, 10–20%, 20–30%, 30–40%, 40–50%, Over 50%
Königsberg	30–39.9k	No Losses
Bremen	20–29.9k	No Losses
Lübeck	20–29.9k	No Losses
Frankfurt am Main	20–29.9k	40–50%
Leipzig	20–29.9k	10–20%
Magdeburg	10–19.9k	40–50%
Hannover	10–19.9k	No Losses
Mannheim	10–19.9k	Over 50%
Daubhausen	<10k	40–50%
Hanau	<10k	40–50%
Leonberg	<10k	Over 50%
Maulburg	<10k	20–30%
Todenhausen	<10k	40–50%
Uckermark	<10k	10–20%
Walldorf	<10k	Over 50%
Halle	<10k	Over 50%
Weimar	<10k	0–25%
Diez	<10k	Over 50%
Hötensleben	<10k	No Losses
Mannheim	<10k	Over 50%
Marburg	<10k	50%
Eilenburg	<10k	10–20%
Meissen	<10k	No Losses
Offenbach	<10k	40–50%
Oschatz	<10k	10–20%
Rohrbach	<10k	30–40%
Heidelberg	<10k	Over 50%
Leipzig	<10k	10–20%
Torgau	<10k	No Losses
Brandenburg	<10k	40–50%
Burg	<10k	40–50%
Bützow	<10k	Over 50%
Calbe	<10k	40–50%
Halberstadt	<10k	n/a
Halle (an der Saale)	<10k	10–20%
Hameln	<10k	10–20%
Mecklenburg	<10k	30–40%
Neustadt	<10k	Over 50%
Prenzlau	<10k	40–50%
Ansbach	<10k	30–40%

City	City Size: De Vries Coding	Population Loss During Thirty Years War: No Losses, 1–10%, 10–20%, 20–30%, 30–40%, 40–50%, Over 50%
Bayreuth	<10k	30–40%
Frankfurt an der Oder	<10k	Over 50%
Quedlinburg	<10k	10–20%
Weferlingen	<10k	10–20%
Wolfenbüttel	<10k	No Losses
Celle	<10k	No Losses
Dornholzhausen	<10k	40–50%
Erlangen	<10k	40–50%
Frankenthal	<10k	Over 50%
Friedrichsdorf	<10k	n/a
Holzappel	<10k	Over 50%
Homburg	<10k	40–50%
Karlsruhe	<10k	40–50%
Kassel	<10k	40–50%
Sieburg	<10k	40–50%
Stettin	<10k	20–30%
Lüneburg	<10k	No Losses
Darmstadt	<10k	Over 50%
Stargard	<10k	Over 50%
Stendal	<10k	Over 50%

Table A7.2 Summary statistics and intercorrelations among variables

Variable	Mean	Median	S.D.	Min.	Max.	Count
City Attitude	1.59	2.00	0.98	0.00	3.00	59
Ruler Attitude	2.45	3.00	0.70	1.00	3.00	60
Longitude	51.16	51.30	1.50	47.64	54.35	57
Latitude	10.74	10.61	2.27	7.21	18.64	57
Trade Distance	9.81	5.81	12.36	0.03	51.22	58
Election	0.17	0.00	0.50	0.00	3.00	58
Guild Power	0.28	0.00	0.56	0.00	2.00	58
Burgher Rep.	0.34	0.00	0.48	0.00	1.00	58
Upper-Tail Human Capital	0.55	0.00	1.42	0.00	8.00	58
Church Ordinance	0.44	0.00	0.50	0.00	1.00	84
City of Residence	0.43	0.00	0.50	0.00	1.00	58
Pop. Loss	0.50	0.50	0.50	0.00	1.00	80
Regional Loss	0.51	1.00	0.50	0.00	1.00	61
City Size	0.13	0.00	0.34	0.00	1.00	63

	City Attitude	Ruler Attitude	Longitude	Latitude	Trade Distance	Election	Guild Power	Burgher Rep.	Upper-Tail Human Capital	Church Ordinance	City of Residence	Pop. Loss	Regional Loss	City Size
City Attitude	1.00	0.25	0.09	−0.07	−0.06	0.22	0.09	−0.22	−0.04	−0.01	0.22	0.11	0.02	−0.11
Ruler Attitude		1.00	−0.12	−0.46	0.14	0.12	−0.24	0.07	−0.11	−0.26	−0.06	0.28	0.17	−0.11
Longitude			1.00	0.60	−0.11	−0.28	−0.09	−0.01	0.17	0.32	−0.10	−0.37	−0.44	0.42
Latitude				1.00	0.07	−0.30	−0.04	−0.22	0.23	0.23	−0.05	−0.47	−0.44	0.17
Trade Distance					1.00	0.03	−0.16	−0.28	−0.25	−0.17	−0.16	−0.18	0.20	−0.29
Election						1.00	0.02	−0.03	−0.09	−0.41	−027	0.15	0.24	0.01
Guild Power							1.00	0.10	−002	0.17	0.16	0.08	−0.17	0.07
Burgher Rep.								1.00	−0.05	0.02	0.12	0.10	−0.12	0.35
Upper-Tail Human Capital									1.00	0.26	−0.06	−0.27	−0.23	0.41
Church Ordinance										1.00	0.22	−0.20	−0.35	0.16
City of Residence											1.00	−0.11	−0.22	0.05
Pop. Loss												1.00	0.31	−0.15
Regional Loss													1.00	−0.18
City Size														1.00

8

When the Endogenous Becomes Exogenous

The Printing Press as a Fifteenth-Century Multiplier of Human Capital

We have seen in an earlier chapter how the Black Death, by decimating the *scriptoria* that produced hand-copied literature and raising its price, created strong incentives to devise a less labor-intensive technology for book production. In this sense, the innovations of Johannes Gutenberg (and likely of several less-known predecessors) were endogenous. Like other revolutionary technological breakthroughs (the railroad, the steamship, the cotton gin), however, it so greatly overshot the original need that it became itself a seemingly exogenous shock to supply – in this case, the supply of human capital.

The printing press expanded the supply of human capital both directly, by rendering the skills of scribes and ancillary professions superfluous; and indirectly, (a) by lowering the costs of literacy and making available a greater wealth of reading matter, and (b) making material available in the vernacular, the language that all but a thin elite spoke. No longer was a command of Latin the prerequisite to the acquisition of literacy, or of new knowledge and skills.

Like all positive supply shocks, this one at first threatened earlier owners of the newly abundant factor of production. Unlike other such shocks, a sudden increase in society's supply of human capital can, after even a few years, raise returns to *all* human capital – and, indeed, to other factors of production. This is because, far more than other factors of production, human capital is characterized by large positive externalities: The social return on human capital appears to be from two to three times as large as the individual return (Acemoglu and Angrist 2000, 11).[1] To put it another way, "the rate of return on human capital of a

[1] Acemoglu offers a convincing theoretical explanation for this result: Where search costs are high but investment in human capital is increasing, potential employers will overinvest in physical capital in anticipation of attracting future workers with more

worker is increasing in the human capital stock of the workforce" (Acemoglu 1996, 780).

In the fifteenth and early sixteenth centuries, Europe faced substantial short-term incentives to restrain or even reverse the sudden and unanticipated surge in human capital – not least, because those who already had human capital were politically powerful both in Church and in government. If, however, at least some regions of Europe could leap over those early impediments, even the previous owners of human capital would soon find it to their advantage to allow a yet greater expansion of supply. To a first approximation, and admitting many exceptions, northern and northwestern Europe surmounted that hurdle and accelerated – not only through increased printing but through a rapid expansion of educational institutions – the growth of human capital. Much of southern and central Europe, by way of contrast, restricted printing and otherwise restrained the expansion of human capital. Our task will be to explain these divergent responses.

In the roughly half-century after the invention of printing, however, opposition was often fierce almost everywhere. Not only the scribes and manuscript workshops, but the whole elite of clerics, university graduates, and Latinate scholars found their skills to be suddenly less valuable. Many others could now do what, before the advent of printing, only they could provide. They were obviously tempted to use their political influence to retard or restrict the new "divine art" of mass-producing literature and literacy – as, indeed, the Ottoman Empire, having drawn its lessons from the European experience, subsequently did, forbidding all printing in Arabic script until the early eighteenth century (Coşgel et al. 2012).[2] While the art spread too widely and with too much speed to allow such a total prohibition in fifteenth and sixteenth century Europe, printing could be severely restricted and censored. That indeed was the outcome in much of southern Europe, with the result that literacy spread there far more slowly. In northern and northwestern Europe by way of contrast, and particularly in the Netherlands, printing and literacy expanded swiftly and censorship remained light. The long-term consequences were profound: Printing contributed centrally to, and plausibly actually caused, the Protestant Reformation (Rubin 2014); the Reformation in turn

human capital. Hence even the workers with less human capital will wind up with more physical capital per unit of labor, hence higher productivity (Acemoglu 1996).

[2] The Ottoman rulers allowed printing in Roman, Armenian, and Hebrew characters – which only a small and unthreatening minority of their subjects could read.

expanded schooling and insured the further growth of "thin upper-tail" human capital; and near-universal literacy and extensive education spurred economic growth.

Why, then, resistance in southern Europe and enthusiastic acceptance in much of northern Europe? In this case, I contend, the explanation lies neither in factor substitution nor in exit, but in *factor mobility*: Northern Europe developed whole new sectors that would employ the newly plentiful holders of human capital, and indeed would encourage a yet greater expansion of supply, while southern Europe did not. That is the story that I shall try to tell in this chapter.

BACKDROP: RISING DEMAND AND HIGHER PRICES

The commercial revival of the thirteenth and early fourteenth centuries had created a prosperous urban elite, which was also predominantly literate, since it would have been difficult to transact business, especially over long distances, or to keep accounts, without the ability to write and read. This growing bourgeoisie quickly developed an appetite for literature[3] – for piety, edification, entertainment, and not least as a mark of prestige.[4] Unlike the Latinate clerical and humanist elites, their taste ran to literature in Europe's vernaculars: the Italian of Dante and Petrarch, the Middle English of Langland and Chaucer, and the French, Catalan, and Provençal in which "histories" and "romances" (e.g., *Chanson de Roland, Roman de la rose*) (Barbier 2017, 44–46) were written.[5] The growing universities – starting with Bologna in 1088, there were some fifteen by 1300, by which time Paris alone enrolled some 10,000 students – added to the burgeoning demand for books, albeit almost exclusively in Latin and Greek (Barbier 2017, 24–26).

The pre-printing book market however resembled today's world of art or high fashion more than of literature: It was a "bespoke" trade. Books were created only on commission: Except for a small market in used

[3] Buringh and Van Zanden find that, up to about the thirteenth century, European demand for books came predominantly from monasteries; thereafter, from urban elites and universities (Buringh and Van Zanden 2009, 429–432).

[4] "Book ownership as much as land ownership was a mark of social status and means" (McKitterick, quoted in Buringh and Van Zanden (2009, 410)). Cf. Barbier (2017, 31).

[5] Since men often still found Latin useful in commerce and were likelier to have had some schooling in the language, it has been suggested that newly literate women supplied much of the demand for literature in the vernacular (Overty 2008, 30–31).

books or rentals (chiefly around universities), the purchaser – usually an individual, but sometimes a monastery or a university library – engaged a *scriptorium* or secular workshop to copy a specific work (Barbier 2017, 70). Details of format, illumination, and binding, often subcontracted to specialists, would also be specified, and of course would affect the price; but on average, at least to judge from the few recorded prices, a book went for between a sixth and a third of a typical worker's annual earnings.[6]

Supply rose to meet demand: According to the (admittedly rough) estimates of Buringh and Van Zanden, total European production of manuscripts rose from about 8,000 per year in the twelfth century to almost 20,000 per year in the thirteenth and over 30,000 annually over the fourteenth century (despite the massive slump in demand in the immediate wake of the Black Death) (Buringh and Van Zanden 2009, 416 and 419).[7] The demand stimulated the expansion of secular workshops, especially around universities, and the introduction of slightly more efficient processes (Barbier 2017, 48, 59–61, and 86–87; Buringh and Van Zanden 2009, 425): part-timers who copied merely to supplement their income from regular jobs; the *pecia* system[8] that divided up the copying of a work and regulated quality and prices; the less ornate and hence more quickly copied *bastarda* script; and, perhaps most importantly, the substitution of paper[9] for the far costlier vellum (calfskin; the

6 Overty finds the average price of a book in the Hereford Cathedral Library (one of the few to have recorded valuations) to have been 97 pence in 1300 (Overty 2008, 5), or about £ 0.4, although values ranged from 24 to 360 pence (£0.1–1.5). [For those too young to recall the rococo features of the pre-decimalization British currency, the pound sterling was divided into twenty shillings and each shilling into twelve pence; hence a pound consisted of 240 pence.] The Statute of Laborers of 1351 stated the pre–Black Death wage of an agricultural worker to have been between 1 and 2 pence per day; hence a 100-pence book would have amounted to between 50 and 100 days of labor, out of an annual total (excluding Sundays) of roughly 300 working days. If Dittmar's estimate is correct, that on average books were priced at about 2 pence per page (Dittmar 2012, 15), each page would have cost one or two days' earnings. By that reckoning also, Overty's average 97-pence volume would have amounted to at least two months' earnings (eight six-day weeks).

7 I have divided Buringh and Van Zanden's century totals by 100 to arrive at average *annual* output over the given century.

8 A *pecia* was a quire, i.e., a "piece" of a book; it normally consisted of eight pages and took four days to copy. For details, see Avrin (1991, 218–219).

9 Paper had been used extensively in the Islamic world, including Moorish Spain. It survived the *Reconquista* and migrated from Iberia into the rest of western Europe. An authoritative and detailed account is Avrin (1991, chap. 12). She attributes the surprisingly slow adoption of paper in Europe to its limited demand for books. Only

word has the same root as veal) and parchment (goat- or sheepskin).[10] Yet, as Dittmar has observed, none of these innovations really succeeded in delivering major cost reductions (J. Dittmar 2012, 4); or, perhaps to put it more precisely, the increase in supply barely kept up with the growth in demand. Prices remained high, only to shoot far higher in the wake of the Black Death.

IMPACT OF THE BLACK DEATH

If, between 1347 and 1352, the Black Death reduced Europe's total population by about a third, it claimed an even higher share in monasteries and university quarters. Students, then as now, lived in close proximity to one other; then, one hopes not as now, also in close proximity to rats and fleas. Monks, even if they did not seek specifically to mortify the flesh, rarely aimed to pamper it; as one historian has eloquently noted, the monasteries' "large complement of unwashed bodies, undiscarded food, and dank corridors, were magnets for rats and fleas." (Kelly 2006, 224). Campbell reports an average death rate in the twelve most important English monasteries of 44 percent (Campbell 2016, 308). At Cambridge University, some 40 percent of faculty, and presumably at least as high a share of students, died over a four-month period (Gottfried 1983, 65). Particularly in the second wave of the plague in 1361, Gottfried notes, "Many skilled, highly trained people perished and could not be replaced" (Gottfried 1983, 130 and 155).

Naturally enough, the returns to human capital rose even more than the wages of low-skill labor (Overty 2008, 10). Literacy and numeracy paid well, and people rushed to acquire them. Grammar schools

in the fourteenth century, "when a middle-class and university-educated readership grew," did paper come into general use (Avrin 1991, 294).

10 Avrin describes in detail the arduous process of hand-curing animal skins and estimates that 200–225 hides of sheep or goats were required to produce one bible (Avrin 1991, 210–213). Paper, produced from rags and employing water-powered machinery, cost by many estimates less than one-sixth as much as parchment. We know, for example, that Gutenberg charged 50 gulden for a vellum copy of his Bible and 20 gulden for a paper copy (Pettegree 2010, 29). If Overty's estimate is correct, that labor constituted 75–85 percent of the cost of a typical book (Overty 2008, 5); and, if labor would have been approximately equal as between the paper and the vellum versions, wages would have accounted for 16 gulden (80 percent of the total cost of the cheaper version's 20 gulden) for either version; hence we can infer that paper for the Gutenberg bible cost about 4 gulden, vellum about 34 gulden (50 – 16), or over eight times as much.

proliferated in urban settings, and some eleven new universities were founded in Europe in the century after 1350. Demand for books rose sharply, even as the supply contracted; books naturally shot up in price. The majority of those inventoried in the Hereford Cathedral Library, for example, roughly tripled in price between 1300 and 1400; but over a quarter of them (nine of thirty-three) increased by a factor of four or five (Overty 2008, 4–5). That considerably exceeded the overall increase in nominal prices of 60 to 75 percent in England in the immediate wake of the Black Death (Munro 2004).[11] Given that, according to her estimates, labor constituted at least 75 percent of the cost of a typical pre-printing book, Overty ascribes the spike in book prices directly to the loss of labor – and, in particular, of the skilled labor of the scribes – during the plague (Overty 2008, 10).

INVENTION AND DIFFUSION OF MOVABLE-TYPE PRINTING

Rising prices and a growing market, plus the knowledge that hand-copying could achieve few further efficiencies, created obvious incentives to a labor-saving technological innovation. Those hardly guaranteed the kind of breakthrough that Gutenberg and his associates achieved in 1451; but, once devised, the new technique spread with startling rapidity. By 1470, seventeen cities, including ones as distant from Mainz as Erlangen and Naples, had at least one press (Barbier 2017, 175); by 1480, 110 cities had established a press (although some were short-lived); by 1500, 240 cities (Sasaki 2017, 1013). By the 1520s, Wittenberg alone (as the birthplace of the Reformation) counted just under forty printing establishments (Kissel 2017).

The new technology required considerable capital – a single press, with its typefaces and other ancillary equipment, cost between four and ten year's wages of a skilled worker (J. Dittmar 2011, 1155) – early printers (and their investors) often succumbed to irrational exuberance, and many enterprises failed (including even Gutenberg's) (Barbier 2017, 181–182). Consolidation, however, meant that the surviving presses quickly achieved minimum efficient scale; and the price of books fell by at least two-thirds

[11] As David Herlihy put it succinctly, "men were dying, but coins were not" (Herlihy 1997, 125). Because the same volume of specie was now chasing fewer goods, prices inevitably rose, probably by more on the Continent (where contemporaries recounted that they doubled or tripled) than in England (Chapter 4). Cf. Farmer (1991).

(J. Dittmar 2011, 1133), consistent with Overty's estimate (above) that labor constituted three-quarters of the cost of a hand-copied book.

Demand proved to be enormous: Over twelve million books were printed between 1450 and 1500 (the so-called *incunabula*); between 1500 and 1550, just under 80 million (Buringh and Van Zanden 2009, 417). By way of contrast, in all of the relatively prosperous thirteenth century, fewer than three million books had been hand-copied; and over the whole period from the sixth through the twelfth century, fewer than 1.5 million (Buringh and Van Zanden 2009, 416). Hand-copied production did not yield to printing until around 1480; but the whole fifteenth century produced only five million manuscript works (Buringh and Van Zanden 2009, 419, 416).

Literacy also exploded. Even in 1450, according to the most generous estimates, between 10 and 15 percent of western Europe's adult population could read and write (Barbier 2017, 21; Buringh and Van Zanden 2009, 434). Cheaper books extended access to the less wealthy and enticed those still illiterate to learn to read, especially as books became available in the vernacular. While up to 1500 the great majority of printed works were still in Latin,[12] thereafter printers discovered and expanded a far larger market in the vernacular (Sasaki 2017).[13] To the horror of some scribes (see below), even many printers had no command of Latin. While university classes were still conducted in Latin, and in bastardized form it remained useful as the lingua franca of international commerce, practical works – on arithmetic, bookkeeping, business, law, and administration[14] – as well as ones that merely entertained or that addressed religious themes, appeared in French, German, Italian, Dutch, and English and found an extensive popular market. Translations of the Bible into the vernacular, beginning as early as 1466 (into old high German), proved especially popular, not to mention socially explosive (see below).

Before 1500, only those who could read Latin were regarded as "lettered" (Barbier 2017, 30). Increasingly, after the turn of the sixteenth

[12] The Universal Short Title Catalog (USTC) lists a total of 31,992 titles published between 1450 and 1500, of which 21,118, or roughly two-thirds, were in Latin. www.ustc.ac.uk , accessed September 16, 2020.

[13] In the comparable half-century between 1550 and 1600, 60 percent of new titles (138,617 of 231,606) were in the vernacular. www.ustc.ac.uk, accessed September 16, 2020.

[14] J. Dittmar and Seabold (2020, esp. 8–9) show the pervasiveness and popularity of business-related books; and they find that the frequency with which such books were printed in a given city relates strongly to its subsequent population growth.

century, Latin became for all except lawyers, leading clerics, and university students and faculty a luxury good: a mark of erudition, but hardly a necessity of everyday life or local commerce. In every major town, "grammar schools" appeared, which in most cases taught predominantly in the vernacular.

All of these trends were accelerated by the Reformation, which itself was in large part a consequence of printing (Kissel 2017). The careful econometric work of Jared Rubin has shown that a western or central European city that had at least one printing press by 1500 – seventeen years before Luther nailed his theses to the church door in Wittenberg – was 23 percentage points likelier than one with no printing press in that year to have become Protestant by 1560, and 29 percentage points likelier to have done so by 1600 (Rubin 2014, 280).[15] Luther was not speaking idly when he called the printing press "*das höchste Geschenk, durch welches Gott die Sache des Evangeliums vorantreibt*," "the greatest gift by which God advances the cause of the Gospel."

Most of the German cities that became Protestant, moreover, adopted (often after intense internal conflict) *Kirchenordnungen* (church ordinances) that secularized and expanded the provision of public goods, including above all education. The cities that took this crucial step not only generated more upper-tail human capital, they induced more of it to immigrate from elsewhere (ittmar and Meisenzahl 2019).

Because Luther himself held that salvation was furthered by personal reading of the scriptures, both girls and boys of all classes were to be taught to read (Becker and Woessmann 2009, 540). Teachers often had the additional assignment of traveling through the countryside to recruit especially talented youngsters (Dittmar and Meisenzahl 2019, 963–964). The Reformation, in other words, worked to enlarge the supply of human capital yet further.

YIELD OR RESIST?

Just as the sharp rise in the land-labor ratio after the Black Death had threatened landowners, this sudden and unanticipated glut of human capital threatened the previous possessors of that factor of production,

[15] Rubin guards against endogeneity by using as an instrumental variable for the diffusion of printing distance from Mainz – which is closely related to the time that printing arrived but bears no direct relation to the likelihood of conversion to Protestantism.

that is, the older Latinate scribes, scholars, and above all the Roman Catholic clergy. Famously, one scribe, described by Pettegree as a "dyspeptic Benedictine" with friends in high places, Filippo de Strata, deeply resented this "creative destruction" and complained to the Doge of Venice, no less, that the printers were

> utterly uncouth types of people who have driven reputable [scribes] from their homes … bewailing the damage which results from the printers' cunning. They shamelessly print, at a negligible price … while a true [scribe] dies of hunger[16]

Worse still, according to Filippo, the new technique cheapened and augmented human capital; and it admitted to the reproduction and reading of books people innocent of Latin:

> This is what the printing presses do … brutes rejoice in the fraudulent title of teachers … "For a small sum, men turn themselves into doctors in three years. Let thanks be rendered to the printers!" Any uncultured person without Latin bawls these things. (Pettegree 2010, 43–44)

Filippo's view may have been that of most scribes, likely including even the secular ones; but it was initially embraced by only a minority of the educated elite. Many indeed, welcomed this "divine art" enthusiastically (Eisenstein 2005, chap. 1) and rushed to stock their own libraries with the new, astonishingly cheap versions.[17] Even the Church at first joined the bandwagon, regarding the standardization of print as a remedy for the frequent errors of hand-copying and a means to uniformity of ritual (Eisenstein 2005, 14). Leading prelates often took the initiative in attracting printers to their sees and monasteries (Eisenstein 2005, 14) (Barbier 2017, 169–172). Much of early book production, even into the early sixteenth century, was of works of the Church fathers, missals, or texts of papal decrees; another large category comprised works of, or on, Roman law. Works of piety or devotion (e.g., Books of Hours) also attracted buyers. And the Church profited hugely from the sale of printed indulgences – certificates that a certain number of years, in return for

[16] (https://www.historyofinformation.com/detail.php?entryid=4741).
The literal term here is "writer," but in contemporary usage that meant scribe, not author.

[17] The acknowledged champion in this endeavor was Hernando Colón (1488–1539), son of Christopher Columbus. As a wealthy and peripatetic official of the Habsburg Empire, he purchased books in cities all over Europe and ordered hundreds sent to him from cities he did not visit. He amassed a library of over 15,000 works, including not only books but such ephemera as pamphlets (Pettegree 2010, 87–88) (J. Dittmar and Seabold 2020, 15 and 60).

value given, had been stricken off a named decedent's time in purgatory (Eisenstein 2005, 14).

The Church approached vernacular translations of the Bible with more trepidation. So long as they were intended for serious scholars and theologians, they were a useful supplement to the Latin Vulgate of St. Jerome; perhaps even individual study of the scriptures by the laity could be countenanced. But a papal decree of 1199 had forbidden the private study of the scriptures by groups of laypersons; and a regional synod of Toulouse in 1229, under the threat of the Albigensian heresy, had outlawed lay ownership of the Bible, presumably with only local effect. As printing made vernacular translations more affordable, and as private ownership expanded, the Church's teaching authority – its *magisterium* – grew shakier. What if a sermon, or perhaps even a settled doctrine of the Church, seemed to contradict the clear meaning of scripture?[18]

These flickers of dissent grew into a conflagration with Luther's publication (in German, not his original Latin) of his Ninety-five Theses (including especially his denunciation of indulgences as contrary to scripture) and his rapid translation, into colloquial and readable German, of first the New and then the Old Testament. The "literature of conflict," as Pettegree has styled it, rapidly came to include a blizzard of pamphlets and flyers, from both the Lutheran and the Catholic side, which were devoured by those who could read and read aloud to those who could not (Rubin 2014, 274). Beginning in the 1540s, adherents of John Calvin joined the fray on the anti-Catholic side in Switzerland and France (Pettegree 2010, 208–212).

The Reformation threatened not only Church doctrine and hierarchy, but Church revenues. The breaking of its monopoly of the means of salvation led to what Dittmar and Meisenzahl call "lower cost provision of religious services" (J. E. Dittmar and Meisenzahl 2019, 965). Even in areas merely in close proximity to a Protestant jurisdiction, the Church had to yield some of its privileges and revenues (Cantoni et al. 2018, 2083). An even stronger blow to Church revenues came when Protestant rulers closed the monasteries and secularized their landholdings.

[18] In Augsburg in the early 1520s, a baker's assistant dared to interrupt a Dominican friar's sermon, demanding to know where in the Bible his assertions could be found. When the city council, in response to the Church's demands that the assistant be punished, administered only a rebuke, and the Church protested that the sentence was too light, the council's secretary explained that "the laity were now in a position to correct their preachers' errors ... 'for the Holy Bible and [other books] are now much read by the laity – women and men, young and old – as has never happened before'" (Creasman 2012, 75).

Certainly by the 1550s both the printing press and the flood of human capital it called forth seemed a decidedly mixed blessing, and not only to the Church and the scribes. The elevation of the vernacular and the proliferation of practical and didactic books challenged the long domination of the thin Latinate elite. Many people no longer saw any need for the services of the traditional secular, or even of the clerical, elite. This was of course especially the case where the Reformation had taken root. The threat seemed dire, above all to the Catholic Church, but what to do? With printing having spread to almost all of Europe except its southern and eastern extremities,[19] and with millions of books having come off European presses between 1500 and 1550 (Buringh and Van Zanden 2009, 417),[20] totally outlawing printing seemed hopeless and counterproductive. The few actual attempts to forbid all printing, for example, in France in 1534 and in Bohemia in 1547 (Barbier 2017, 245), proved the point; the prohibitions lapsed within a year. Printing was too useful – in commerce, in administration, and as a tool of Church indoctrination – to be completely suppressed.

Instead, one could to some extent choke off the growing supply of human capital by censoring the press and maintaining strict control of education. The Church turned to licensing and censorship of the press even before the Reformation (Barbier 2017, 261–267),[21] but both intensified as the Reformation challenge deepened. Where previously only pre-publication censorship or post-publication seizure and fines were imposed (Creasman 2012, 53), now authors and printers faced the death penalty (Barbier 2017, 265); and mere possession of forbidden works[22] could be treated as evidence of heresy (Pettegree 2010, 206).

Certainly Protestants also imposed censorship. Both Luther and Calvin regarded it as necessary (Barbier 2017, 266–267). The Protestant touch however was lighter, its penalties less severe; and, lacking the central authority of the papacy, Protestants could rarely agree on *which* books

[19] Otherwise large and thriving cities, such as Lisbon, Granada, Naples, and Prague had either no presses or minuscule output from very few (Barbier 2017, 178).

[20] Against the 80 million volumes that Buringh and van Zanden estimate, the USTC counts some 112,000 distinct titles; so the average press run for a given title, if both estimates are correct, must have been about 700.

[21] Papal bulls of 1501 and 1515 instituted prior censorship; the latter decreed that no book should be published without the authorization of the Church (Barbier 2017, 263).

[22] Regional indices of forbidden books began to proliferate after 1545; the first papal index appeared in 1558 and "included some 8000 forbidden titles and a list of sixty-one printers whose entire production was prohibited" (Barbier 2017, 264).

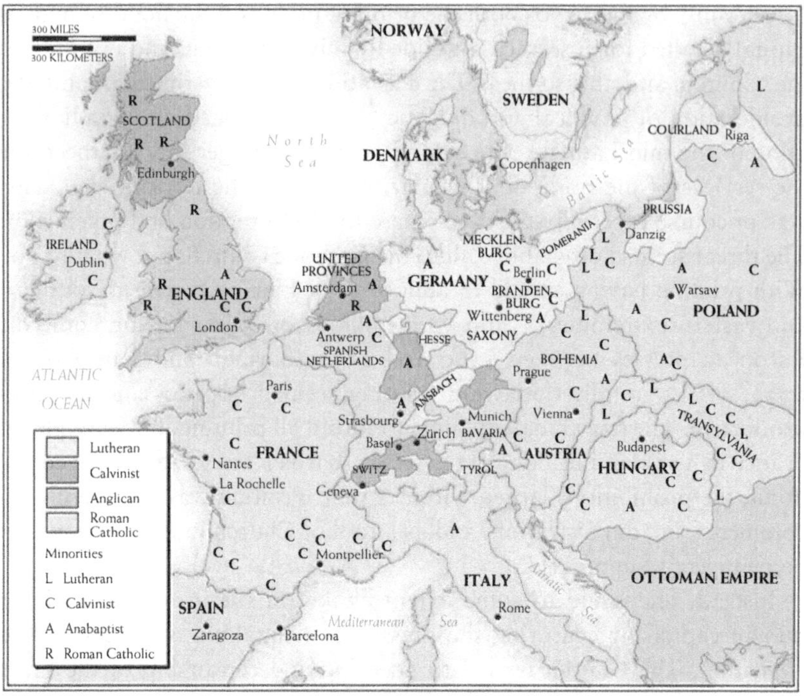

Map 8.1 Religious boundaries in Europe, ca. 1600[23]

to forbid. The Holy Roman Empire, to be sure, nominally introduced centralized censorship (Eisenhardt 1970). But the Empire was fragmented and decentralized, and books could easily cross borders. Because enforcement of the central prohibitions was left to the regional authorities (*Landesfürsten*), some of whom drew prestige and revenue from annual book fairs (Frankfurt, Leipzig), in northern European reality only the most scandalous books were suppressed (Creasman 2012, 5 and 135).

With some exceptions, then, most of Catholic Europe censored; most of Protestant Europe did so only lightly or ineffectively. The increasing geographical division along religious lines led to a massive movement of people, and of printers, fleeing persecution (Pettegree 2010, 207). By 1600 the religious map of Europe showed how much self-sorting had occurred (Map 8.1). The Protestant areas were those in which publishing was relatively free and human capital grew rapidly; the Catholic ones

[23] Source: (Kagan et al. (2010, 315), reprinted by permission of Prentice-Hall publishers.

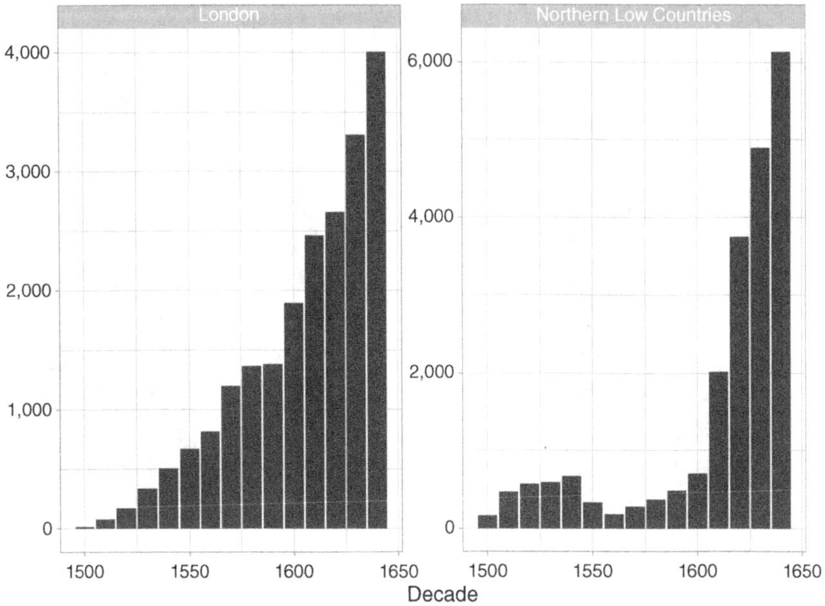

Figure 8.1 Number of titles printed each decade in Protestant region or city, 1500–1650

were subject to censorship (especially rigid in Spain) and saw a smaller increase in human capital, if any.

Predictably, the center of European publishing began to move. Growth was clearly most rapid in the Protestant (northern) parts of the Low Countries and London. The USTC allows one to generate timelines of decadal production of distinct titles. In the half-century between 1600 and 1650, production in London more than doubled (from fewer than 200 titles to 400 annually) and in the northern Low Countries more than sextupled (from fewer than 100 to over 600 annually) (Figure 8.1).

By contrast, the issuance of new titles fell sharply in the Italian City-States (including Venice, one of Europe's early centers of printing).[24] After peaking at over 1200 volumes annually between 1610 and 1620, production there had fallen by 1650 by 25 percent. Production in Paris stagnated at about 500 volumes annually, albeit with sharp fluctuations.[25] In Madrid, production grew rapidly from an initially risible level

[24] In the last five years of the fifteenth century, Venice had printed the second highest number of titles of all European cities (Barbier 2017, 179).

[25] After increasing in the late 1640s, printing in Paris fell rapidly again in the 1660s, as Colbert imposed strict censorship and limited the number of print shops to thirty

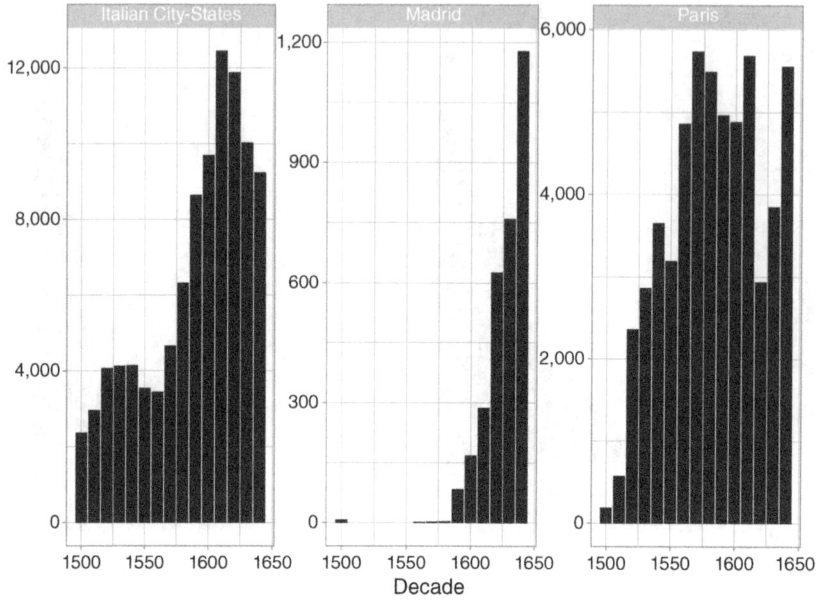

Figure 8.2 Number of titles printed each decade in Catholic region or city, 1500–1630

but by the 1640s amounted to only 120 titles annually (Figure 8.2). The overall pattern seems clear: rapid growth in the Netherlands and London, stagnation in Paris, decline in Italy; and, in Madrid, growth only to a level that was dwarfed by that of other major cities.[26] Martin, in his magisterial overview of European printing in the seventeenth century, notes the "singular contrast" between the "relative vacuum" in Spain or the "stagnation" in Italy, and "what one can observe to the north and the east of France," that is, in the Low Countries and Germany (Martin 1984, 28).

Reading shifted even more rapidly than printing. By the first half of the seventeenth century, the Protestant Netherlands had become the undisputed center of European readership, consuming a then astonishing 140 books annually per thousand, or one book for every seven, persons; England came second, purchasing eighty annually per thousand; and

(from an initial total of seventy-nine). The result, as Soll notes concisely, was that "Colbert's state regulation succeeded in strangling the once great Parisian book industry" (Soll 2009, 130–131). Moreover, of the volumes from this period that have survived in the holdings of the *Bibliothèque nationale*, a steadily rising share (after 1680, over 40 percent) are on religious topics, as against roughly 15 percent in arts and sciences (Martin 1984, 1065).

[26] All results are from USTC, accessed September 6, 2022, by Jacob Morrier.

Germany, despite the plunder and bloodshed of the Thirty Years War (1618–1648), stood third, at fifty-four per thousand souls annually. Italy had fallen to fifth place in book consumption: Forty-two volumes annually per thousand inhabitants. Even backward (but Protestant) Sweden managed forty volumes annually per thousand, roughly the average for western Europe as a whole. Among Catholic states, France was the signal exception: Fifty-two volumes annually per thousand of population, or one for every twentieth person (Buringh and Van Zanden 2009, 421).[27] As early as 1500, eight of the ten German cities that printed the most were ones that later became Protestant (Rubin 2014, 273). Northern Europe welcomed both the growth of human capital and the Reformation; southern and southeastern Europe remained largely Catholic and did not.

WHAT CAN EXPLAIN THE GEOGRAPHICAL SPLIT?

In this instance, as in the others studied here, we see divergent responses to a common supply shock. Here, however, we must bear in mind three important differences.

1. Because of human capital's large positive externalities, any move to accept an augmented supply will, despite initial resistance, almost certainly become self-sustaining. As the supply of human capital grows, so do its social benefits, the uses to which it is put, and the demand for it.
2. Precisely because of the inexorable tendency of human capital to multiply – what we might call its "sorcerer's apprentice" character – the answer cannot lie simply in using human capital more intensively in existing sectors and technologies. Existing production technologies will certainly adjust to use newly cheap human capital more intensively, but that hardly suffices to solve the problem. It is as if the European landowners, after the Black Death, faced not only a sudden relative abundance of land, but a seemingly endless proliferation of land: a supply that grew at a steadily accelerating pace.

[27] Because of Colbert's strict censorship, however, many of the books that were read in France had been smuggled in from the Netherlands. Sporadic attempts at border control were largely evaded. Colbert considered attempting to ban *all* imports of books but was eventually persuaded that such a blanket prohibition would be inimical to learning and – more importantly – would be almost impossible to enforce (Soll 2009, 132–133).

3. In contrast to sudden shortages that create incentives to adopt or invent factor-saving technologies, this kind of sudden abundance invites no obvious technological "fix." Even if new technologies could make better use of the other factors, rendered relatively scarce by the surge in human capital, that could hardly alleviate the threat that the elite of priesthood and learning perceived.

As indicated in Chapter 2, there remains one other salient path of adjustment: *factor mobility*, the movement of overabundant factors into other sectors or regions where they are in greater demand. The sudden cheapening of human capital incentivized the creation of whole new sectors that could use it productively. Two such sectors indeed arose fortuitously in this period in northern Europe: *state bureaucracy* and *long-range commerce*. The former was likely the more important of the two and was unique to northern Europe. Bureaucratic absolutism, indeed, may have arisen in northern Europe in this period precisely because human capital had suddenly become so abundant – and because ambitious rulers saw how that capital could be used to build the strong states that their survival required.

State bureaucracy. In southern, or "Latin," Europe (France, Italy, and Iberia) states arose early – in France and Spain, as early as the thirteenth century – from the rubble of the Carolingian Empire and its welter of small principalities. Notoriously, however, these early states suffered, despite their outward pomp, from serious weaknesses. Desperate for money to fight their frequent wars, they had often resorted to the sale of offices and had even (for payment of a yet higher price) permitted those offices to become hereditary. Moreover, in their rush to enlarge their domains, these rulers often incorporated new territories only by granting them substantial administrative and legal autonomy. The rulers neither fully controlled their "proprietary" bureaucracies – ones in which the holders of the positions in some sense "owned" their offices – nor imposed anything resembling uniform law and administration throughout their nominal domains.

The nascent states of northern Europe, and particularly of Germany, emerged by contrast only later, beginning in the last decade of the fifteenth century (Ertman 1997, 243).[28] Out of the literally hundreds of

[28] The first, according to Ertman (*loc. cit.*), were the Austrian domains of Maximilian I (reforms carried out 1493–1497), Saxony (1499), and Bavaria (1501). Maximilian's reforms emulated in many respects ones that the Netherlands had pioneered.

small principalities,[29] often with unclear and overlapping jurisdictions, there swiftly emerged some two dozen increasingly sovereign states (Ertman 1997, 237). Their ambitious rulers were intent on avoiding what they saw as the mistakes of the Latin monarchies, and they faced heavy external threats, not least from each other. Each ruler, if he wanted to survive, sought unwaveringly to create a strong and independent state, staffed by bureaucrats (*Beamten*) who would be both highly skilled and loyal only to him.[30]

The opportunity that these emerging rulers saw lay precisely in the sudden abundance of human capital. The most important reason for the rapid emergence of these strong, non-proprietary bureaucracies was that

> ... the administrative and legal skills which government officials possessed [and required] were no longer the rare commodities they had been in the thirteenth and fourteenth centuries, and hence could not be used to extort concessions from their rulers. (Ertman 1997, 244)

The surge in the supply of human capital had so cheapened it, in contrast to earlier centuries, that every aspiring ruler could avail himself of it. Not only could those skilled in law and administration no longer demand privileges or high compensation, but rulers could pick and choose. In the realm of human capital, it was suddenly a buyer's market.

At the same time, the emergence of military and geopolitical contestation among these rapidly expanding states forced each, once any had begun the process, to develop as swiftly as possible these powerful administrative instruments to enforce their rule, raise revenues, and sustain a military.[31] Any ruler who hesitated might see his principality sink into insignificance – or, likelier, be annexed to some more powerful neighboring state.

The process of state formation was further accelerated by the Reformation, which – by confiscating the extensive lands of the monasteries – greatly expanded the revenues of the secular rulers (Cantoni, Dittmar, and Yuchtman 2018, 2054–2058). While part of the revenues

[29] In 1500 there were just over 300 principalities (just under half ecclesiastical, the rest lay) and 85 free (i.e., self-governing) Imperial cities, but over 2000 autonomous "knightly" (*Reichsritterliche*) domains (Ertman 1997, 233).

[30] The "laicization" of the governmental elite had begun in some areas as early as the thirteenth century and had accelerated in the wake of the Black Death (Gottfried 1983, 145–146); bureaucratic absolutism, however, emerged only in the course of the sixteenth century (Anderson 1979, 15).

[31] Note the remarkable speed with which Saxony and Bavaria emulated the example of Austria.

went to the construction of lavish palaces, rulers for the most part "demanded more labor ... for the administration of their territory" (Cantoni, Dittmar, and Yuchtman 2018, 2060). Now, at least in Protestant Europe, the supply of human capital rose again to meet growing demand. In the Protestant universities, but only in them, enrollments in theology fell, to be supplanted by the study of law and the other secular subjects that would fit graduates for temporal and administrative offices[32] – to which, by all evidence, they increasingly turned. Moreover, new universities continued to be founded – between the Black Death and 1600, some twenty-eight in all, including such renowned institutions as Tübingen, Uppsala, Edinburgh, and Leiden – "producing a steady stream of graduates trained in Roman and canon law suitable for positions in government service" (Ertman 1997, 244).[33]

Long-range commerce. While southern Europe, and particularly Italy, had long been Europe's entrepôt for the lucrative Silk Road trade in Asian spices and fabrics, the last decade of the fifteenth century also, fortuitously, began Italy's precipitous decline, to be supplanted briefly by Portugal and soon thereafter by the Netherlands and England. Vasco da Gama's opening of a sea route to Asia in 1498 drastically reduced profits from the arduous overland journey through central Asia to the Red Sea and the Mediterranean, which had been the backbone of Italy's long-range commerce (Neal and Cameron 2016, 126). That, coupled with Columbus's voyages to the Americas in the 1490s, began a rapid shift of Europe's long-range commerce to Atlantic seaports, which soon concentrated on the flourishing harbors of the Netherlands – first Bruges, then Antwerp, and finally Amsterdam – and the secondary ones of London and Hamburg (Neal and Cameron 2016, 132). From these, trade radiated out in all directions, but it remained most intense in northern Europe.[34]

[32] Before the Reformation, in the universities that later became Protestant, as well as those that remained Catholic, approximately 10 percent of students majored in theology. By 1600, theology enrolled in Protestant universities fewer than 2 percent of students, but in Catholic universities (despite an initial dip to about 5 percent) still about 9 percent (Cantoni, Dittmar, and Yuchtman 2018, 2072).

[33] For a comprehensive list, see https://en.wikipedia.org/wiki/List_of_oldest_universities_in_continuous_operation#Founded_as_universities_before_1500.

[34] Spain of course rapidly established its presence in the New World in the early sixteenth century. But the aim of the aptly named conquistadors was plunder rather than commerce. By stealing so much of South America's gold and silver, they both set off a Europe-wide inflation (the "price revolution" of the sixteenth century) and inflicted on their homeland a severe bout of "Dutch disease" that stunted Spanish

Long-distance trade, as the Italians had already learned, demanded an extensive array of skills: double-entry bookkeeping, a variety of languages (still including Latin as the European lingua franca), banking, the writing of binding contracts, knowledge of foreign markets and mores. Here, in short, any excess of human capital could find employment, likely even more lucrative (if riskier) than in rulers' expanding bureaucracies.

Again, however, this alternative employment of human capital, long available in Italy and then for a short time in Portugal, soon came to be specific to northern Europe. There, it remained a predominantly Protestant pursuit,[35] although the Netherlands, as the center of long-distance trade, practiced even in the sixteenth century extensive religious toleration.

CONCLUSION

The printing press responded to an acute shortage of a particular kind of human capital, that of the scribes who hand-copied books, coupled with steeply rising demand for books and correspondingly high prices. By bringing the price of books down to a third or less of their previous level, printing broadened readership, encouraged literacy (especially in the vernacular), and – particularly after the Reformation – made education more widely available. In short, the press turned what had been a shortage of human capital into an exponentially growing abundance – a positive shock to its supply.

That shock, and the cheapening of human capital that it entailed, threatened not only the wealth and incomes, but the status and authority, of that asset's previous monopolists: above all the clerics, but also the scribes and scholars who read and wrote chiefly (often only) in Latin. As the threat deepened, they were inevitably tempted to restrict printing, if not by prohibiting it, then by keeping it under the strict limitations of censorship. Those fears became acute after 1517, when the Reformation threatened – by further expanding education and mandating the reading of the Bible in the vernacular – not only the Church's "monopoly of salvation" but its extensive wealth and landholdings and, to boot, the

manufacturers and made them importers, rather than traders, of goods (Drelichman 2005). The parallel to today's petrostates is both accurate and illuminating.

[35] Max Weber was supposedly inspired to begin his research for *The Protestant Ethic and the Spirit of Capitalism* by noticing, somewhat to his surprise, that the students enrolled in *Betriebswirtschaft* (business administration) at Heidelberg were overwhelmingly Protestant. See also Weber (2013, 3).

livelihoods of the rest of the Latinate elite. That the Reformation had been propagated, and perhaps even caused, by printing argued additionally for its strict control.

Censorship indeed came to prevail, and the Catholic Church's monopoly of salvation to persist, in southern Europe and France – a.k.a. "Latin" Europe.[36] Censorship was practiced lightly and ineffectually, if at all, in most of Protestant Europe – least of all in the Netherlands.[37]

The divergent responses had profound long-term effects, chiefly because human capital has large positive externalities: Its social return, as noted earlier, appears to be two to three times as large as its individual return. Where it was encouraged to multiply, it rapidly stimulated economic growth; where it was choked off, economic growth was much slower. Southern Europe remained poorer and less literate than the North.

So why this disparate reaction to a common supply shock? The answer advanced here is *factor mobility*: Demand for human capital grew so rapidly in previously small or non-existent sectors that not only was the shock quickly absorbed, but demand began again to outstrip supply – leading to a further expansion of education at all levels.

The two sectors that absorbed the most human capital, indeed provided voracious demand for it, were (a) the nascent *administrative structures* of bureaucratic absolutism and (b) *long-range commerce*. The former likely responded directly to the sudden abundance of human capital and spread rapidly, by a sort of "domino effect," because of geopolitical pressures. Out of the hundreds of late Medieval jurisdictions within the Holy Roman Empire, some two dozen began suddenly to emerge as powerful, increasingly sovereign, states with pronounced expansionist ambitions. As relative "latecomers" to state-building, they sought to avoid the weaknesses – in particular, limited sovereignty and a proprietary bureaucracy characterized by *vénalité des offices* – of the states of Latin Europe that had consolidated earlier; and the abundance of human capital gave them a way: recruit, for manageable compensation, able "non-proprietary" administrators of proven ability and undoubted loyalty. Doing so greatly expanded a state's extractive capacities and its

36 The strictness of censorship of course varied within Catholic Europe: extremely restrictive in the Spain of the Inquisition and in the papal states, less so in France.

37 Even Protestant jurisdictions that attempted to censor found themselves undermined by the fragmentation of sovereignty and the porousness of borders: Ostensibly forbidden works could usually be smuggled in.

military power; and, precisely for that reason, most states quickly emulated the first to do so. That this wave of state formation, bureaucratization, and strengthening began precisely in the last decade of the fifteenth century suggests its link – which historians have expressly noted – to that period's abundance of human capital.

More fortuitously, long-range commerce, first with Asia and then with Americas, began to shift its center from Italy to northern Europe in that same final decade of the fifteenth century. Improved ships and navigation, allowing longer-range voyages, were – no less than the printing press – an indirect result of the Black Death's labor shortages. With these new tools, however, Vasco da Gama and Christopher Columbus opened the new routes of trade and conquest that allowed Atlantic ports to displace Mediterranean ones as the main channels of Europe's growing commerce. Where the rise of bureaucratic absolutism was likely in large part endogenous – it came about *because* of the abundance of human capital – the shift of long-range commerce to northern Europe, and particularly to the Netherlands, was exogenous. It nonetheless developed a voracious appetite for human capital: for correspondence, contracting, litigating, and bookkeeping.

Taken together, these new and expanding sectors could absorb all of the sudden abundance of human capital and demand yet more – from schools, apprenticeships, and universities. These new sectors supported, benefited from, and furthered the Reformation; and it was in the Protestant universities that students increasingly devoted themselves to precisely the subjects that the new sectors required. Hence, far from resisting either printing or the explosion of human capital, Protestant northern Europe embraced both. First Amsterdam, and later London, became Europe's great centers of publishing, commerce, and Protestantism.

The exogenous shock of printing was welcomed where the burgeoning factor of human capital proved itself to be mobile to new sectors of employment; it was resisted and suppressed, to the region's long-term detriment, where human capital – largely for exogenous reasons – revealed itself to be immobile.

9

Conclusion

The Role of Other Factors, Including Institutions, Ideas, and Human Agency

What determines, then, how people and governments react to supply shocks? Why do their responses to the same shock often differ so radically, across and within regions? Do variables other than the three I have emphasized – the possibilities of factor substitution, of exit (to another sector or jurisdiction), or of a factor-saving new technology – affect how, or whether, they will adjust? In all of the cases studied here, exogenous factors – or, at any rate, ones outside any immediate control by the actors – have proven determinative: whether soil and climate permitted factor substitution; how external military threat compelled railroads, industrialization, and the opening of new lands; why the trauma of wartime starvation might have opened minds to the sanguinary fantasy of *Lebensraum*; how the emergence of new trade routes and of competition among nascent states absorbed and encouraged the flood of human capital unleashed by the printing press.

What of institutions, which surely a political scientist ignores at his peril? Or culture and ideas, whose importance even economists nowadays often stress? Are some cultures more open to innovation, hence likelier to conjure up a technological response to a supply shock? What role do leaders – good or bad, wise or foolish – play? And, ultimately, don't ordinary individuals decide – to rebel or to acquiesce, to stay or to leave, to support or to reject some political movement? What is the role of human agency in responding to supply shocks?

My short answer is that, yes, all of these things matter – but, except for one kind of idea, only at the margins. In the face of the kinds of extreme and unanticipated shocks on which this book has focused, the others prove surprisingly, perhaps even depressingly, malleable. In short, institutions and ideas are largely endogenous; and leaders and ordinary individuals are mostly compelled by circumstances. The possibilities of factor substitution, exit, and technology are almost always determinative.

Preliminarily, we must consider what "making a difference" in the face of a supply shock means. In a bad sense, it could mean avoiding or obstructing a readily available non-coercive adaptation. We saw in Chapter 4 one example in miniature: the English abbey of Bury St. Edmunds, which stubbornly clung to labor-intensive agriculture when labor had become scarce – and which lost ground, economically and politically, as a result. We know that, in the wake of the print revolution and the Reformation, theology enrollments declined sharply in Protestant universities; but some students continued to major in theology, and perhaps even some universities retained it as their principal course of study. Failing to fit themselves, or their students, to the hugely expanding demand for human capital in chancelleries and commerce, they renounced the adaptive avenue of intersectoral mobility. Even, or perhaps especially, a technological solution to a supply shock often fails to bea-dopted among some individuals and rulers. Firearms, as we have seen, were a technological response to the labor shortage that followed the Black Death: They made each individual soldier far more effective. Despite the intense competitive pressures, however, some rulers doubtless held back and retained older methods of warfare. Most are lost to history, for the good reason that others conquered them and annexed their territories.

"Making a difference" in the good sense would mean either (a) rapidly adapting to the shock by one of our three standard ways or (b) in circumstances where no such adaptation is possible, either (1) accepting reduced circumstances or (2) seeking the least costly coercive solution. Weimar Germany, as analyzed in Chapter 6 and discussed more summarily below, provides a cautionary example.

So: Do institutions, ideas, culture, leaders, or human agency really matter, for good or ill? Faced with a large, exogenous, and unanticipated shock to the supply of some crucial factor of production, do any of these otherwise important features of society discern or obscure, significantly accelerate or impede, a least costly response?

INSTITUTIONS

Institutions strongly affect response to a change in supply that is (a) endogenous or otherwise foreseeable or (b) of modest proportions. The flood of New World grain and meat onto the markets of Europe after 1875 was both endogenous – it resulted from improvements in transportation (steamships, refrigeration) that had been expressly devised to allow those profitable flows – and foreseeable in its consequences, at least to all with even a rudimentary knowledge of markets.[1] And here, as has often been observed, institutions mattered greatly: The entrenched power of the Prussian landowning elite in the institutions of the German Empire allowed the adoption of protective tariffs that, in all likelihood, no more democratic system would have countenanced; while the wider franchise in the United Kingdom, instituted by the Second Reform Act of 1867, quashed from the outset any movement toward reviving the Corn Laws – as Benjamin Disraeli patiently explained to choleric Tory landowners (Blake 1966, 664). In France, too, the broad franchise of the Third Republic empowered smallholding peasants – heirs of the Revolutionary land settlement – to force the adoption of the Méline Tariff in 1892. German and French farmers could access the coercive power of the state at low cost and hence did not adjust; British landowners, many of whom were farsighted enough to have done so in advance, diversified their portfolios and moved out of sole dependence on land rents (Schonhardt-Bailey 1991).

We have also seen, however, how institutions can be neutered, ignored, or swept aside in the face of a large and unanticipated shock. Neither royal power nor parliamentary enactment could suppress wages or strengthen serfdom in post–Black Death England; nor, in eastern Europe, did the nominal right of peasants to appeal to the territorial ruler avail much against the depredations of the landowners. Less than a century ago, the unanticipated shock of the Great Depression toppled democracies – admittedly, young and often feeble ones – in favor of dictatorships not only in Weimar Germany but in Yugoslavia, Romania, Latvia, Estonia, Bulgaria, Greece, and Spain (Frieden 2006, 209).

Perhaps the most tenacious institutions, for reasons that North and Thomas expounded a half-century ago, are property rights (North and Thomas 1973, 4–8). In Europe between the two World Wars, as we have seen, amalgamating tiny peasant holdings into farms of efficient size – that is, ones that could have taken advantage of newly available mechanized tillage (Juma 2019, chap. 5)[2] – proved too slow and politically too

[1] The drop in British wheat prices of over 50 percent between the late 1860s and the mid-1890s inevitably entailed a similar decline in the market value of cropland suitable only for wheat.

[2] The first commercially successful tractor, the small Fordson, appeared on the US market only in 1917; the much more versatile McCormick-Deering Farmall, in 1924.

daunting.[3] Nonetheless, under extreme pressure and often at high cost, property rights do change: The breaking up of large manors revolutionized Dutch farming; enclosures, somewhat later, did the same for English agriculture (North and Thomas 1973, 142–144, 150–151). From the eighteenth through the twentieth centuries, seizure by eminent domain made possible the canals, railroads, and motor roads that revolutionized transportation.

Institutions, then – or so I contend – are "sticky" but endogenous. They may channel or impede reaction to a moderate or foreseeable shock; but an extreme enough exogenous supply shock will alter institutions, albeit often with some delay.

IDEAS AND IDEOLOGIES

In perhaps the most famous passage of the *General Theory of Employment, Interest, and Money*, Keynes asserted that "the world is ruled by little else" than "the ideas of economists and political philosophers" (Keynes 1936, 383). Even allowing for professional hubris, Keynes was at most half-right. Ideas are powerful only when they accord with, and account for, experience.

It will be helpful first to distinguish two kinds of ideas, which I'll label "passionate" and "systemic." *Passionate* ideas simply express strong preferences and are inherently prescriptive: Using fewer fossil fuels, financing better infrastructure, expanding higher education, or liberalizing trade are (to use the common parlance) "good ideas." Ideas of this kind are highly malleable: When one discovers that abandoning fossil fuels or financing infrastructure would cost far more than imagined, or that greater trade openness would threaten one's own livelihood, a formerly "good" idea quickly becomes "bad" and is opposed or abandoned. Thus the passion of Prussian *Junker* for free trade and the ideas of Adam Smith quickly became in less than a year an equally passionate embrace of protection and more specifically the ideas of Friedrich List (Gerschenkron 1966, 42–43). Passionate ideas are little more than an expression of interest and can shift quickly when interests change.

As late as 1928, only about one US farm in every eight had a tractor (782,000 tractors, 6.5 million farms) (Juma 2019, 126) (US Bureau of the Census 1920, 24).

[3] In Weimar Germany, the payoff not only seemed too distant and too small, but the "export powerhouse" strategy seemed far more promising. See Chapter 6 in this volume.

Systemic ideas, which are what Keynes had in mind, are what Lippman called the "pictures in our heads" that tell us how the world works (Lippmann 1922, chap. 1). Ideas of this kind describe an interlocking and internally self-consistent mechanism with definite predictions about how changing one aspect will inevitably change others. Classical economics, including Say's Law, was emphatically such an idea (and, of course, the one that Keynes repudiated). A smoothly running economy depended on the gold standard, a frugal government, free markets, security of property, and reliable enforcement of contracts. Abandon any of these, and disaster would follow: uncontrolled inflation, capital flight, and ultimately economic collapse. Thus, the defenders of orthodox policy were not just (or even) expressing their own interests (certainly Britain's minority Labour government in 1929–1931 understood that their deflationary policies were harming their own constituents) but doing what seemed imperative to prevent systemic collapse.

As the Great Depression persisted and deepened, belying the classical economists' assurances that it would quickly resolve, leaders in several countries – Sweden, the USA, and not least Nazi Germany – began to experiment with heterodox policies, even before Keynes's intellectual revolution could take hold (Frieden 2006, 202–205; Weir and Skocpol 1985). Nor is it an accident that the world was so receptive, precisely in those years, to Keynes's radical rejection of the systemic ideas of classical economics.

Similarly, from the time of Hippocrates into the later nineteenth century, disease was explained by "miasma," or "bad air," in which the odors of decomposition sickened people (Winslow 1943, 256).[4] Even after the work of Louis Pasteur, indeed well into the twentieth century in the USA, many physicians and epidemiologists continued to reject the germ theory of disease (Gordon 2016, 232; Winslow 1943, chap. 15).[5] The miasmatic theory was abandoned only as it became clear that no amount of greenery could prevent disease, but that vaccines – based on attenuated versions of the causative microbes – were highly effective in doing so.

As both examples demonstrate, systemic ideas can be remarkably tenacious. They yield only to contrary experience, and to an equally comprehensive systemic idea that accords better with experience.

[4] A surprising side benefit of the "miasmatic" theory was the nineteenth-century movement to establish urban green spaces, including Frederick Law Olmstead's Central Park in Manhattan (Szczygiel and Hewitt 2000).

[5] In 1892, a Munich professor and several of his students publicly swallowed virulent cultures of the bacillus that Robert Koch had already identified as the cause of cholera, to "prove" that, absent other factors, the bacillus was harmless (Winslow 1943, 312).

The most comprehensive kind of systemic idea is an *ideology* – or, to use what was originally a German term, a "world view" (*Weltanschauung*). An ideology constitutes almost a "theory of everything," a comprehensive explanation of whole domains of historical development. Friedrich Engels was not wrong when, in his speech at the graveside of Marx, he asserted that, "Just as Darwin discovered the law of development of organic nature, so Marx discovered the law of development of human history" (Marx and Engels 1978, 681). The more comprehensive such an edifice is, the harder it is to abandon; indeed, the first reaction to seemingly contradictory evidence is often to invent the equivalent of Ptolemaic epicycles.[6] Actual abandonment entails what Thomas Kuhn labeled a "paradigm shift," that is, displacement of one ideology by another that is more accurate and at least equally comprehensive (Kuhn 1996).

Yet here, too, "more difficult to displace" is not the same as "impossible to displace." The extreme supply shock that ensued from the introduction of movable-type printing (See Chapter 7 in this volume) sufficed to dislodge, at least in much of Europe, the seemingly impregnable edifice of Roman Catholic theology and papal authority.

To sum up: Passionate ideas are easily overthrown, systemic ideas much harder to dislodge, ideologies (in the sense of *Weltanschauungen*) even more tenacious. At the margin, and in the face of mild shocks or the early stages of larger ones, they are indeed likely to channel or impede responses. Yet a big enough supply shock suffices to dislodge even the most comprehensive ideology. Ideas are impediments, but not insuperable obstacles, to action.

On the other hand, as we have seen in the case of the Huguenots, early adopters of a more accurate systemic idea – in that case, rulers who rejected the importance of craft guilds and embraced free competition and the rapid accumulation of human capital – can gain a powerful advantage over those who cling to the obviated ideology.

CULTURE

The late Alberto Alesina pioneered the field now known as the Political Economy of Culture and moved the National Bureau of Economic Research (NBER), as early as 2010, to begin an ongoing series of conferences

[6] In response to Darwin, and as geological and fossil evidence accumulated, traditional Christianity resorted to increasingly convoluted efforts to rescue the Biblical account of creation (Wood 2019, 7–17).

on the "Economics of Culture and Institutions" (https://www.nber.org/conferences/economics-culture-and-institutions-spring-2021). Among the leading practitioners of this field, "culture" is understood, not in the nebulous sense common to anthropologists and sociologists, but as evolved norms and practices that serve as mental shortcuts – in Daniel Kahneman's trenchant phrase, ways of "thinking fast" (Kahneman 2011) – to prescribe socially optimal conduct.

Aspects of culture often have ancient roots and long lives – and, over time, can become markedly suboptimal. People of African ancestry whose forebears came from regions that were heavily raided for slaves continue to exhibit lower levels of interpersonal trust (Nunn and Wantchekon 2011); populations whose ancestors adopted the plow (which demanded more physical strength, and hence favored males), or who come from regions whose climate and soil favored use of the plow, are characterized even today by lower female participation in the labor market and fewer women in leadership roles (Alesina et al. 2013).

Despite their antiquity and persistence, these norms, too, can change under large shocks. We have seen earlier how the Black Death, by moving western Europe toward sedentary animal husbandry, expanded women's opportunities despite that region's history of plow-based agriculture. Two World Wars dramatically increased the share of women in the workforce in belligerent nations, regardless of ancestral ties to the plow (Economics Focus: The Plough and the Now 2011).

It must be admitted, however, that culture in this sense is likely one of the strongest factors that can retard or channel adaptation to supply shocks. However desperate the Nazis' plight became in their effort to conquer *Lebensraum*, for example, they never emulated their Soviet opponents in drafting women into combat. Future research will have necessarily to attend more to this aspect of how societies respond (or fail to respond) to supply shocks.

TECHNOLOGICAL INNOVATION

We have seen that a factor-saving technological innovation can permit a society to adjust non-violently to a supply shock, even as it may through overshooting occasion yet other supply shocks. The printing press (Chapter 8) not only alleviated the acute shortage of skilled labor occasioned by the Black Death's heavy toll on *scriptoria*; it in turn precipitated a rapid and accelerating growth of human capital through its effects on literacy and education. More often, no such technological solution arises:

We saw in the case of interwar Europe that the kinds of "green revolution" or genetically modified organisms that could have alleviated the Continent's post-1914 food shortages certainly did not arise, and almost certainly could not have arisen; the technological leap that would have been required was simply too vast.

We have also seen, however, in Chapter 3, that the probability of innovation rises with the number of potential innovators and with their ability to communicate with one another. Hence the world's burgeoning population, the rise of almost universal literacy, and the prevalence of a common scientific language (English,[7] alas[8]) makes it far likelier that future supply shocks will find a technological solution: Perhaps the "warp speed" development of successful COVID vaccines, and the extraordinarily rapid communication of research results and genomes, is an example. Even where rapid innovation provides such a solution, however, problems of collective action or collective ignorance may retard its adoption. We know how to combat global warming, but nations (not to mention factions within nations) resist doing so; and the willfully ignorant resist vaccinations that could quickly have alleviated the disruptions of COVID. The good news is that technological answers are likelier to be found; the bad news is that human frailty often obstructs their adoption.[9]

LEADERSHIP

In an age in which monarchs mattered, whether the monarch was bright or dim (or, in the worst cases, feeble-minded from inbreeding) strongly affected her or his country's prosperity and security (Ottinger and Voigtländer 2020). Arthur Schlesinger, Jr., the hagiographer of Franklin

[7] A conservative but admittedly imprecise estimate holds that the world contains 1.35 billion speakers of English as a first or second language, only slightly ahead of the 1.12 billion with a primary or secondary command of Chinese. Only 370 million have English as their native tongue, as against 920 million native speakers of Chinese. https://en.wikipedia.org/wiki/List_of_languages_by_total_number_of_speakers.

[8] For obscure historical reasons (above, p. 61), English orthography is a disaster that must drive non-native speakers to distraction. Almost any other alphabetical language, and possibly some that employ syllabaries or ideograms, would have provided a more accessible and more easily mastered form of communication.

[9] Long after the lightning rod became available and had proven its efficacy, many regarded its use as an impiety: an attempt to thwart the will of God (A. D. White 1932, chap. 11).

Roosevelt, was convinced that leaders had played the same critical role in the twentieth century.[10] Under the pressure of extreme supply shocks, however, leadership fades into insignificance. Edward III, usually accounted one of the abler English monarchs, failed utterly to impose wage controls in the wake of the Black Death. The Holy Roman Emperor Charles V lacked neither ability nor energy, yet his best efforts could not hold back the Reformation that the printing press had unleashed. Nor is it easy to imagine that Gustav Stresemann, even had he lived beyond 1929, could have held back the Nazi onslaught unleashed by the 1929 Crash and the Great Depression.[11]

To be sure, bad leaders bring bad results (and are often replaced as a result) (Croco 2011). Good leaders can perhaps negotiate a smoother response to a major supply shock, as Stresemann did between 1924 and 1929. But even the best leaders seem powerless to stem the consequences of a severe shock that cannot be addressed by factor substitution, factor mobility, or factor-saving technology.

HUMAN AGENCY

If leaders are usually powerless against major supply shocks, perhaps their subjects – the ordinary people – carry greater weight; and, by virtue of a kind of Aristotelean "wisdom of crowds," may discern an optimal course of action more clearly and have the massed power to pursue it. Just as possibly, the masses can be too conflicted, or too pig-headed, to accept readily even a minimally costly adaptation.

Probably the clearest evidence for collective wisdom is the working of markets, even where those markets are weakly developed or morally suspect. We have seen that, even in the superstitious and dogma-ridden fourteenth century, peasants responded to the post-plague labor shortage by holding out for higher wages or moving (or trying to move) to regions where wages

[10] "Would the next two decades have been the same had the automobile that hit him killed Winston Churchill in 1931, and the bullet that missed him killed Franklin Roosevelt in 1933? Would Neville Chamberlain or Lord Halifax have rallied Britain in 1940? Would John Garner have produced the New Deal and the Four Freedoms? Suppose in addition that Lenin had died of typhus in Siberia in 1895, and Hitler had been killed on the western front in 1916? Would the 20th century have looked the same? Individuals do make a difference in history" (1931: One Year, Two Accidents 2012).

[11] Stresemann died on October 3, 1929, exactly three weeks before the Black Thursday (October 24, 1929) that marked the onset of the Wall Street crash.

were higher. If any peasants felt so bound by tradition or deference to continue to accept pre-plague wages, they were far outnumbered.

The impersonal forces unleashed by supply shocks, however, just as often impel large segments of the population toward welfare-reducing policies. However much the arrival of the Huguenots might have contributed to the overall prosperity of a seventeenth-century German city, its citizens frequently allowed their short-term self-interest to dominate their prospects of long-term growth and to oppose the refugees' entry. Two centuries later, upstanding German citizens, whose moral and religious values forbade cruelty and killing, acquiesced in the genocidal pursuit of *Lebensraum* because they embraced the delusion that no other means could guarantee their own survival.

In short, the impersonal forces unleashed by supply shocks can easily triumph over notions of the common good or personal morality – or, more precisely, can bend those concepts to accommodate what self-interest, in the face of a supply shock, dictates. Crowds are no wiser, and often less wise, than leaders.

Supply shocks severely constrain human agency. In almost theological terms, such shocks can easily overwhelm free will. Few Eastern European landlords declined to enserf their peasants in the wake of the Black Death; few German cities, even if they were devoutly Protestant, welcomed the competition of Huguenot refugees; many Russians in areas cut off from railroad access revolted, despite the growing prosperity and opportunities of Russia as a whole; depressingly few Germans, by the late 1930s, recoiled from the idea of eastern conquest and ethnic cleansing.

Supply shocks bring opportunity and tragedy. Against their impersonal force, institutions, culture, and leadership avail little, the "wisdom of crowds" even less. Only systemic ideas matter, and then but rarely. Factors and developments beyond our control – soil, climate, trade routes, historical memory – condition, and in most cases determine, our response. We can hope to understand supply shocks, perhaps even to adapt to them; we cannot resist or control them.

References

"1931: One Year, Two Auto Accidents That Could Have Changed the World." 2012. *International Churchill Society*. https://winstonchurchill.org/publications/churchill-bulletin/bulletin-047-may-2012/1931-one-year-two-auto-accidents-that-could-have-changed-the-world/ (Accessed August 15, 2021).

Acemoglu, Daron. 1996. "A Microfoundation for Social Increasing Returns in Human Capital Accumulation." *The Quarterly Journal of Economics* 111 (3): 779–804.

Acemoglu, Daron, and Joshua Angrist. 2000. "How Large Are Human-Capital Externalities? Evidence from Compulsory Schooling Laws." *NBER Macroeconomics Annual* 15: 9–59.

Acemoglu, Daron, and Pascual Restrepo. 2019. "Automation and New Tasks: How Technology Displaces and Reinstates Labor." *Journal of Economic Perspectives* 33(2): 3–30.

2020. "Robots and Jobs: Evidence from US Labor Markets." *Journal of Political Economy* 128(6): 2188–2244.

Acemoglu, Daron, and James A. Robinson. 2006. "Economic Backwardness in Political Perspective." *American Political Science Review* 100(1): 115–131.

2012. *Why Nations Fail: The Origins of Power, Prosperity and Poverty*. 1st ed. New York: Crown Publishers.

Acemoglu, Daron, and Alexander Wolitsky. 2011. "The Economics of Labor Coercion." *Econometrica* 79(2): 555–600.

Acharya, Avidit, Maya Sen, and Matthew Blackwell. 2018. *Deep Roots: How Slavery Still Shapes Southern Politics*. Princeton, NJ; Oxford: Princeton University Press.

Alesina, Alberto, Paola Giuliano, and Nathan Nunn. 2013. "On the Origins of Gender Roles: Women and the Plough." *The Quarterly Journal of Economics* 128(2): 469–530.

Alfani, Guido. 2017a. "The Rich in Historical Perspective: Evidence for Preindustrial Europe (c. 1300–1800)." *Cliometrica* 11(3): 321–348.

2017b. "The Top Rich in Europe in the Long Run of History (1300 to Present Day)." *VOX: CEPR Policy Portal*. https://voxeu.org/article/europe-s-rich-1300 (Accessed April 3, 2020).

Allen, Robert C. 2009. *The British Industrial Revolution in Global Perspective.* Cambridge; New York: Cambridge University Press.

2011. *Global Economic History: A Very Short Introduction.* Oxford; New York: Oxford University Press.

Ames, Edward. 1947. "A Century of Russian Railroad Construction: 1837–1936." *The American Slavic and East European Review* 6(3/4): 57–74.

Anderson, Perry. 1979. *Lineages of the Absolutist State.* London: Verso.

Ansell, Ben W., and David Samuels. 2014. *Inequality and Democratization: An Elite-Competition Approach.* New York: Cambridge University Press.

Antonopoulos, John. 1992. "The Great Minoan Eruption of Thera Volcano and the Ensuing Tsunami in the Greek Archipelago." *Natural Hazards* 5(2): 153–168.

Aston, T. H., and C. H. E. Philpin. 1985. *The Brenner Debate: Agrarian Class Structure and Economic Development in Pre-industrial Europe.* Cambridge, UK; New York: Cambridge University Press.

Augustine, Wilson R. 1965. "Russia's Railwaymen, July–October 1917." *Slavic Review* 24(4): 666–679.

Avrin, Leila. 1991. *Scribes, Script, and Books: The Book Arts from Antiquity to the Renaissance.* Chicago, IL; London: American Library Association; The British Library.

Bailey, Brian J. 1998. *The Luddite Rebellion.* New York: University Press.

Barbier, Frédéric. 2017. *Gutenberg's Europe: The Book and the Invention of Western Modernity.* Cambridge, UK; Malden, MA: Polity Press.

Barro, Robert J., and Jong Wha Lee. 2013. "A New Data Set of Educational Attainment in the World, 1950–2010." *Journal of Development Economics* 104(C): 184–198.

Barro, Robert J., and Xavier I. Sala-I-Martin. 2003. *Economic Growth.* Cambridge, MA: MIT Press.

Bates, Robert H., and Da-Hsiang Donald Lien. 1985. "A Note on Taxation, Development, and Representative Government." *Politics & Society* 14(1): 53–70.

Beck, Jan, and Andrea Sieber. 2010. "Is the Spatial Distribution of Mankind's Most Basic Economic Traits Determined by Climate and Soil Alone?" ed. Anna Dornhaus. *PLoS ONE* 5(5): e10416.

Becker, Sascha O.; Irena Grosfeld, Pauline Grosjean, Nico Voigtländer, and Ekaterina Zhuravskaya. 2020. "Forced Migration and Human Capital: Evidence from Post-WWII Population Transfers." *American Economic Review* 110(5): 1430–1463.

Becker, Sascha O., Francesco Cinnirella, Erik Hornung, and Ludger Woessmann. 2014. "IPEHD: The ifo Prussian Economic History Database." *Historical Methods: A Journal of Quantitative and Interdisciplinary History* 47(2): 57–66.

Becker, Sascha O., and Ludger Woessmann. 2009. "Was Weber Wrong? A Human Capital Theory of Protestant Economic History." *The Quarterly Journal of Economics* 124(2): 531–596.

Beckert, Sven. 2014. *Empire of Cotton: A Global History.* 1st ed. New York: Alfred A. Knopf.

Beloff, Max. 1971. *The Age of Absolutism: 1660–1815*. London: Hutchinson.
Benedictow, Ole Jørgen. 2004. *The Black Death, 1346–1353: The Complete History*. Woodbridge, UK; Rochester, NY: Boydell Press.
Benson, L. D. 2000. "The Great Vowel Shift." *The Geoffrey Chaucer Page*. https://chaucer.fas.harvard.edu/pages/great-vowel-shift (Accessed February 21, 2020).
Bernstein, William J. 2008. *A Splendid Exchange: How Trade Shaped the World*. 1st ed. New York and Berkeley, CA: Atlantic Monthly Press; Distributed by Publishers Group West.
Blackbourn, David. 1977. "The *Mittelstand* in German Society and Politics, 1871–1914." *Social History* 2(4): 409–433.
Blake, Robert. 1966. *Disraeli*. London: Eyre & Spottiswoode.
Blaydes, Lisa, and Christopher Paik. 2019. "Muslim Trade and City Growth Before the Nineteenth Century: Comparative Urbanization in Europe, the Middle East and Central Asia." *British Journal of Political Science* 51(2): 1–24.
Blum, Jerome. 1957. "The Rise of Serfdom in Eastern Europe." *The American Historical Review* 62(4): 807–836.
1971. *Lord and Peasant in Russia: From the Ninth to the Nineteenth Century*. Princeton, NJ: Princeton University Press.
Boix, Carles. 2003. *Democracy and Redistribution*. Cambridge, UK; New York: Cambridge University Press.
"Booming Sugar in Hawaii." 1898. *Wall Street Journal*, June 30, 1898: 1.
Borodkin, Leonid, Brigitte Granville, and Carol Scott Leonard. 2008. "The Rural/Urban Wage Gap in the Industrialisation of Russia, 1884–1910." *European Review of Economic History* 12(1): 67–95.
Bottomley, Sean. 2014. *The British Patent System during the Industrial Revolution 1700–1852: From Privilege to Property*. Cambridge: Cambridge University Press.
Bourguignon, François. 2015. *The Globalization of Inequality*. Princeton, NJ: Princeton University Press.
Boustan, Leah Platt. 2017. *Competition in the Promised Land: Black Migrants in Northern Cities and Labor Markets*. Princeton, NJ: Princeton University Press.
Bowman, Shearer. 1980. "Antebellum Planters and 'Vormärz' Junkers in Comparative Perspective." *The American Historical Review* 85(4): 779–808.
Braudel, Fernand. 1981. *Civilization and Capitalism, 15th–18th Century*. London: Collins.
Braun, Guido, and Susanne Lachenicht, eds. 2007. *Hugenotten und deutsche Territorialstaaten: Immigrationspolitik und Integrationsprozesse = Les Etats allemands et les huguenots: politique d'immigration et processus d'intégration*. [Huguenots and German Territorial States : Immigration Policies and Integration Processes] Munich: Oldenbourg.
Brooks, Jeffrey. 1985. *When Russia Learned to Read: Literacy and Popular Literature, 1861–1917*. Princeton, NJ: Princeton University Press.
Burds, Jeffrey. 1998. *Peasant Dreams and Market Politics: Labor Migration and the Russian Village, 1861–1905*. Pittsburgh, PA: University of Pittsburgh Press.

Burgess, Robin, and Dave Donaldson. 2012. "Railroads and the Demise of Famine in Colonial India." In *Working Paper*, http://dave-donaldson.com/wp-content/uploads/2015/12/Burgess_Donaldson_Volatility_Paper.pdf. (Accessed November 2, 2019).

Buringh, Eltjo, and Jan Luiten van Zanden. 2009. "Charting the 'Rise of the West': Manuscripts and Printed Books in Europe, a Long-Term Perspective from the Sixth through Eighteenth Centuries." *The Journal of Economic History* 69(2): 409–445.

Campbell, B. M. S. 2016. *The Great Transition: Climate, Disease and Society in the Late Medieval World*. Cambridge, UK; New York: Cambridge University Press.

Cantoni, Davide, Jeremiah Dittmar, and Noam Yuchtman. 2018. "Religious Competition and Reallocation: The Political Economy of Secularization in the Protestant Reformation." *The Quarterly Journal of Economics* 133(4): 2037–2096.

Casella, Alessandra. 1996. "On Market Integration and the Development of Institutions: The Case of International Commercial Arbitration." *European Economic Review* 40: 155–186.

Castañeda Dower, Paul, Evgeny Finkel, Scott Gehlbach, and Steven Nafziger. 2018. "Collective Action and Representation in Autocracies: Evidence from Russia's Great Reforms." *American Political Science Review* 112(1): 125–147.

2017. "Replication Data for 'Collective Action and Representation in Autocracies: Evidence from Russia's Great Reforms'" ed. American Political Science Review. https://doi.org/10.7910/DVN/X7AMNO.

Central Intelligence Agency. 2018. *The CIA World Factbook 2018–2019*. La Vergne: Skyhorse Publishing.

Central Statistical Committee. [Russia] 1901. *Posevnye ploshchadi prinimaemye Tsentral'nym Statisticheskim Komitetom pri razrabotke urozhaev 1881, 1887 i 1893–1899 gg. po 50 guberniiam Evropeiskoi Rossii*. St. Petersburg: Vremennik TsSK MVD (Central Statistical Committee of the Ministry of Internal Affairs). Statistical Bulletin.

Chang, Eric C. C., Mark Andreas Kayser, Drew A. Linzer, and Ronald Rogowski. 2011. *Electoral Systems and the Balance of Consumer-Producer Power*. New York: Cambridge University Press.

Chernow, Ron. 2017. *Grant*. London: Head of Zeus.

Chertoff, Mariela. 2015. "Protein Malnutrition and Brain Development." *Brain Disorders & Therapy* 04(03).

Cheung, Christina et al. 2019. "Stable Isotope and Dental Caries Data Reveal Abrupt Changes in Subsistence Economy in Ancient China in Response to Global Climate Change." *PLoS ONE* 14(7): e0218943.

Cinnirella, Francesco, and Erik Hornung. 2016. "Landownership Concentration and the Expansion of Education." *Journal of Development Economics* 121: 135–152.

Clancy, Tom. 1986. *Red Storm Rising*. New York: Putnam.

Clark, Christopher M. 2006. *Iron Kingdom: The Rise and Downfall of Prussia, 1600–1947*. Cambridge, MA: Belknap Press of Harvard University Press.

Clark, Gregory. 2005. "The Condition of the Working Class in England, 1209–2004." *Journal of Political Economy* 113(6): 1307–1340.

2007. *A Farewell to Alms: A Brief Economic History of the World*. Princeton; Oxford: Princeton University Press.

Cohn, Samuel. 2007. "After the Black Death: Labour Legislation and Attitudes towards Labour in Late-Medieval Western Europe." *The Economic History Review* 60(3): 457–485.

Colantone, Italo, and Piero Stanig. 2018. "Global Competition and Brexit." *American Political Science Review* 112(2): 201–218.

Coşgel, Metin M., Thomas J. Miceli, and Jared Rubin. 2012. "The Political Economy of Mass Printing: Legitimacy and Technological Change in the Ottoman Empire." *Journal of Comparative Economics* 40(3): 357–371.

Creasman, Allyson F. 2012. *Censorship and Civic Order in Reformation Germany, 1517–1648: "Printed Poison and Evil Talk."* Farnham, Surrey, England: Ashgate Pub.

Crisp, Olga. 1976. *Studies in the Russian Economy before 1914*. London: Macmillan; The School of Slavonic and East European Studies, University of London.

Croco, Sarah E. 2011. "The Decider's Dilemma: Leader Culpability, War Outcomes, and Domestic Punishment." *The American Political Science Review* 105(3): 457–747.

Curtin, Philip D. 1984. *Cross-Cultural Trade in World History*. Cambridge: Cambridge University Press.

Dalgaard, Carl-Johan, Nicolai Kaarsen, Ola Olsson, and Pablo Selaya. 2018. "Roman Roads to Prosperity: Persistence and Non-Persistence of Public Goods Provision." No. 722, Working Papers in Economics from University of Gothenburg, Department of Economics. https://econpapers.repec.org/paper/hhsgunwpe/0722.htm.

De Vries, Jan. 2008. *The Industrious Revolution: Consumer Behavior and the Household Economy, 1650 to the Present*. Cambridge; New York: Cambridge University Press.

Deaton, Angus. 2013. *The Great Escape: Health, Wealth, and the Origins of Inequality*. Princeton: Princeton University Press.

Dermineur, Elise, ed. 2018. *Women and Credit in Pre-industrial Europe*. Turnhout, Belgium: Brepols Publishers.

Desborough, V. R. d'A. 1972. *The Greek Dark Ages*. London: Benn.

Deutsche Hugenotten-Gesellschaft e.V. 2021. "Das internationale und das deutsche Refuge." www.hugenotten.de/hugenotten/refuge.php (Accessed February 2, 2021).

Diamond, Jared M. 1997. *Guns, Germs, and Steel: The Fates of Human Societies*. 1st ed. New York: W. W. Norton.

Dittmar, Jeremiah. 2011. "Information Technology and Economic Change: The Impact of The Printing Press." *The Quarterly Journal of Economics* 126(3): 1133–1172.

2012. "The Welfare Impact of a New Good: The Printed Book."

Dittmar, Jeremiah E., and Ralf R. Meisenzahl. 2020. "Public Goods Institutions, Human Capital, and Growth: Evidence from German History." *The Review of Economic Studies* 87(2): 959–996,

Dittmar, Jeremiah, and Skipper Seabold. 2019. "New Media and Competition: Printing and Europe's Transformation after Gutenberg." Center for Economic Performance, London School of Economics, Discussion Paper 1600.

Dölemeyer, Barbara. 1997. "Die Aufnahmeprivilegien Für Hugenotten Im Europäischen Refuge." In *Das Privileg Im Europäischen Vergleich*, Ius commune. Sonderhefte; 93, 125, Frankfurt: V. Klostermann.

2006. *Die Hugenotten*. Stuttgart: Kohlhammer.

Domar, Evsey D. 1970. "The Causes of Slavery or Serfdom: A Hypothesis." *The Journal of Economic History* 30(1): 18–32.

Donaldson, Dave. 2018. "Railroads of the Raj: Estimating the Impact of Transportation Infrastructure." *American Economic Review* 108(4–5): 899–934.

Drelichman, Mauricio. 2005. "The Curse of Moctezuma: American Silver and the Dutch Disease." *Explorations in Economic History* 42(3): 349–380.

Duby, Georges. 1998. *Rural Economy and Country Life in the Medieval West*. Philadelphia, PA: University of Pennsylvania Press.

Easterly, William. 2007. "Inequality Does Cause Underdevelopment: Insights from a New Instrument." *Journal of Development Economics* 84(2): 755–776.

"Economics Focus: The Plough and the Now." 2011. *The Economist*, July 21.

Eisenhardt, Ulrich. 1970. *Die kaiserliche Aufsicht über Buchdruck, Buchhandel und Presse im Heiligen Römischen Reich Deutscher Nation (1496–1806); ein Beitrag zur Geschichte der Bücher- und Pressezensur*. Karlsruhe: C. F. Müller.

Eisenstein, Elizabeth L. 2005. *The Printing Revolution in Early Modern Europe*. 2nd ed. Cambridge; New York: Cambridge University Press.

Ejrnaes, M., and K. G. Persson. 2010. "The Gains from Improved Market Efficiency: Trade before and after the Transatlantic Telegraph." *European Review of Economic History* 14(3): 361–381.

Eklof, B., J. Bushnell, and L.G. Zakharova. 1994. *Russia's Great Reforms, 1855–1881*. Indiana University Press.

Eltis, David. 1995. *The Military Revolution in Sixteenth-Century Europe*. London; New York: Tauris Academic Studies; St Martin's Press distributor.

Emmons, Terence. 1968. *The Russian Landed Gentry and the Peasant Emancipation of 1861*. Cambridge, UK: Cambridge University Press.

Epstein, Stephan R. 2000. *Freedom and Growth: The Rise of States and Markets in Europe, 1300–1750*. London: Routledge.

Ertman, Thomas. 1997. *Birth of the Leviathan: Building States and Regimes in Medieval and Early Modern Europe*. Cambridge, UK; New York: Cambridge University Press.

European Environment Agency. 2020. "Large Rivers and Large Lakes." https://www.eea.europa.eu/data-and-maps/data/wise-large-rivers-and-large-lakes.

Falkus, Malcolm E. 1966. "Russia and the International Wheat Trade, 1861–1914." *Economica* 33(132): 416.

1972. *The Industrialisation of Russia, 1700–1914*. London: Macmillan.

Falter, Jürgen W. 2020a. *Hitlers Parteigenossen: die Mitglieder der NSDAP 1919–1945*. Frankfurt: Campus Verlag.

2020b. *Hitlers Wähler: die Anhänger der NSDAP 1924–1933*. Überarbeitete und erweiterte Neuauflage. Frankfurt: Campus Verlag.

2022. *"Wie ich den Weg zum Führer fand": Beitrittsmotive und Entlastungsstrategien von NSDAP-Mitgliedern*. Frankfurt; New York: Campus Verlag.

Farmer, David L. 1991. "Prices and Wages, 1350–1500." In *The Agrarian History of England and Wales*, Cambridge: Cambridge University Press, 431–525.

Ferejohn, John A., and Frances McCall Rosenbluth. 2017. *Forged through Fire: War, Peace, and the Democratic Bargain*. New York: Liveright Publishing Corporation, a Division of W. W. Norton & Company.

Finkel, Evgeny, Scott Gehlbach, and Dmitrii Kofanov. 2017. "(Good) Land and Freedom (for Former Serfs): Determinants of Peasant Unrest in European Russia, March–October 1917." *Slavic Review* 76(3): 710–721.

Fischer, David Hackett. 1996. *The Great Wave: Price Revolutions and the Rhythm of History*. New York: Oxford University Press.

Flaherty, Thomas M., and Ronald Rogowski. 2020. "Replication Data for: Rising Inequality as a Threat to the Liberal International Order." https://dataverse.harvard.edu/citation?persistentId=doi:10.7910/DVN/TYX3UE (Accessed February 24, 2021).

Franz, Günther. 1961. *Der Dreissigjährige Krieg und das Deutsche Volk; Untersuchungen zur Bevölkerungs- und Agrargeschichte*. 3. verm. Aufl. Stuttgart: G. Fischer.

Freeman, John R., and Dennis P. Quinn. 2012. "The Economic Origins of Democracy Reconsidered." *American Political Science Review* 106(1): 58–80.

Frieden, Jeffry A. 1994. "International Investment and Colonial Control: A New Interpretation." *International Organization* 48(4): 559–593.

2006. *Global Capitalism: Its Fall and Rise in the Twentieth Century*. 1st ed. New York: Norton.

Frieden, Jeffry, and Arthur Silve. 2022. "The Political Reception of Innovations." *Economics & Politics*: https://doi.org/10.1111/ecpo.12228

Galofré-Vilà, G. et al. 2021. "A Lesson from History? Worsening Mortality and the Rise of the Nazi Party in 1930s Germany." *Public Health* 195: 18–21.

Gasquet, Francis Aidan. 1908. *The Black Death of 1348 and 1349*. 2nd ed. London: George Bell and Sons.

Gatrell, Peter. 1994. "The Meaning of the Great Reforms in Russian Economic History." In Ben Eklof, John Bushnell, and Larissa Zakharova (eds.). *Russia's Great Reforms, 1855–1881, Indiana-Michigan Series in Russian and East European Studies*, Bloomington, IN: Indiana University Press.

Gerschenkron, Alexander. 1962. *Economic Backwardness in Historical Perspective*. Cambridge, MA: Belknap Press of Harvard University Press.

1966. *Bread and Democracy in Germany*. New York: Howard Fertig.

"Geschichte des Memellandes von 1525 bis 1722." 2021. *Geschichte des Memellandes*. http://wiki-de.genealogy.net/Geschichte_des_Memellandes#Von_1525_bis_1722_-_die_Zeit_des_Hauptamts (Accessed March 5, 2021).

Giles, John, Albert Park, and Meiyan Wang. 2019. "The Great Proletarian Cultural Revolution, Disruptions to Education, and the Returns to Schooling in Urban China." *Economic Development and Cultural Change* 68(1): 131–164.

Gingerich, Daniel W., and Jan P. Vogler. 2020. "Pandemics and Political Development: The Electoral Legacy of the Black Death in Germany." *World Politics* 73(3): 393–440.

Goldin, Claudia. 1998. "America's Graduation from High School: The Evolution and Spread of Secondary Schooling in the Twentieth Century." *The Journal of Economic History* 58(2): 345–374.

Gordon, Robert J. 2016. *The Rise and Fall of American Growth: The US Standard of Living since the Civil War*. Princeton: Princeton University Press.

Gottfried, Robert. 1982. *Bury St. Edmunds and the Urban Crisis, 1290–1539*. Princeton, NJ: Princeton University Press.

1983. *The Black Death: Natural and Human Disaster in Medieval Europe*. New York: The Free Press.

Graham, Loren R. 1993. *Science in Russia and the Soviet Union: A Short History*. Cambridge; New York: Cambridge University Press.

Gregory, Paul R. 1994. *Before Command: An Economic History of Russia from Emancipation to the First Five-Year Plan*. Princeton, NJ, Baltimore, MD: Princeton University Press, Project MUSE.

Greif, Avner. 1993. "Contract Enforceability and Economic Institutions in Early Trade: The Maghribi Traders' Coalition." *The American Economic Review* 83(3): 525–48.

Grendler, Paul F. 2004. "The Universities of the Renaissance and Reformation." *Renaissance Quarterly* 57(1): 1–42.

Guillemenot-Ehrmantraut, Dominique. 2007. "L'immigration des huguenots dans le Palatinat entre 1649 et 1685." In *Hugenotten und deutsche Territorialstaaten = Les Etats allemands et les huguenots: politique d'immigration et processus d'integration* [Huguenots and German Territorial States : Immigration Policies and Integration Processes], Pariser historische Studien, Munich: Oldenbourg, 17–34.

Hagen, William W. 2002. *Ordinary Prussians: Brandenburg Junkers and Villagers, 1500–1840*. Cambridge, UK; New York: Cambridge University Press.

Hager, Thomas. 2008. *The Alchemy of Air: A Jewish Genius, a Doomed Tycoon, and the Scientific Discovery That Fed the World but Fueled the Rise of Hitler*. 1st ed. New York: Harmony Books.

Hainmueller, Jens, and Michael J. Hiscox. 2010. "Attitudes toward Highly Skilled and Low-Skilled Immigration: Evidence from a Survey Experiment." *American Political Science Review* 104(1): 61–84.

Hale, John R. 2009. *Lords of the Sea: The Epic Story of the Athenian Navy and the Birth of Democracy*. New York: Viking.

Hall, Peter A., and David W. Soskice. 2001. *Varieties of Capitalism: The Institutional Foundations of Comparative Advantage*. Oxford; New York: Oxford University Press.

Hastie, T. J., and R. J. Tibshirani. 2017. *Generalized Additive Models*. 1st ed. Abingdon: Routledge.

Hellie, Richard. 1971. *Enserfment and Military Change in Muscovy*. Chicago: University of Chicago Press.

1992. "The Impact of the Southern and Eastern Frontiers of Muscovy on the 'Ulozhenie' (Law Code) of 1649 Compared with the Impact of the Western Frontier." *Russian History* 19(1/4): 75–95.

Herlihy, David. 1997. *The Black Death and the Transformation of the West*. Cambridge, MA: Harvard University Press.

Hicks, John. 1963. *The Theory of Wages*. [2d ed.]. London: Macmillan.

Hilton, R. H. 1977. *Bond Men Made Free: Medieval Peasant Movements and the English Rising of 1381*. London; New York: Methuen.

Hintze, Otto. 1906. *Staatsverfassung und Heeresverfassung. Vortrag gehalten in der Gehe-stiftung zu Dresden am 17. Februar 1906,*. Dresden: Zahn & Jaensch.

Hitler, Adolf. 2003. *Hitler's Second Book: The Unpublished Sequel to Mein Kampf*. 1st English language ed. New York: Enigma.

2016. *Mein Kampf: eine kritische Edition*. München: Institut für Zeitgeschichte.

Hobsbawm, Eric, and George Rudé. 1973. *Captain Swing*. Harmondsworth: Penguin Books.

Hoch, Steven L. 1986. *Serfdom and Social Control in Russia: Petrovskoe, a Village in Tambov*. Chicago: University of Chicago Press.

Hoffman, Philip T. 2015. *Why Did Europe Conquer the World?* Princeton: Princeton University Press.

Hornung, Erik. 2014. "Immigration and the Diffusion of Technology: The Huguenot Diaspora in Prussia." *American Economic Review* 104(1): 84–122.

Iversen, Torben, and David W. Soskice. 2019. *Democracy and Prosperity: Reinventing Capitalism through a Turbulent Century*. Princeton, NJ: Princeton University Press.

Jensen, J. Bradford, Dennis P. Quinn, and Stephen Weymouth. 2017. "Winners and Losers in International Trade: The Effects on US`Presidential Voting." *International Organization* 71(3): 423–457.

Jensen, Richard L. 1994. "British Immigrants and Life in Utah." *Utah History Encyclopedia*. https://www.uen.org/utah_history_encyclopedia/b/BRITISH_IMMIGRANTS.shtml (December 19, 2019).

Jones, A. H. M. 1953. "Inflation under the Roman Empire." *The Economic History Review* 5(3): 293–318.

Jordà, Òscar, Sanjay R. Singh, and Alan M. Taylor. 2020. "Longer-Run Economic Consequences of Pandemics." Washington, DC. NBER Working Paper 26934. https://www.nber.org/papers/w26934 (Accessed April 19, 2020).

Juma, Calestous. 2019. *Innovation and Its Enemies: Why People Resist New Technologies*. paper. Oxford; New York: Oxford University Press.

Kaak, Heinrich. 1991. *Die Gutsherrschaft: theoriegeschichtliche Untersuchungen zum Agrarwesen im ostelbischen Raum*. Berlin; New York: Walter de Gruyter.

Kagan, Donald, Steven E. Ozment, and Frank M. Turner. 2010. *The Western Heritage*. Teaching and learning classroom edition, 6th ed. Upper Saddle River, NJ: Prentice Hall.

Kahneman, Daniel. 2011. *Thinking, Fast and Slow*. New York: Farrar, Straus and Giroux.

Kelly, John. 2006. *The Great Mortality: An Intimate History of the Black Death, the Most Devastating Plague of All Time*. 1st Harper Perennial ed. New York: Harper Perennial.

Keynes, John Maynard. 1920. *The Economic Consequences of the Peace*. New York: Harcourt, Brace, and Howe. https://oll.libertyfund.org/titles/303.

1936. *The General Theory of Employment, Interest and Money*. New York: Harcourt, Brace.

Kindleberger, C. P. 1951. "Group Behavior and International Trade." *Journal of Political Economy* 59(1): 30–46.

Kissel, Theodor. 2017. "Luther, der Medienrevolutionär; der rechte Zeitpunkt für die Reformation." *Spektrum – Die Woche* (36). https://www.spektrum.de/news/luther-der-medienrevolutionaer/1497505 (Accessed August 18, 2020).

Klebnikov, Paul G. 1991. "Agricultural Development in Russia, 1906–17: Land Reform, Social Agronomy, and Cooperation." PhD dissertation. London School of Economics and Political Science.

Klingebiel, Thomas. 1990. "Aspekte zur Ansiedlung von Hugenotten in den norddeutschen Territorien." In *Die Hugenotten und das Refuge: Deutschland und Europa: Beiträge zu einer Tagung*, Berlin: Colloquium Verlag, 67–80.

Kocka, Jurgen. 1988. "German History before Hitler: The Debate about the German Sonderweg." *Journal of Contemporary History* 23(1): 3–16.

Kopsidis, Michael, Katja Bruisch, and Daniel W. Bromley. 2015. "Where Is the Backward Russian Peasant? Evidence against the Superiority of Private Farming, 1883–1913." *The Journal of Peasant Studies* 42(2): 425–447.

Kronmal, Richard A. 1993. "Spurious Correlation and the Fallacy of the Ratio Standard Revisited." *Journal of the Royal Statistical Society. Series A (Statistics in Society)* 156(3): 379–392.

Kuhn, Thomas S. 1996. *The Structure of Scientific Revolutions*. Chicago, IL: University of Chicago Press.

Lachenicht, Susanne. 2005. "Migration, Migrationspolitik und Integration: Hugenotten in Brandenburg-Preußen, Irland, und Großbrittanien." In *Hugenotten zwischen Migration und Integration: Neue Forschungen zum Refuge in Berlin und Brandenburg*, Berlin: Metropol, 37–58.

La Croix, Sumner J., and Christopher Grandy. 1997. "The Political Instability of Reciprocal Trade and the Overthrow of the Hawaiian Kingdom." *The Journal of Economic History* 57(1): 161–189.

Landa, Janet T. 1981. "A Theory of the Ethnically Homogeneous Middleman Group: An Institutional Alternative to Contract Law." *The Journal of Legal Studies* 10(2): 349–362.

Landes, David S. 1983. *Revolution in Time: Clocks and the Making of the Modern World.* Cambridge, MA: Belknap Press of Harvard University Press.

Lienhard, John. 1988. "The Black Death." *Engines of our Ingenuity.* https://uh.edu/engines/epi123.htm (Accessed February 21, 2020).

Lindberg, Erik. 2009. "Club Goods and Inefficient Institutions: Why Danzig and Lübeck Failed in the Early Modern Period." *The Economic History Review* 62(3): 604–628.

Lippmann, Walter. 1922. *Public Opinion.* New York: Harcourt, Brace and Company.

Lis, Catharina, and Hugo Soly. 1997. "Different Paths of Development: Capitalism in the Northern and Southern Netherlands during the Late Middle Ages and the Early Modern Period." *Review (Fernand Braudel Center)* 20(2): 211–42.

Lucas, Robert. 1990. "Why Doesn't Capital Flow from Rich to Poor Countries?" *The American Economic Review* 80(2): 92–96.

Magdelaine, Michelle. 2007. "Francfort-sur-le-Main et les réfugiés huguenots." In *Hugenotten und deutsche Territorialstaaten: Immigrationspolitik und Integrationsprozesse = Les Etats allemands et les huguenots: politique d'immigration et processus d'integration* [Huguenots and German Territorial States : Immigration Policies and Integration Processes], Pariser historische Studien, Munich: Oldenbourg, 35–50.

Maier, Charles S. 1975. *Recasting Bourgeois Europe Stabilization in France, Germany, and Italy in the Decade after World War I.* Princeton, NJ; Baltimore, MD: Princeton University Press, Project MUSE.

Markevich, Andrei, and Ekaterina Zhuravskaya. 2018. "The Economic Effects of the Abolition of Serfdom: Evidence from the Russian Empire." *American Economic Review* 108(4–5): 1074–1117.

Martin, Henri Jean. 1984. *Livre, pouvoirs et société a Paris au XVIIe siècle: (1598–1701).* Réimpression de l'édition de Genève, 1969. Geneva: Droz.

Marx, Karl, and Friedrich Engels. 1978. *The Marx-Engels Reader.* 2nd ed. Robert C. Tucker. New York: Norton.

Matranga, Andrea, and Timur Natkhov. 2019. "All Along the Watchtower: Defense Lines and the Origins of Russian Serfdom." Presented at the Economic History and Historical Political Economy of Russia (Мэдисон, Moscow. www.hse.ru/en/staff/natkhov#sci (Accessed July 11, 2020).

McCaffray, Susan P. 2005. "Confronting Serfdom in the Age of Revolution: Projects for Serf Reform in the Time of Alexander I." *The Russian Review* 64(1): 1–21.

McElroy, Brendan. 2020. "Peasants and Parliaments: Agrarian Reform in Eighteenth Century Europe." PhD dissertation. Harvard.

McNeill, William Hardy. 1976. *Plagues and Peoples.* Garden City, NY: Anchor Press/Doubleday.

Medema, Steven G. 2020. "The Coase Theorem at Sixty." *Journal of Economic Literature* 58(4): 1045–1128.

Melton, Edgar. 2015. "The Agrarian East." In Hamish Scott (ed.) *The Oxford Handbook of Early Modern European History, 1350–1750*. Oxford: Oxford University Press, 428–454.

Middell, Katharina. 2007. "Hugenotten in Kursachsen. Einwanderung und Integration." In *Hugenotten und deutsche Territorialstaaten: Immigrationspolitik und Integrationsprozesse = Les Etats allemands et les huguenots: politique d'immigration et processus d'integration* [Huguenots and German Territorial States : Immigration Policies and Integration Processes]. Pariser historische Studien, Munich: Oldenbourg, 51–70.

Mironov, Boris. 1991. "The Development of Literacy in Russia and the USSR from the Tenth to the Twentieth Centuries." *History of Education Quarterly* 31(2): 229.

Mironov, Boris Nikolaevich. 2012. *The Standard of Living and Revolutions in Russia, 1700–1917*. Abingdon: Routledge.

Moon, David. 1996. "Estimating the Peasant Population of Late Imperial Russia from the 1897 Census: A Research Note." *Europe-Asia Studies* 48(1): 141–153.

1997. "Peasant Migration and the Settlement of Russia's Frontiers, 1550–1897." *The Historical Journal* 40(4): 859–893.

1999. *The Russian Peasantry, 1600–1930: The World the Peasants Made*. London; New York: Longman.

2013. *The Plough That Broke the Steppes: Agriculture and Environment on Russia's Grasslands, 1700–1914*. 1st ed. Oxford: University Press.

Münkler, Herfried. 2013. *Der Grosse Krieg: die Welt 1914 bis 1918*. 1. Auflage. Berlin: Rowohlt.

Munro, John. 2004. "Before and after the Black Death: Money, Prices, and Wages in Fourteenth-Century England." In *New Approaches to the History of Late Medieval and Early Modern Europe*, Copenhagen, Denmark: Munich Personal RePEc Archive, 335–364. https://mpra.ub.uni-muenchen.de/15748/ (Accessed August 10, 2020).

Natkhov, Timur, and Natalia Vasilenok. 2022. "Ethnic-specific Infant Care Practices and Infant Mortality in Late Imperial Russia." *The Economic History Review: ehr.13210*.

Navaneetham, Kannan. 2011. "Demography and Development: Preliminary Interpretations of the 2011 Census." *Economic and political weekly* XLVI: 13–17.

Neal, Larry. 2000. "A Shocking View of Economic History." *The Journal of Economic History* 60(2): 317–334.

Neal, Larry, and Rondo E. Cameron. 2016. *A Concise Economic History of the World: From Paleolithic Times to the Present*. 5th ed. New York: Oxford University Press.

Nhem, Boraden. 2013. *The Khmer Rouge: Ideology, Militarism, and the Revolution That Consumed a Generation*. Santa Barbara, CA: Praeger, an Imprint of ABC-CLIO, LLC.

Nordhaus, William. 2004. *Schumpeterian Profits in the American Economy: Theory and Measurement*. Cambridge, MA: National Bureau of Economic Research. www.nber.org/papers/w10433 (Accessed July 10, 2020).

North, Douglass C. 1991. "Institutions." *The Journal of Economic Perspectives* 5 (1): 97–112.

North, Douglass C., and Robert Paul Thomas. 1973. *The Rise of the Western World: A New Economic History*. Cambridge, UK: Cambridge University Press.

Nunn, Nathan. 2007. "Relationship-Specificity, Incomplete Contracts, and the Pattern of Trade." *The Quarterly Journal of Economics* 122(2): 569–600.

Nunn, Nathan, and Nancy Qian. 2011. "The Potato's Contribution to Population and Urbanization: Evidence from a Historical Experiment." *The Quarterly Journal of Economics* 126(2): 593–650.

Nunn, Nathan, and Leonard Wantchekon. 2011. "The Slave Trade and the Origins of Mistrust in Africa." *American Economic Review* 101(7): 3221–3252.

Onorato, Massimiliano, Kenneth Scheve, and David Stasavage. 2014. "Technology and the Era of the Mass Army." *The Journal of Economic History* 74(2): 449–481.

O'Rourke, Kevin H., and Jeffrey G. Williamson. 1999. *Globalization and History: The Evolution of a Nineteenth-Century Atlantic Economy*. Cambridge, MA: MIT Press.

Ostrom, Elinor. 1990. *Governing the Commons: The Evolution of Institutions for Collective Action*. Cambridge; New York: Cambridge University Press.

Ottinger, Sebastian, and Nico Voigtländer. 2020. "*History's Masters: The Effect of European Monarchs on State Performance.*" Cambridge, MA: National Bureau of Economic Research. www.nber.org/papers/w28297.pdf (Accessed August 15, 2021).

Overty, Joanne Filippone. 2008. "The Cost of Doing Scribal Business: Prices of Manuscript Books in England, 1300–1483." *Book History* 11(1): 1–32.

Pamuk, S. 2007. "The Black Death and the Origins of the 'Great Divergence' across Europe, 1300–1600." *European Review of Economic History* 11(3): 289–317.

Parker, Geoffrey. 1996. *The Military Revolution: Military Innovation and the Rise of the West, 1500–1800*. 2nd ed. New York: Cambridge University Press.

Peters, Margaret E. 2022. "Government Finance and Imposition of Serfdom after the Black Death." *European Review of Economic History*: 1–25.

Pettegree, Andrew. 2010. *The Book in the Renaissance*. New Haven, CT: Yale University Press.

Pincus, Steven C. A. 2009. *1688: The First Modern Revolution*. New Haven, CT: Yale University Press.

Pinker, Steven. 2018. *Enlightenment Now: The Case for Reason, Science, Humanism, and Progress*. New York: Viking, an imprint of Penguin Random House LLC.

Piotrowski, Thaddeus M. 1998. *Poland's Holocaust: Ethnic Strife, Collaboration with Occupying Forces and Genocide in the Second Republic, 1918–1947*. Jefferson, NC: McFarland.

Prestwich, Menna. 1988. "The Revocation of the Edict of Nantes." *History* 73: 63–73.

Pritchett, Lant. 1997. "Divergence, Big Time." *The Journal of Economic Perspectives*: 3–17.

Rasmussen, Carsten Porskrog. 2010. "Innovative Feudalism. The Development of Dairy Farming and 'Koppelwirtschaft' on Manors in Schleswig-Holstein in the Seventeenth and Eighteenth Centuries." *The Agricultural History Review* 58(2): 172–190.

Raster, Tom. 2019. "Serfs and the Market: Second Serfdom and the East-West Goods Exchange, 1579–1857." MA thesis. Paris School of Economics. http://piketty.pse.ens.fr/files/Raster2019.pdf (Accessed April 18, 2020).

Reichman, Henry. 1987. *Railwaymen and Revolution: Russia, 1905*. Berkeley, CA: University of California Press.

Renger, Johannes M., Michaël North, and Charles W. Calomiris. 2003. "Banking." http://www.oxfordreference.com/view/10.1093/acref/9780195105070.001.0001/acref-9780195105070-e-0058 (Accessed December 16, 2019).

Robinson, Geroid Tanquary. 1949. *Rural Russia under the Old Régime: A History of the Landlord-Peasant World and a Prologue to the Peasant Revolution of 1917*. New York: Macmillan Co.

Romer, Paul M. 1996. "Why, Indeed, in America? Theory, History, and the Origins of Modern Economic Growth." *The American Economic Review* 86(2): 202–206.

Rosenberg, Hans. 1943. "The Rise of the Junkers in Brandenburg-Prussia, 1410–1653: (Part I)." *The American Historical Review* 49(1): 1–22.

1944. "The Rise of the Junkers in Brandenburg-Prussia, 1410–1563: Part II." *The American Historical Review* 49(2): 228–242.

Rosensprung, Jan. 2022. "'Für den Nationalsozialismus reif gemacht.' Politische Einflüsse in der Sozialisationsphase früher Nationalsozialisten." In "*Wie ich den Weg zum Führer fand": Beitrittsmotive und Entlastungsstrategien von NSDAP-Mitgliedern*. Frankfurt; New York: Campus Verlag, 83–94.

Rubin, Jared. 2014. "Printing and Protestants: An Empirical Test of the Role of Printing in the Reformation." *The Review of Economics and Statistics* 96(2): 270–286.

Russell, Josiah C. 1976. "Population in Europe 500–1500." In Carlos Cipolla (ed.) *The Middle Ages, Fontana Economic History of Europe*, Brighton; New York: Harvester Press and Barnes & Noble.

Sarit Cohen and Chang-Tai Hsieh. 2001. "Macroeconomic and Labor Market Impact of Russian Immigration in Israel." Bar-Ilan University, Department of Economics. Working Paper. https://ideas.repec.org/p/biu/wpaper/2001-11.html (Accessed December 19, 2019).

Sasaki, Yu. 2017. "Publishing Nations: Technology Acquisition and Language Standardization for European Ethnic Groups." *The Journal of Economic History* 77(4): 1007–1047.

Scheidel, Walter. 2004. "Human Mobility in Roman Italy, I: The Free Population." *Journal Of Roman Studies* 94: 1–26.

2017. *The Great Leveler: Violence and the History of Inequality from the Stone Age to the Twenty-First Century*. Princeton, NJ: Princeton University Press.

Schencking, J. Charles. 2008. "The Great Kanto Earthquake and the Culture of Catastrophe and Reconstruction in 1920s Japan." *The Journal of Japanese Studies* 34(2): 295–331.

Schmidt, Georg. 2003. *Der Dreissigjährige Krieg*. 6. Aufl. Munich: Beck.

Schonhardt-Bailey, Cheryl. 1991. "Specific Factors, Capital Markets, Portfolio Diversification, and Free Trade: Domestic Determinants of the Repeal of the Corn Laws." *World Politics* 43(4): 545–569.

Scott, Hamish, and Brendan Simms, eds. 2007. *Cultures of Power in Europe during the Long Eighteenth Century*. Cambridge; New York: Cambridge University Press.

Scott, James C. 2017. *Against the Grain: A Deep History of the Earliest States*. New Haven, CT: Yale University Press.

Scoville, Warren. 1952a. "The Huguenots and the Diffusion of Technology, I." *The Journal of Political Economy* 60: 294.

1952b. "The Huguenots and the Diffusion of Technology. II." *The Journal of Political Economy* 60: 392.

1953. "The Huguenots in the French Economy, 1650–1750." *Quarterly Journal of Economics* 67(3): 423–444.

1960. *The Persecution of Huguenots and French Economic Development, 1680–1720*. Berkeley, CA: University of California Press.

Scullard, H. H. (Howard Hayes). 1970. *From the Gracchi to Nero: A History of Rome from 133 B.C. to A.D. 68*. 3rd ed. London; New York: Methuen.

2013. *A History of the Roman World: 753 to 146 BC. Routledge classics ed.* Abingdon; New York: Routledge.

Seckendorff, Veit Ludwig von. 1711. *Herrn Veit Ludwigs von Seckendorff. Teutscher fürstenstaat, mit einer gantz neuen zugabe ... üm ein grosses theil verm*. Franckfurt und Leipzig: J. Meyers Wittwe. https://link.gale.com/apps/doc/U0110690182/MOME?u=uclosangelessid=bookmark-MOMExid=acbfec39pg=1 (Accessed August 25, 2021).

Seely, Bruce E. 1986. "Good Roads and Motor Vehicles: Managing Technological Change." *Railroad History* (155): 34–63.

Sen, Amartya. 1982. *Poverty and Famines: An Essay on Entitlement and Deprivation*. Oxford: Oxford University Press.

Smil, Vaclav. 2001. *Enriching the Earth: Fritz Haber, Carl Bosch, and the Transformation of World Food Production*. Cambridge, MA: MIT Press.

Smith, Roger C. 1993. *Vanguard of Empire: Ships of Exploration in the Age of Columbus*. New York: Oxford University Press.

Sobel, Dava. 1995. *Longitude: The True Story of a Lone Genius Who Solved the Greatest Scientific Problem of His Time*. New York: Walker.

Soll, Jacob. 2009. *The Information Master: Jean-Baptiste Colbert's Secret State Intelligence System*. Ann Arbor, MI: University of Michigan Press.

Soto, Hernando de. 2000. *The Mystery of Capital: Why Capitalism Triumphs in the West and Fails Everywhere Else*. 1st paperback ed. New York: Basic Books.

Sporhan-Krempel, L. and Von Stromer. 1960. "Das Handelshaus Der Stromer von Nürnberg Und Die Geschichte Der Ersten Deutschen Papiermühle. Nach

Neuen Quellen." *Vierteljahrschrift Für Sozial- Und Wirtschaftsgeschichte* 47 (1): 81–104.

Spufford, Peter. 1988. *Money and Its Use in Medieval Europe*. Cambridge, UK; New York: Cambridge University Press.

Starns, Karl E. M. 2012. "The Russian Railways and Imperial Intersections in the Russian Empire." MA thesis. University of Washington.

Statistisches Reichsamt. 1916. 1915 *Statistisches Jahrbuch für das Deutsche Reich*. Berlin: Puttkammer & Mühlbrecht. www.digizeitschriften.de/dms/resolveppn/?PID=PPN514401303_1915 (Accessed December 3, 2020).

1921. 1920 *Statistisches Jahrbuch für das Deutsche Reich*. Berlin: Puttkammer & Mühlbrecht. www.digizeitschriften.de/dms/resolveppn/?PID=PPN514401303_1920 (Accessed December 3, 2020).

Steinwender, Claudia. 2018. "Real Effects of Information Frictions: When the States and the Kingdom Became United." *American Economic Review* 108 (3): 657–696.

Swetzer, Alexandra. 1996. "Foreign Investment and Economic Development in Tsarist Russia." In Patrick Artisien-Maksimenko and Yuri Adjubei (eds.), *Foreign Investment in Russia and Other Soviet Successor States*. London: Palgrave Macmillan, 23–40.

Szczygiel, Bonj, and Robert Hewitt. 2000. "Nineteenth-Century Medical Landscapes: John H. Rauch, Frederick Law Olmsted, and the Search for Salubrity." *Bulletin of the History of Medicine* 74(4): 708–734.

Taylor, Philip A. M. 1965. *Expectations Westward: The Mormons and the Emigration of Their British Converts in the Nineteenth Century*. Edinburgh: Oliver & Boyd.

Thomas, Alex M. 2018. "Adam Smith on the Philosophy and Provision of Education." *Journal of Interdisciplinary Economics* 30(1): 105–116.

Tilly, Charles. 1990. *Coercion, Capital, and European States, AD 990–1990*. Oxford, UK; Cambridge, MA: Blackwell.

Tollin, Henri. 1886. *Geschichte der französischen Colonie von Magdeburg: Jubiläumsschrift*. Halle: Niemeyer.

Tooze, J. Adam. 2008. *The Wages of Destruction: The Making and Breaking of the Nazi Economy*. New York: Penguin Books.

Torp, Cornelius. 2005. *Die Herausforderung der Globalisierung: Wirtschaft und Politik in Deutschland 1860–1914*. Göttingen: Vandenhoeck & Ruprecht.

Turner, Frederick Jackson. 1993 [1893]. *History, Frontier, and Section: Three Essays*. 1st ed. Albuquerque, NM: University of New Mexico Press.

Unger, Richard W. 1997. *Ships and Shipping in the North Sea and Atlantic, 1400–1800*. Aldershot; Brookfield, WI: Ashgate/Variorum.

US Bureau of the Census. 1920. *Farms and Farm Property*. Washington, DC: US Department of Agriculture. Census of Agriculture.

1949. *Historical Statistics of the United States, 1789–1945, Chap. D*. Washington, DC: US Department of Commerce.

US Bureau of Economic Analysis (BEA). 2019. *Gross Domestic Product by Industry: Second Quarter 2019 Annual Update: 2014 through First Quarter 2019*.

Voigtländer, Nico, and Hans-Joachim Voth. 2013. "How the West 'Invented' Fertility Restriction." *The American Economic Review* 103(6): 2227–2264.
Volckart, Oliver. 2002. *Wettbewerb und Wettbewerbsbeschränkung im Vormodernen Deutschland 1000–1800*. Tübingen: Mohr Siebeck.
de Vries, Jan. 1981. "Patterns of Urbanisation in Pre-industrial Europe, 1500–1800." In Henk Schmal (ed.), *Patterns of European Urbanisation Since 1500*. London: Croom Helm, 79–109.
Wagret, Paul. 1968. *Polderlands*. London: Methuen.
Wahl, Fabian. 2016. "Participative Political Institutions in Pre-modern Europe: Introducing a New Database." *Historical Methods: A Journal of Quantitative and Interdisciplinary History* 49(2): 67–79.
Walker, Edward Ronald. 1943. *From Economic Theory to Policy*. Chicago, IL.: The University of Chicago Press.
Walker, Mack. 1971. *German Home Towns: Community, State, and General Estate, 1648–1871*. Ithaca, NY, and Baltimore, MD: Cornell University Press, Project MUSE.
Ward-Perkins, Bryan. 2005. *The Fall of Rome: And the End of Civilization*. Oxford; New York: Oxford University Press.
Weir, Margaret, and Theda Skocpol. 1985. "State Structures and the Possibilities for 'Keynesian' Responses to the Great Depression in Sweden, Britain, and the United States." In Dietrich Rueschemeyer, Peter B. Evans, and Theda Skocpol (eds.), *Bringing the State Back In*. Cambridge: Cambridge University Press, 107–164.
Westwood, J. N. 1964. *A History of Russian Railways*. London: G. Allen and Unwin.
White, Andrew Dickson. 1932. *A History of the Warfare of Science with Theology in Christendom*. New York: D. Appleton and company.
White, Lynn. 1962. *Medieval Technology and Social Change*. Oxford: Clarendon Press.
Wilkes, John. 2001. "The Pen behind the Sword: Power, Literacy and the Roman Army." *Archaeology International* 5: 32.
Williams, Eric Eustace. 1944. *Capitalism and Slavery*. Chapel Hill: University of North Carolina Press.
Williamson, Jeffrey G. 2005. *The Political Economy of World Mass Migration: Comparing Two Global Centuries*. Washington, DC: AEI Press.
Williamson, Oliver E. 1985. *The Economic Institutions of Capitalism: Firms, Markets, Relational Contracting*. New York: London: Free Press; Collier Macmillan.
Winslow, C.-E. A. 1943. *The Conquest of Epidemic Disease: A Chapter in the History of Ideas*. Princeton, NJ: Princeton University Press.
Wood, Bernard A. 2019. *Human Evolution: A Very Short Introduction*. 2nd ed. Oxford; New York: Oxford University Press.
Woytinsky, W. S., and Emma Shadkhan Woytinsky. 1955. *World Commerce and Governments: Trends and Outlook*. New York: Twentieth Century Fund.
Yue, Ricci P. H., Harry F. Lee, and Connor Y. H. Wu. 2017. "Trade Routes and Plague Transmission in Pre-industrial Europe." *Scientific Reports* 7(1): 12973.

Zechini, Mariana. 2017. "Beneath Berlin: Interpreting Dietary Responses to the Black Death in Medieval Berlin Using Stable Isotope Analysis." MA thesis. University of West Florida.

Zhu, Susan Chun, and Daniel Trefler. 2005. "Trade and Inequality in Developing Countries: A General Equilibrium Analysis." *Journal of International Economics* 65(1): 21–48.

Ziblatt, Daniel. 2009. "Shaping Democratic Practice and the Causes of Electoral Fraud: The Case of Nineteenth-Century Germany." *American Political Science Review* 103(01): 1–21.

Zimmer, Ben. 2010. "On Language: Ghoti." *New York Times Magazine*: 14.

Zipf, George Kingsley. 1949. *Human Behavior and the Principle of Least Effort; an Introduction to Human Ecology*. Cambridge, MA: Addison-Wesley Press.

Index

Index

***Other books in the series** (continued from page iii)*

Faisal Ahmed, *Conquests and Rents: A Political Economy of Dictatorship and Violence in Muslim Societies*

Alberto Alesina and Howard Rosenthal, *Partisan Politics, Divided Government and the Economy*

Lee J. Alston, Thrainn Eggertsson and Douglass C. North, eds., *Empirical Studies in Institutional Change*

Lee J. Alston and Joseph P. Ferrie, *Southern Paternalism and the Rise of the American Welfare State: Economics, Politics, and Institutions, 1865–1965*

James E. Alt and Kenneth Shepsle, eds., *Perspectives on Positive Political Economy*

Josephine T. Andrews, *When Majorities Fail: The Russian Parliament, 1990–1993*

Jeffrey S. Banks and Eric A. Hanushek, eds., *Modern Political Economy: Old Topics, New Directions*

Yoram Barzel, *Economic Analysis of Property Rights, 2nd edition*

Yoram Barzel, *A Theory of the State: Economic Rights, Legal Rights, and the Scope of the State*

Robert Bates, *Beyond the Miracle of the Market: The Political Economy of Agrarian Development in Kenya*

Jenna Bednar, *The Robust Federation: Principles of Design*

Charles M. Cameron, *Veto Bargaining: Presidents and the Politics of Negative Power*

Kelly H. Chang, *Appointing Central Bankers: The Politics of Monetary Policy in the United States and the European Monetary Union*

Tom S. Clark *The Supreme Court: An Analytical History of Constitutional Decision Making*

Peter Cowhey and Mathew McCubbins, eds., *Structure and Policy in Japan and the United States: An Institutionalist Approach*

Gary W. Cox, *The Efficient Secret: The Cabinet and the Development of Political Parties in Victorian England*

Gary W. Cox, *Making Votes Count: Strategic Coordination in the World's Electoral System*

Gary W. Cox, *Marketing Sovereign Promises: Monopoly Brokerage and the Growth of the English State*

Gary W. Cox and Jonathan N. Katz, *Elbridge Gerry's Salamander: The Electoral Consequences of the Reapportionment Revolution*

Tine De Moore, *The Dilemma of the Commoners: Understanding the Use of Common-Pool Resources in Long-Term Perspective*

Adam Dean, *From Conflict to Coalition: Profit-Sharing Institutions and the Political Economy of Trade*

Adam Dean *Opening Up by Cracking Down: Labor Repression and Trade Liberalization in Democratic Developing Democracies*

Mark Dincecco, *Political Transformations and Public Finances: Europe, 1650–1913*

Mark Dincecco and Massimiliano Gaetano Onorato, *From Warfare to Wealth: The Military Origins of Urban Prosperity in Europe*

Raymond M. Duch and Randolph T. Stevenson, *The Economic Vote: How Political and Economic Institutions Condition Election Results*

Jean Ensminger, *Making a Market: The Institutional Transformation of an African Society*

David Epstein and Sharyn O'Halloran, *Delegating Powers: A Transaction Cost Politics Approach to Policy Making under Separate Powers*

Kathryn Firmin-Sellers, *The Transformation of Property Rights in the Gold Coast: An Empirical Study Applying Rational Choice Theory*

Clark C. Gibson, *Politicians and Poachers: The Political Economy of Wildlife Policy in Africa*

Daniel W. Gingerich, *Political Institutions and Party-Directed Corruption in South America*

Avner Greif, *Institutions and the Path to the Modern Economy: Lessons from Medieval Trade*

Jeffrey D. Grynaviski, *Partisan Bonds: Political Reputations and Legislative Accountability*

Stephen Haber, Armando Razo, and Noel Maurer, *The Politics of Property Rights: Political Instability, Credible Commitments, and Economic Growth in Mexico, 1876–1929*

Ron Harris, *Industrializing English Law: Entrepreneurship and Business Organization, 1720–1844*

Anna L. Harvey, *Votes Without Leverage: Women in American Electoral Politics, 1920–1970*

Shigeo Hirano and James M. Snyder, Jr. *Primary Elections in the United States*

Murray Horn, *The Political Economy of Public Administration: Institutional Choice in the Public Sector*

John D. Huber, *Rationalizing Parliament: Legislative Institutions and Party Politics in France*

Sean Ingham, *Rule of Multiple Majorities: A New Theory of Popular Control*

John E. Jackson, Jacek Klich, Krystyna Poznanska, *The Political Economy of Poland's Transition: New Firms and Reform Governments*

Jack Knight, *Institutions and Social Conflict*

Michael Laver and Kenneth Shepsle, eds., *Cabinet Ministers and Parliamentary Government*

Michael Laver and Kenneth Shepsle, eds., *Making and Breaking Governments: Cabinets and Legislatures in Parliamentary Democracies*

Margaret Levi, *Consent, Dissent, and Patriotism*

Brian Levy and Pablo T. Spiller, eds., *Regulations, Institutions, and Commitment: Comparative Studies of Telecommunications*
Leif Lewin, *Ideology and Strategy: A Century of Swedish Politics (English Edition)*
Gary Libecap, *Contracting for Property Rights*
John Londregan, *Legislative Institutions and Ideology in Chile*
Arthur Lupia and Mathew D. McCubbins, *The Democratic Dilemma: Can Citizens Learn What They Need to Know?*
C. Mantzavinos, *Individuals, Institutions, and Markets*
Mathew D. McCubbins and Terry Sullivan, eds., *Congress: Structure and Policy*
Gary J. Miller, *Above Politics: Bureaucratic Discretion and Credible Commitment*
Gary J. Miller, *Managerial Dilemmas: The Political Economy of Hierarchy*
Ilia Murtazashvili, *The Political Economy of the American Frontier*
Douglass C. North, *Institutions, Institutional Change, and Economic Performance*
Elinor Ostrom, *Governing the Commons: The Evolution of Institutions for Collective Action*
Sonal S. Pandya, *Trading Spaces: Foreign Direct Investment Regulation, 1970–2000*
John W. Patty and Elizabeth Maggie Penn, *Social Choice and Legitimacy*
Daniel N. Posner, *Institutions and Ethnic Politics in Africa*
J. Mark Ramseyer, *Odd Markets in Japanese History: Law and Economic Growth*
J. Mark Ramseyer and Frances Rosenbluth, *The Politics of Oligarchy: Institutional Choice in Imperial Japan*
Stephanie J. Rickard *Spending to Win: Political Institutions, Economic Geography, and Government Subsidies*
Meredith Rolfe, *Voter Turnout: A Social Theory of Political Participation*
Jean-Laurent Rosenthal, *The Fruits of Revolution: Property Rights, Litigation, and French Agriculture, 1700–1860*
Michael L. Ross, *Timber Booms and Institutional Breakdown in Southeast Asia*
Shanker Satyanath, *Globalization, Politics, and Financial Turmoil: Asia's Banking Crisis*
Alberto Simpser, *Why Governments and Parties Manipulate Elections: Theory, Practice, and Implications*
Norman Schofield, *Architects of Political Change: Constitutional Quandaries and Social Choice Theory*
Norman Schofield and Itai Sened, *Multiparty Democracy: Elections and Legislative Politics*
Alastair Smith, *Election Timing*
Pablo T. Spiller and Mariano Tommasi, *The Institutional Foundations of Public Policy in Argentina: A Transactions Cost Approach*
David Stasavage, *Public Debt and the Birth of the Democratic State: France and Great Britain, 1688–1789*

Charles Stewart III, *Budget Reform Politics: The Design of the Appropriations Process in the House of Representatives, 1865–1921*

George Tsebelis and Jeannette Money, *Bicameralism*

Georg Vanberg, *The Politics of Constitutional Review in Germany*

Nicolas van de Walle, *African Economies and the Politics of Permanent Crisis, 1979–1999*

Stefanie Walter, *Financial Crises and the Politics of Macroeconomic Adjustments*

John Waterbury, *Exposed to Innumerable Delusions: Public Enterprise and State Power in Egypt, India, Mexico, and Turkey*

David L. Weimer, ed., *The Political Economy of Property Rights Institutional Change and Credibility in the Reform of Centrally Planned Economies*

Other books in the series *(continued from page iii)*

Faisal Ahmed, *Conquests and Rents: A Political Economy of Dictatorship and Violence in Muslim Societies*

Alberto Alesina and Howard Rosenthal, *Partisan Politics, Divided Government and the Economy*

Lee J. Alston, Thrainn Eggertsson and Douglass C. North, eds., *Empirical Studies in Institutional Change*

Lee J. Alston and Joseph P. Ferrie, *Southern Paternalism and the Rise of the American Welfare State: Economics, Politics, and Institutions, 1865–1965*

James E. Alt and Kenneth Shepsle, eds., *Perspectives on Positive Political Economy*

Josephine T. Andrews, *When Majorities Fail: The Russian Parliament, 1990–1993*

Jeffrey S. Banks and Eric A. Hanushek, eds., *Modern Political Economy: Old Topics, New Directions*

Yoram Barzel, *Economic Analysis of Property Rights, 2nd edition*

Yoram Barzel, *A Theory of the State: Economic Rights, Legal Rights, and the Scope of the State*

Robert Bates, *Beyond the Miracle of the Market: The Political Economy of Agrarian Development in Kenya*

Jenna Bednar, *The Robust Federation: Principles of Design*

Charles M. Cameron, *Veto Bargaining: Presidents and the Politics of Negative Power*

Kelly H. Chang, *Appointing Central Bankers: The Politics of Monetary Policy in the United States and the European Monetary Union*

Tom S. Clark *The Supreme Court: An Analytical History of Constitutional Decision Making*

Peter Cowhey and Mathew McCubbins, eds., *Structure and Policy in Japan and the United States: An Institutionalist Approach*

Gary W. Cox, *The Efficient Secret: The Cabinet and the Development of Political Parties in Victorian England*

Gary W. Cox, *Making Votes Count: Strategic Coordination in the World's Electoral System*

Gary W. Cox, *Marketing Sovereign Promises: Monopoly Brokerage and the Growth of the English State*

Gary W. Cox and Jonathan N. Katz, *Elbridge Gerry's Salamander: The Electoral Consequences of the Reapportionment Revolution*

Tine De Moore, *The Dilemma of the Commoners: Understanding the Use of Common-Pool Resources in Long-Term Perspective*

Adam Dean, *From Conflict to Coalition: Profit-Sharing Institutions and the Political Economy of Trade*

Adam Dean *Opening Up by Cracking Down: Labor Repression and Trade Liberalization in Democratic Developing Democracies*
Mark Dincecco, *Political Transformations and Public Finances: Europe, 1650–1913*
Mark Dincecco and Massimiliano Gaetano Onorato, *From Warfare to Wealth: The Military Origins of Urban Prosperity in Europe*
Raymond M. Duch and Randolph T. Stevenson, *The Economic Vote: How Political and Economic Institutions Condition Election Results*
Jean Ensminger, *Making a Market: The Institutional Transformation of an African Society*
David Epstein and Sharyn O'Halloran, *Delegating Powers: A Transaction Cost Politics Approach to Policy Making under Separate Powers*
Kathryn Firmin-Sellers, *The Transformation of Property Rights in the Gold Coast: An Empirical Study Applying Rational Choice Theory*
Clark C. Gibson, *Politicians and Poachers: The Political Economy of Wildlife Policy in Africa*
Daniel W. Gingerich, *Political Institutions and Party-Directed Corruption in South America*
Avner Greif, *Institutions and the Path to the Modern Economy: Lessons from Medieval Trade*
Jeffrey D. Grynaviski, *Partisan Bonds: Political Reputations and Legislative Accountability*
Stephen Haber, Armando Razo, and Noel Maurer, *The Politics of Property Rights: Political Instability, Credible Commitments, and Economic Growth in Mexico, 1876–1929*
Ron Harris, *Industrializing English Law: Entrepreneurship and Business Organization, 1720–1844*
Anna L. Harvey, *Votes Without Leverage: Women in American Electoral Politics, 1920–1970*
Shigeo Hirano and James M. Snyder, Jr. *Primary Elections in the United States*
Murray Horn, *The Political Economy of Public Administration: Institutional Choice in the Public Sector*
John D. Huber, *Rationalizing Parliament: Legislative Institutions and Party Politics in France*
Sean Ingham, *Rule of Multiple Majorities: A New Theory of Popular Control*
John E. Jackson, Jacek Klich, Krystyna Poznanska, *The Political Economy of Poland's Transition: New Firms and Reform Governments*
Jack Knight, *Institutions and Social Conflict*
Michael Laver and Kenneth Shepsle, eds., *Cabinet Ministers and Parliamentary Government*
Michael Laver and Kenneth Shepsle, eds., *Making and Breaking Governments: Cabinets and Legislatures in Parliamentary Democracies*
Margaret Levi, *Consent, Dissent, and Patriotism*